The Army of Tennessee
in Retreat

The Army of Tennessee in Retreat

*From Defeat at Nashville through
"the Sternest Trials of the War"*

O. C. HOOD

McFarland & Company, Inc., Publishers
Jefferson, North Carolina

LIBRARY OF CONGRESS CATALOGUING-IN-PUBLICATION DATA

Names: Hood, O. C., 1949– author.
Title: The Army of Tennessee in retreat : from defeat at Nashville
through "the sternest trials of the war" / O.C. Hood.
Description: Jefferson, North Carolina : McFarland & Company,
Inc., Publishers, 2019 | Includes bibliographical references and
index.
Identifiers: LCCN 2018048627 | ISBN 9781476672922 (softcover :
acid free paper) ∞
Subjects: LCSH: Confederate States of America. Army of Tennessee—
History. | United States—History—Civil War, 1861–1865—
Campaigns. | Tennessee—History—Civil War,
1861–1865—Campaigns.
Classification: LCC E470.5 .H66 2019 | DDC 973.7/468—dc23
LC record available at https://lccn.loc.gov/2018048627

BRITISH LIBRARY CATALOGUING DATA ARE AVAILABLE

ISBN (print) 978-1-4766-7292-2
ISBN (ebook) 978-1-4766-3190-5

Front cover image of Hood during the course of the battle at
Nashville, Tennessee, December 15–16, 1864 (Jacob F. Coonley,
photographer, Library of Congress)

Printed in the United States of America

McFarland & Company, Inc., Publishers
Box 611, Jefferson, North Carolina 28640
www.mcfarlandpub.com

To the rebel rear guard,
that starving, shivering band of saviors
who bled for their country every step of the way
from Nashville to Tuscumbia and beyond.

Table of Contents

Acknowledgments

To Cousin Sam Hood and historian Dave Fraley, who were always on hand with an encouraging word, inspiration, and sound guidance. Thanks guys. You're the best!

Although every effort has been made to avoid inaccuracies and blunders, I take full responsibility for all errors found herein, great or small.

David, thanks especially for the outstanding photos. They add a dimension into the story that nothing else could; and for your first class resources, I'm indebted to you a great deal. I only hope that the finished product meets your high standards of approval, both professionally and in remembrance of those threadbare brigades of butternut and grey that tramped the ice covered fields from Nashville to Tupelo in search of a dream that had become a nightmare.

GENERAL FIELD ORDERS, HDQRS. ARMY OF TENNESSEE,

Near Nashville, Tenn. December 6, 1864.

I. The general commanding desires to call the attention of the officers and men to the fact that success and safety in battle consists in piercing the enemy's lines as quickly as possible after coming under his fire. No halts should be made, except those temporary ones necessary for partial rectification of the alignment.

II. Commanding officers will forward, with as little delay as possible, the names of those officers and soldiers who passed over the enemy's interior line of works at Franklin, on the evening of the 30th of November, that they may be forwarded to the War Department and placed upon the roll of honor.

By command of General Hood:

A.P. Mason,
Colonel and Assistant Adjutant-General
OR, Series I, Part II, Vol. XLV, p. 653

"On this retreat came the sternest trials of the war."
—Luke Finlay, 4th Tennessee Infantry, CSA

Preface

"What have you done?"

Places where dramatic events have taken place leave a lasting, distinct impression within its immediate surroundings. There is something in the air in such places; a stillness, a wonder, and admiration of those who long ago performed the most noble (and at times the most cruel) of deeds. This is doubly true at sites where blood had been shed to preserve life.

Whether blood is spilled in vicious criminality or in self sacrifice, there must always follow an accountability. In the ancient record of the Book of Genesis it is written that, subsequent to the murder of Abel by his brother Cain, the Lord Himself came forth to judge, demanding an answer, an explanation from Cain: "What have you done? The voice of your brother's blood cries to me from the ground." Perhaps this is one reason we feel a profound sense of solemnity when entering a battlefield.

Those who take the time to visit such places often experience identical sensations: a certain numbness coupled with an embarrassing lack of inner response, an all-pervasive powerlessness to measure up, a chasm of ignorance when attempting to relate to the participants and their era, a dismal lack of understanding of the event that took place beneath their feet, a frustrating inability to sufficiently grasp the enormity of what happened as well as to truly believe that it did actually happen, and a peculiar, uneasy smallness in stark contrast to the magnitude of the story and the larger-than-life personalities who contributed to it. At such a time there's only so much the average visitor can take in. And when he's had enough he quietly slips away, back into his own familiar, safe, and comfortable world. Yet, something intangible but very real has silently penetrated his soul. He's all too aware that for a brief moment he has stood on ground where greatness showed itself to the world. Here heroes were immortalized. History was made. It is humbling to face up to it. Although these were men, much like all other men in many

1

ways, the fact remains that there is a select number who have proven themselves worthy of immortal memory. Standing in the very spot where those men gave all for a purpose greater than themselves allows the onlooker a rare glimpse into the unseen. Somehow, through this experience that observer sees past the veil, from the temporal into the eternal, and again is humbled.

On the northern bank of the Harpeth River in middle Tennessee, a literal stone's throw from the streets of battle-scarred Franklin, the traveler has found such a place. At this modestly unassuming site the visitor at once feels the impact of long-ago events. Here on a cold, rainy December 17, 1864, a most bloody and ferocious conflict ensued. On the mid-morning of that fateful day, swarms of Federal cavalry units suddenly and unexpectedly crashed headlong into the stubborn line of the Confederate rear guard positioned at the river's edge. The full range of weaponry on hand was put to immediate use, from artillery posted across the stream to muskets, carbines, pistols, sabers, and gun-butts. Whatever was available was put to work—and a deadly work it was.

The scene is impossible to justly convey and equally impossible to fully comprehend. But it can be forgotten, all too easily. The following chapters were written to prevent that from ever happening.

Out of Step

Most students familiar with the various battle scenarios of the Civil War are accustomed to a fairly common, recognizable setting. After a long period of planning and strategic movement, two opposing armies suddenly meet face to face on a field of battle. The lines are drawn. Each side makes careful preparations, taking every advantage of terrain, manpower, maneuverability, and skill in positioning itself to confront the enemy. Over a period of usually not more than a day, the battle is waged. The ebb and flow of combat sways back and forth until one side has clearly defeated the opponent or a draw has occurred. In either case, in the closing stages both armies have suffered greatly and are temporarily unable to engage in further combat. In typical fashion, at battle's end each will withdraw from the field to care for the respective wounded, collect scattered remnants, resupply, and prepare for the next round of fighting, generally weeks away.

The story of General John Bell Hood's retreat from Tennessee is altogether different. To many who may be unaware of the particular character of this phase of the war and the nature of this episode, the storyline may seem altogether unusual, out of step with the familiar setting so many of us are accustomed to. Due to the unique character of the historical narrative, a short note of clarification is required.

The engagements depicted herein during Hood's retreat were not fought as pitched battles of two opposing forces facing each other over standing ground. Similar to Johnston's withdrawal from Dalton, the narrative of this retreat is one of a long series of conflicts taking place over a combined distance of a hundred miles and lasting over a period of ten consecutive days in the depths of an unusually severe winter. This is a running battle. Each army is fast on the move, every day. The Southerners are retreating as rapidly as possible. The Northerners are equally determined in pursuit. Various rounds of fighting break out along the way as the two armies periodically collide with one another in fierce and dramatic contests.

Each day, each hour, the scenario changes. Here we are met with constant, fluid movement. With both armies stretching out to a length of twenty to thirty miles and each one on the move, it must be kept in mind that at any given point on any given day, what one section of either army is experiencing may be altogether different from another section.

U.S. Cavalry Background and a Tribute to the Faithful

The development of the U.S. Cavalry from that of frontier service and garrison duty out in the far west into a much larger and highly effective fighting force capable of standing the rigors of strenuous prolonged armed conflict on a vast scale was forced upon the U.S. military establishment during the Civil War out of an obvious sense of pressing necessity. Although the American soldier (the mounted volunteer as well as the Regulars) who met the enemy on horseback had a long history behind him prior to the War Between the States, it was this conflict that eventually brought into being a heightened level of professionalism and expertise—and that on a much grander stage. At no other time in the nation's young history had there been such a desperate need for the combination of sledgehammer manpower and quick mobility. As huge armies met together on the field of battle the meager intelligence services of both Northern and Southern commanders relied in great measure on the ability of its cavalry corps to perform accurate reconnaissance. Without the aid of a swift and well-trained cavalry the commanding general was left to conjecture as to the whereabouts and probable intentions of his enemy, in addition to the lay of the land that surrounded him.

The army also relied heavily on an able-bodied functioning cavalry to swiftly move on the offensive and wreak havoc in the disruption of the enemy's supply and communication lines. The highly mobile nature of the cavalry had no equal in its capacity to protect the flanks and rear of the infantry, both on the march and in combat, as well as possessing a unique and somewhat terrifying talent for rapid and dogged pursuit of an enemy in retreat. Because of his advanced potential for rapid movement as a quick-strike force, the cavalryman (carrying his supplies and equipment with him) was called upon to cover vast regions of territory, frequently encountering comparable if not greater hazards than that of the infantryman.

While it was a comparatively inferior fighting force for most of the war, by late 1864 the arm of the Union cavalry had become a foe to be reckoned with, claiming equality with the ingrained ingenuity and dash that had so well characterized the Confederate horsemen from the beginning. Possessing the superior weapons technology of the era, the Union cavalry facing Hood's depleted ranks in the winter of 1864 could boast of having not only the customary light cavalry saber with its slightly curved blade designed for cutting and slashing effectiveness (which had replaced the original military issue, the long, straight style of the Prussian model) but also the tremendously advantageous edge that the lightweight breech-loading repeating carbine gave over the single-shot musket borne by enemy infantry or the single-shot smoothbore pistol carried by Confederate cavalrymen.

The familiar U.S. standard-issue, breech-loading .52 caliber model 1859 Sharps rifle in time was replaced by the Spencer repeating carbine available to the Union cavalry. The Spencer, in good hands, could load (somewhat awkwardly) a total of seven rounds per load (in contrast to the comparatively agonizing slowness of the one-shot per load of a rifled musket), multiplying the repeater's efficiency many times over. The weapon of choice in either army for men on horseback for convenience, quick maneuverability, and short-range use was the surprisingly accurate and highly prized cap and ball Colt revolver, either the .44 caliber army model or the earlier (and more readily available) .36 caliber navy model. Any cavalryman who valued his life and had a measure of common sense would strap as many of these guns, cylinders preloaded, around his waist or have them stuffed in his saddlebags, as practicality would permit. The Federal cavalry (in like manner to its cousin, the well-supplied infantry) at the beginning of the war was so weighed down with nonessentials as to practically disable the trooper's effectiveness by reason of the overwhelming amount of gear that was piled upon him. The following quote is an illustration: "The trials of many of the newly recruited organizations, until the beginning of the third year of the war, are illustrated in the following extract from a typical regimental history: Captain Vanderbilt describes in graphic terms his first experience in escort duty (December 10, 1862)" (*History of the Tenth New York Cavalry* (Preston, NY):

> Please remember that my company had been mustered into the service only about six weeks before, and had received horse month prior to this march; and in the issue we drew everything on the list—watering-bridles, lariat ropes, and pins—in fact, there was nothing on the printed list of supplies that we did not get. Many men had extra blan-

kets, nice large quilts presented by some fond mother or maiden aunt (dear souls), sabers and belts, together with the straps that pass over the shoulders, carbines and slings, pockets full of cartridges, nose bags and extra little bags for carrying oats, haversacks, canteens, and spurs—some of them of the Mexican pattern as large as small windmills, and more in the way than the spurs of a young rooster, catching in the grass when they walked, carrying up briers, vines, and weeds, and catching their pants, and in the way generally—curry-combs, brushes, ponchos, button tents, overcoats, frying-pans, cups, coffee-pots, etc. Now the old companies had become used to these things and had got down to light-marching condition gradually, had learned how to wear the uniform, saber, carbine, etc.; but my company had hardly, time to get into proper shape when "the general" was sounded, "boots and saddles" blown.

Within the space of a year's training, mostly on hand in the school of combat, the newly recruited cavalryman had discarded much if not all of his unnecessary equipment for a lighter, more effective means of preparing himself for the rigors of war. Freed from such distractions he was "at home in the saddle, able to deliver telling blows with the saber, and to ride boot-to-boot in battle charges."[1] As for the supplying of the Confederate cavalry with the essential equipment necessary for waging war on horseback, it was quite the opposite. Rather than being overwhelmed with gear, as was the case with the Federal cavalry, the Southern horse soldier shared the same fate as his inadequately equipped companion, the regular infantry: "In 1861 the Confederate cavalry had no Colt revolvers, no Chicopee sabers, and no carbines that were worth carrying. Their arms were of the homeliest type and of infinite variety." As the war progressed the Southern cavalry was supplied for the most part by what it could carry away from a deserted battlefield or by what could be obtained from prisoners.[2]

The brand of American horse soldier in late 1864, both Union and Confederate, produced by the changing conditions of the time had become one of proficient flexibility. He was adaptable and resourceful, ready and able to fight a saber duel, exchange blows on the ground as dismounted cavalry or as mounted troops charging the ranks of standing infantry, a most unwelcome and dangerous prospect for the cavalryman, veteran or new recruit.

The Unsung Hero of Battle: The Warhorse

In all the vast dialogue over the War Between the States we have failed to give proper recognition due to that loyal host of friends that for four long years faithfully fought alongside the armies of blue and gray. Whether he was pulling caissons filled with desperately needed supplies of ammunition; hauling wagonloads of food, clothing, equipment, and wounded men; dragging howitzers into position; or carrying the cavalry on their backs, the horse went anywhere and everywhere the army ventured.

It may seem a strange thing to consider. Although the war was fought man to man, the horse waged war just as well, just as long and just as hard, was exposed to the same dangers on the march and on the field, and endured the same sufferings and privations as his human counterpart, if not more. When the army starved, the horses starved. When the soldiers faced "the deadly hail," so did the horses. When the men broke into a charge, the horses carried them. And when they fell back in disarray the horses led them out.

The horse was indispensable during the war. Without that animal it could not have been successfully waged. As a consequence, a great number of them died alongside their riders. Not surprisingly, scripture provides a fascinating and rare glimpse into the personality of the battle horse. In the ancient biblical record an unusual discourse is set forth between the Lord and Job. In it, God illustrates to Job the awe-inspiring attributes of the warhorse:

> Hast thou given the horse strength? Hast thou clothed his neck with thunder? Canst thou make him afraid as a grasshopper? The glory of his nostrils is terrible. He paweth in the valley, and rejoiceth in his strength: he goeth on to meet the armed men. He mocketh at fear, and is not frightened; neither turneth he back from the sword. The quiver rattleth against him, the glittering spear and the shield. He swalloweth the ground with fierceness and rage: neither believeth he that it is the sound of the trumpet. He saith among the trumpets, Ha, ha; and he smelleth the battle afar off, the thunder of the captains, and the shouting.[3]

In the winter of 1864 in middle Tennessee that was certainly the case, time and time again. The pounding hoofbeats of well over ten thousand warhorses rushing into battle thundered down the roads and fields between Nashville and the Alabama border for ten terrifying days without letup. At times the earth must have shaken, but no more than the trembling hearts of the participants.

From time to time reports emerge from the American Civil War that push credibility to its absolute limits. The record of the Confederate Army of Tennessee's retreat from Nashville in the winter of 1864 is one of those accounts. The pages herein depict an exceptional story, a recounting of extreme suffering mixed with unflinching courage and fortitude. While at times it may seem brutal and even ugly to the modern reader in respect to the degree of misery and affliction produced by the war, it must be clearly understood that in the minds and hearts of 19th century America some things were worth dying for. For them such sacrifice was not to be shunned. It was a matter of duty and honor. Love of country and American heritage drove them to the fore. And before they knew what had hit them, a mighty hard wind had begun to sweep over the land, carrying all before it.

Introduction

Nashville is the key to independence—Gen. John Bell Hood to Gen. Patrick Cleburne, Winstead Hill, overlooking Franklin, Tennessee, November 30, 1864, *Augusta Constitutionalist,* December 16, 1864

Late in the third year of the War Between the States, prospects in the South for the hope of Confederate independence had unexpectedly plummeted to a state of sober desperation. Despite his largely unfavorable reputation in the North, President Abraham Lincoln was seeking reelection. And after a series of fierce military engagements, by late summer the major Southern railway supply hub of Atlanta, Georgia, had fallen to the onslaught of the Federal army. Abandoning all semblance of human decency, Union general W.T. Sherman's infamous "march to the sea" that was soon to follow would be remembered as being among the most treacherous and barbaric acts a civilized nation's government has ever inflicted upon its own people.

These events boded very darkly for the South, casting a pall across the entire Confederate nation. The probability of Lincoln's reelection to a second term afforded a strengthening of Federal resolve in its overwhelming military might to crush this so-called rebellion and obliterate it from the face of the earth, regardless of the Northern lives it took to accomplish it. With the loss of Atlanta's supply base in the summer of 1864, the already poorly supplied Southern armies would have to subsist on even less. And the Southern civilian population suffered even more (if that were possible), their homes, crops, livestock, and towns devastated in the wake of Sherman's marauding army. Times were indeed distressing for the Confederacy. Desperate measures seemed the only viable solution to the war-ravaged South.

As an intended counterstroke, on November 21, 1864, Confederate general John Bell Hood and his newly inherited (as of the previous July) Army of Tennessee embarked from northern Alabama upon an audacious campaign to retake the city of Nashville, Tennessee, from Federal occupation. With

Tennessee once more in Southern hands, Hood's army would launch an uncontested, aggressive invasion into Northern territory. Foremost in a long list of grand objectives built into the plan included the crossing of the Cumberland River well out of range of the Union gunboats patrolling it, and a drive deep into Kentucky and Ohio, which wolud threaten Cincinnati. Throughout the advance Hood would be resupplying and recruiting his army as well as rebuilding its sagging morale and fighting spirit, all at the expense of Union resources.once these goals were accomplished, Hood's army, deeply entrenched behind Federal lines, would gain the offensive, throwing the Union government off balance and temporarily halting any military objectives directed against the South.

While from the Federal government's standpoint U.S. troops tramping Southern soil was acceptable, satisfactory policy, Hood well knew the Washington authorities could never countenance a Confederate army on the loose in Northern territory. If he could succeed as planned the war would immediately assume drastically different perspectives. In a vital communiqué dated December 2, 1864, to General E. Kirby Smith, commanding the Department of Trans-Mississippi, General P.G.T. Beauregard outlined the critical nature and objective of Hood's bold plan, stressing the vital necessity of General Smith sending him reinforcements from the Trans-Mississippi region:

GENERAL: You are probably aware that the Army of Tennessee, under General J.B. Hood, has penetrated into Middle Tennessee as far as Columbia, and that the enemy is concentrating all his available forces, under General Thomas, to oppose him. It is even reliably reported that the forces under [Union] Generals A.J. Smith, in Missouri, and Steele, in Arkansas, have been sent to re-enforce Thomas [at Nashville]. It becomes, then, absolutely necessary, to insure the success of Hood, either that you should send him two or more divisions, or that you should at once threaten Missouri, in order to compel the enemy to recall the re-enforcements he is sending to General Thomas.

I beg to urge upon you prompt and decisive action. The fate of the country may depend upon the result of Hood's campaign in Tennessee. Sherman's army has lately abandoned Atlanta on a venturesome march across Georgia to the Atlantic coast about Savannah. His object is, besides the destruction of public and private property, probably to re-enforce Grant and compel Lee to abandon Richmond. It is hoped that Sherman may be prevented from effecting his object, but, should it be otherwise, the success of Hood in Tennessee and Kentucky would counterbalance the moral effect of the loss of Richmond. Hence the urgent necessity of either re-enforcing Hood or making a diversion in Missouri in his favor.[1]

A few days later, on the 6th of December, in a letter of reply to President Jefferson Davis, Beauregard spelled out his personal rationale behind his authorization for the Confederate army's invasion of Tennessee.

After the fall of Atlanta Sherman's plans to decimate middle Georgia had begun in earnest. With Sherman's army consisting of superior numbers and traveling over comparatively good roads, he had an extensive advance, outdistancing Hood some 275 miles, due to the fact that Hood had moved his forces to the northwest, far from the scene of action. Understandably, Beauregard was convinced of the impracticable nature of an attempted pursuit of Sherman—and that for a number of reasons. "To pursue Sherman, the march of the Army of Tennessee would necessarily have been over roads with all the bridges destroyed, and through a desolated country, affording neither subsistence nor forage, while a retrograde movement of the [Confederate] army must have seriously depleted its ranks by desertions. Moreover, to have recalled the army to follow Sherman would have opened to Thomas [situated in Nashville] the richest portions of Alabama. Montgomery, Mobile, and Selma would have easily fallen, without insuring the defeat of Sherman."[2]

Through the conquest and liberation of federally occupied Tennessee, and with Nashville once again firmly in Confederate hands, Southern morale would undoubtedly rise and with it a renewal of the hope of a well-deserved, satisfactory end to the hostilities. A Confederate victory in Nashville carried the potential to thoroughly undermine Northern political resolve, ideally forcing Federal capitulation and eventually paving the way for the reclamation of Southern sovereignty over its states, seaports, and borders. The South had paid the dearest price to obtain political independence. As the opportunity came within reach, nothing would be spared to secure it. One major Confederate victory in Nashville with the conquering "rebel" army threatening the Union's rear unopposed would pose as a knife to the throat of Lincoln's administration. Under these conditions the likelihood of a Confederate advance on Washington could not be ruled out.

With only a scaled-down Union presence to resist him in his advance into Tennessee and with Sherman on the move far to the Southeast, Hood could move freely while resting and resupplying his beleaguered army at the expense of Northern storehouses. And, more important, after a Confederate victory in Nashville the whole country north of the Mason-Dixon line would be open before him, its major cities lying directly in his path unprotected. As proposed, with Nashville retaken and pushing northward to Louisville, Kentucky, Hood's plan centered on a bold attempt to force an unavoidable withdrawal of Sherman from Georgia in the pursuit of Hood's army, denying Grant reinforcements and taking pressure off Lee's besieged troops in nearby Virginia.

To offset Hood's plan to lure him out, the Federal Fourth and Twenty-third corps, including Major General James Wilson's Federal Cavalry Corps, were detached by Sherman and sent to Nashville as reinforcements under Thomas. Sherman and the bulk of his army would in time continue southeast on their devastating march through Georgia to the sea. From Hood's perspective, should Sherman follow through with his plan to march to the coast and thereafter join Grant, "Hood calculated that he could make his [own] movement through Tennessee and Kentucky and strike Grant in the rear two weeks before Sherman could reach Virginia."[3]

In the process of designing his preparations for the proposed invasion of Tennessee, Hood took careful deliberations before making his final decision. Throughout the first weeks of October 1864 the Army of Tennessee had been on the move. After the sober realization that Sherman had won the day in the hard-fought battles around Atlanta, Hood's army had eased off, slowly backtracking up the main roads northwest of Atlanta, occupying itself in the breaking up of Sherman's supply lines and communications in an attempt to lure him out.

On the 15th of October, while debating on the projected success of enticing Sherman to forsake his plan to march through Georgia and force him instead into a head-on confrontation, Hood brought his army into northwest Georgia to a small place known as Cross Roads located "in a beautiful valley about nine miles south of Lafayette." To many a mind the surrounding countryside must have kindled frightful memories of those never-to-be-forgotten days of September 1863, when only a few short miles up the Lafayette road the battle of Chickamauga, the most costly fight in the Western theatre, was waged. "At this time I received intelligence that on the 13th Sherman had reached Snake Creek Gap, where the right of his line had rested in the early spring of this year; also that he was marching in our pursuit, whilst [Confederate] General Wheeler was endeavoring to retard his advance as much as possible. I here determined to advance no farther toward the Tennessee River, but to select a position and deliver battle, since Sherman, at an earlier date than anticipated, had moved as far north as I had hoped to allure him."

At this point Hood was optimistic, as he was in a favorable position tactically. His disheartened troops had in his estimation recently received a noticeable improvement in morale. Not moving on impulse, he diligently sought out the advice of his general staff and junior officers regarding the question of entering into an all-out confrontation with Sherman. Did they agree with him as to the improved state of morale? Was the army geared up for combat? Without their consent he would not order battle. After consultation the verdict was clear, unanimous among the officer corps: "although the army had much improved in spirit it was not in condition to risk battle." According to intelligence reports indicating that Sherman's numerical strength far exceeded that of the Confederates (in addition to the poor state of morale it had found itself in for weeks), the "rebel General Hood" had to concede that his army was not yet ready for a full-on encounter with the Federals.

Although disappointed by the consensus, Hood well understood the difficulty, having observed the army's retrograde movements in northwest Georgia for weeks prior to his promotion to full command. In his judgment the element of prolonged, continuous back-tracking over the past months had badly weakened the army's confidence. The policy of surrendering valuable territory (which could not be regained) on a regular basis was insufferable and not to be tolerated. Alert to the fact that morale had seriously fallen far below anything previously experienced (as well as having thoroughly infected the army), Hood was quite uncertain that his soldiers would ever again regain their original, renowned fighting spirit. Working through it all, he chose to remain at Cross Roads for two days, engrossed "in serious thought and perplexity."

The stakes were high indeed, higher than he had ever dreamed. The fact that the destiny of an army now rested on his ability to coordinate his forces into the most effective plan possible weighed heavily on him. It had to work—and work well. Alternative options were thoroughly scrutinized and weighed for ultimate effectiveness. The general commanding the Army of Tennessee was entering into a high-risk arena of potential disaster. One serious slip could bring it all down around him. Never given to hesitation, Hood considered his viable options and pushed on:

> I could not offer battle [to Sherman] while the officers were unanimous in their opposition. Neither could I take an entrenched position with likelihood of advantageous results, since Sherman could do the same, repair the railroad, amass a large army, place [General George] Thomas in my front in command of the forces he afterward assembled at Nashville, and then, [Sherman] himself, move southward; or, as previously suggested, he could send Thomas into Alabama, whilst he marched through Georgia, and left me to follow in his rear. This last movement upon our part would be construed by the troops into a retreat, and could but result in disaster. In this dilemma I conceived the plan of marching into Tennessee with the hope to establish our line eventually in Kentucky, and determined to make the campaign which followed, unless withheld by General Beauregard or the authorities at Richmond.

In light of the fact that for the moment, battle with Sherman was an unwise and possibly dangerous move, Hood's plan for the Tennessee Campaign began to gel. He would "order a heavy reserve of artillery to accompany the army in order to overcome any serious opposition by the Federal gun-boats; to cross the Tennessee [River] at or near Guntersville, and again destroy Sherman's communications at Stevenson and Bridgeport; to move upon Thomas and Schofield, and to attempt to rout and capture their army before it could reach Nashville."

After the liberation of Nashville he would resupply and, if possible, reinforce the army from the surrounding countryside. If Sherman, instead of taking the bait and pursuing Hood's army (a preference General Hood reasoned he would not opt for), would "cut loose and move south," Hood would then move into Kentucky, forcing his opponent to eventually be encumbered with a host of logistical problems in the attempt to counteract Hood's move. Should Sherman decide instead to enforce Grant in Virginia it would be equally time consuming, involving journeys by both land and sea. Such tedious and pro-longed movements would allow Hood the time he needed to maneuver behind enemy lines unchecked. On the other hand, should Sherman take up the pursuit to follow Hood into Tennessee, Hood would be in position to offer battle. If Hood were successful in Sherman's defeat, the options would be open for Hood to send reinforcements to General Lee. Should Sherman either defeat him or refuse to do battle Hood would pass through the Cum-berland Mountains and "attack Grant in the rear." In the event Sherman should move to join forces with Grant, Hood would "pass through the Cum-berland gaps to Petersburg and attack Grant in the rear at least two weeks before Sherman could render him assistance."

Working in conjunction with General Lee's Army of Northern Virginia, the arrival of Hood's army on the field of battle would doubtless spell the end of Northern military aggression in Virginia. This particular strategy involving the merging together of the two great Confederate armies would in all prob-ability defeat Grant. Afterward, Hood would combine forces with the Army of Northern Virginia into one vast army on a permanent basis, with Lee in total command. The Confederate army would then be in perfect position to "march upon Washington or turn upon and annihilate Sherman."

It seemed that whatever course Sherman took, Hood was well prepared to retain the offensive. In any case that evolved, Hood would act immediately, according to a prearranged plan thoroughly approved by his staff and the Richmond authorities: "Such is the plan which during the 15th and 16th [of October], as we lay in bivouac near Lafayette, I maturely considered, and determined to carry out." The next day Hood crossed the Alabama line, in conformity with his preparations. After his arrival at Gadsden he met with Beauregard to hammer out the details: "I at once unfolded to him my plan, and requested that he confer apart with the corps commanders, Lieutenant Generals [S.D.] Lee and Stewart and Major General Cheatham. If after calm deliberation he deemed it expedient we should remain upon the Alabama line and attack Sherman, or take position, entrench, and finally follow on his rear when he should move south, I would of course acquiesce, albeit with reluctance. If, contrariwise, he should agree to my proposal into Tennessee, I would move immediately to Guntersville, thence to Stevenson, Bridgeport, and Nashville."

Throughout the remainder of the night, Hood, in consultation with his superior, analyzed the proposed plan. With maps spread before them and with no time to lose, the command structure of the Army of Tennessee exam-ined every detail of the proposition to take the war again into Northern ter-ritory. Knowing by personal experience the unsuccessful outcomes of two prior attempts made by General Lee to accomplish a similar objective, Hood was indeed striking out boldly:

> After he [Beauregard] had held a separate conference with the corps commanders, we again debated several hours over the course of action to be pursued; and, during the interview, I discovered that he had gone to work in earnest to ascertain, in person, the true condition of the army that he had sought information not only from the corps commanders, but from a number of officers and had reached the same conclusion I had formed at Lafayette: that we were not competent to offer pitched battle to Sherman, nor could we follow him south without causing our retrograde movement to be construed by the troops into a recurrence of retreat, which would entail desertions and render the army of little or no use in its opposition to the enemy's march through Georgia.
>
> After two days' deliberation General Beauregard authorized me, on the evening of the 21st of October, to proceed to the execution of my plan of operations into Tennessee. General Beauregard's approval of a forward movement into Tennessee was soon made known to the army. The prospect of again entering that state created great enthusiasm and from the different encampments arose at intervals that genuine Confederate shout so familiar to every Southern soldier, and which then betokened an improved state of feeling among the troops.[4]

So it was that in those fateful days of autumn 1864 the two opposing armies of the Western theatre of the war encamped within close proximity of each other, watching and waiting. General Hood, after a series of daring adventures that baffled all Sherman's calculations ("He can turn and twist like a fox," said Sherman, "and wear out my army in pursuit"), concentrated his entire force except Forrest's cavalry at Gadsden, Alabama, on the 22d of October, while General Sherman established his headquarters at Gaylesville, a "position," he wrote to General Halleck, "very good to watch the enemy."[5]

Though General Hood's plan had considerable merit it would ultimately fail. After enduring several unusually vicious and costly battles at Franklin, Murfreesboro, and Nashville, Tennessee, the surviving remnant of the Army of Tennessee would soon find itself crippled, limping and staggering and withdrawing down the long miles southward, leaving bloody footprints in the snow, defending itself from the relentless attacks of the massive Federal cavalry corps. The final days of the Tennessee Campaign, fraught with terribly severe weather, would be as miserable and trying as any American soldiers would ever be called upon to suffer.

Despite the brutal hardships the Southern army would prove over the coming days of mid–December 1864 that while badly beaten it was by no means conquered. Collective Southern resolve and fortitude would rise with each encounter, skillfully fending off the repeated attempts of a ruthless, pursuing Federal cavalry of enormous numerical magnitude determined to surround and finish them off. Trudging back in a humiliating retreat over the frozen landscape and far from the lofty objective of carrying the war into

Northern territory, the Confederate army's only goal in the end would be
sheer survival: Across the Alabama line and the Tennessee River to safety.
Would they make it or die in the attempt?

Thomas, Ice, and U.S. Grant: December 11, 1864, Nashville, Tennessee

In mid–December, caught in the throes of a brutal ice storm, Union
General George Thomas, within earshot of Hood's defiant troops entrenched
on the surrounding Nashville hills, pondered his options of attacking Hood.
Having withheld his assault on Hood's forces due to the persistent presence
of inclement weather, he had sufficiently provoked the Washington authorities
for what they perceived as his customary practice of being excessively cautious. Lt. General U.S. Grant, located in far-off Virginia, soon entered the
picture by way of telegraph. Despite the unusually harsh weather, he wanted
action. There would be no further postponement of troop movement, regardless of the dangers involved:

> Major General George Thomas
> Nashville, Tennessee
>
> If you delay [to] attack [Hood] longer, the mortifying spectacle will be witnessed of a
> rebel army moving for the Ohio River and you will be forced to act, accepting such
> weather as you find. Let there be no further delay.
>
> U.S. Grant
> Lieutenant General
> City Point, VA. December 11, 1864

George Thomas's reply was brief and to the point. He would obey. But being
on hand at the battle site and therefore personally apprised of the situation,
he was keenly aware of the ill-advised council:

> Lt. General U.S. Grant; City Point
>
> … I will obey the order as promptly as possible, however much I may regret it, as the
> attack [upon Hood] will have to be made under every disadvantage. The whole coun-
> try is covered with a perfect sheet of ice and sleet, and it is with difficulty the troops
> are able to move about on level ground. It was my intention to attack Hood as soon
> as the ice melted, and would have done so yesterday had it not been for the storm.
>
> Geo. H. Thomas U.S. Volunteers Commanding
> Nashville, December 11, 1864.[6]

With a momentary lull in the severe weather now in view, Thomas prepared
for the long-awaited attack. Against the advice of his military superiors in
distant Washington he had chosen to wait for the most advantageous moment.
That moment was soon to arrive.

NASHVILLE, TENN. December 12, 1864 10.30 p.m.

Major General H.W. Halleck,

Washington, D. C.:

I have the troops ready to make the attack on the enemy as soon as the sleet which now covers the ground has melted sufficiently to enable the men to march. As the whole country is now covered with a sheet of ice so hard and slippery it is utterly impossible for troops to ascend the slopes, or even move over level ground in anything like order. It has taken the entire day to place my cavalry in position, and it has only been finally effected with imminent risk and many serious accidents, resulting from the number of horses falling with their riders on the roads. Under these circumstances I believe an attack at this time would only result in a useless sacrifice of life.[7]

Geo. H. Thomas,
Major General, U.S. Volunteers, Commanding.

Nevertheless, he had no choice. The order was given, the die cast. Union commander George Henry Thomas would soon move upon Hood's threadbare army in full force, setting off a most remarkable and decisive chain of events.

1

Friday, December 16, 1864

Hood's Devasted Confederate Army in Full Retreat

The suffering of the winter of 1864–65 ... these [Confederate] veterans encountered, cannot be forgotten.[1]

"The sleet and severe freezes had made the surface of the earth a sheet of ice. Nearly one-fourth of the men were still barefooted, yet plodded "their weary way" under these adverse circumstance (many with bleeding feet)…. I pressed every pair of shoes which could be found for them, and in many instances the citizens gave them second-hand shoes, which but partially supplied the demand"[2] (Reports of Major General William B. Bate, CSA).

Friday, December 16, 1864, the Second and Final Day of the Battle for Nashville

"December 16.—A general attack was commenced early this morning on our entire [Confederate] line, and all the enemy's assaults repulsed, with heavy loss, till 3.30 p.m., when our line suddenly gave way to the left of the center, causing in a few moments our lines to give way at all points, our troops retreating rapidly and in some confusion down the Franklin pike"[3] (Journal of the Army of Tennessee). The weather in middle Tennessee fit the solemn occasion on the morning of the 16th of December 1864, "a gloomy, drizzly, dark day."[4] The dim sunlight had barely broken through the thick fog as a murky, foreboding day slowly unfolded for the Confederacy. The ominous, shadowy morning of the 16th was doubtless similar in character to the previous day. Almost surreal, the first light of dawn crept slowly over the dark forms of two armies spread out on the hillsides south of Nashville. "The morning of the 15th was dark and somber; a heavy fall of fog and smoke rested on the face of the earth and enveloped every object in darkness"[5] (Report of Brig. Gen. T.J. Wood, USA, commanding Fourth Army Corps).

Following months of extreme privation, the wretched state of affairs for the Army of Tennessee had at last culminated in a prolonged siege by General George Henry Thomas's well-fortified city of Nashville, commencing from the 2nd of December as the ragged, tenacious Confederate army shivered in frozen ditches through the icy grip of one of the worst winters on record: "The weather was very severe and the suffering of the men was great. There was no supply of shoes, and the men covered their bare feet with rawhide taken from animals freshly slaughtered. Hundreds of Tennesseans passed their own doors on the march without halting, and many were in sight of their homes when the guns opened."[6]

> December 11, 10:00 a.m.—There is a meeting of corps commanders at General Thomas' headquarters. It is decided that we cannot attack the enemy with any show of success until the weather moderates and the snow and sleet now on the ground thaws. The ground is yet covered with a cake of ice, and it is very difficult to move over it. The weather still continues very cold below the freezing point[7] [Journal of the Fourth Army Corps].

"[O]wing to the whole surface of the country being covered with ice … it [was] almost impossible for men or animals to move over uneven ground"[8] (Report of Major General James B. Steedman, U.S. Army). "Both armies were ice-bound for a week previous to the 14th of December, when the weather moderated[9] (Major General George Thomas)." "[A] heavy rain setting in General Thomas delayed his operations. Snow, sleet, and intense cold followed, covering the ground so thickly with ice as to render it impossible to move cavalry not specially shod for such an occasion. In fact, neither infantry nor cavalry could have marched over a country so undulating and broken as that separating our lines from those of the enemy"[10] (Reports of General James H. Wilson, USA, commanding Cavalry Corps).

At approximately 9:00 a.m. on that eventful morning of the 16th of December, Lt. General Stephen D. Lee, CSA—located with his divisions of Maj. General Carter L. Stevenson and Maj. General Henry D. Clayton in the center of Hood's line just south of Nashville along the Franklin pike—directed his attention to his immediate front. Menacing forms barely visible through the thick fog were forming opposite. A considerable force was gathering strength against him. Another deadly engagement, similar to that of the day before, would soon break upon the defiant Southern army.

As the second days' battle opened, the men of Hood's army rose to meet it. For the next several hours Lee's Corps dug in hard as the fighting began in earnest all along Hood's front. Bracing for the coming Federal assault, S.D. Lee's corps waited out the deafening bombardment—an awful combination of severe, prolonged Federal artillery barrages followed by a series of reckless infantry assaults several ranks deep moving upon the right flank, approaching within thirty yards of the Confederate line of battle. "[T]he enemy, having placed a large number of guns in position, opened a terrible artillery fire upon my [Lee's] line, principally on the Franklin Pike.... They came up in several lines of battle. My men reserved their fire until they [the advancing Federals] were within easy range, and then delivered it with terrible effect. The assault was easily repulsed"[11] (Report of Lieutenant General Stephen D. Lee, CSA, commanding Army Corps of operations, November 2–December 17, 1864).

Suffering grievous losses with each failed attempt, by 3:30 that afternoon the Union advance ultimately stalled, being repelled with decisive force. Clayton's division of Lee's Corps (the brigades of Holtzclaw, Gibson, and Stovall, with Pettus's brigade of Stevenson's, each destined to figure prominently in the days just ahead) had performed admirably. Highly praised in later reports for their "conspicuous and soldierly conduct" in countering the recurring Federal advances made upon their lines, the Confederate position in the center had remained unmoved. Clayton had held. The Federal charge in Lee's front was broken[12] (Report of Lieutenant General Stephen D. Lee, CSA, commanding Army Corps of operations, November 2–December 17, 1864).

"Their success the previous day had emboldened them, and they rushed forward with great spirit, only to be driven back with dreadful slaughter. Finding at last that they could make no impression upon our lines, they relinquished their attempt and contented themselves with keeping up an incessant fire of small-arms at long-range and an artillery fire which I have never seen surpassed for heaviness, continuance, and accuracy. This state of things continued until evening, doing, however, but little damage, my men keeping closely in the trenches and perfectly cool and confident." In a moment the storm had broken upon them in all its ferocity, lashing their defenseless bodies with icy hail and shrapnel. The lurid flash of artillery guns piercing through the thick haze gave a mere seconds warning of what was to come. As if drawn up from the deep, from the belly of some terrifying prehistoric monster, shot and shell burst forth, shrieking overhead and exploding in every direction. Growling and hissing, the beast roared, shaking the very earth and raining fire down upon them, indiscriminately slashing to bits anything and everything in its path.[13] (Report of Major General Carter L. Stevenson, CSA, commanding Division of operations, September 29–December 17, 1864). J.A. Dozier, a private in Co. B, 18th Alabama Infantry, Brigadier General James Holtzclaw's brigade, which was positioned behind a "stone fence" on the left of the Franklin pike, witnessed the desperate but ineffective charges of the United States Colored Troops of the 19th Indiana advancing upon the Confederate lines in waves, only to be repulsed and driven back. "The ground was almost covered with [the USCT troops], and in other places they lay in heaps."[14] "The [Union] dead lay thick on the ground as we could see, and we kept up the firing.... They seemed at last to be convinced that we could not

be driven out of our line, and they retired beyond the reach of our guns...."[15]
Wave upon wave the Federal regiments advanced, pushing forward into the
Confederate works. But for most of them, they never again saw the light of
day. They came only to die.

> At 12 p.m. the enemy made a most determined charge on my [Holtzclaw's] right.
> Placing a Negro brigade in front, they gallantly dashed up to the abatis, forty feet in
> front, and were killed by hundreds. Pressed on by their white brethren in the rear
> they continued to come up in masses to the abatis, but they came only to die. I have
> seen most of the battlefields of the West, but never saw dead men thicker than in
> front of my two right regiments; the great masses and disorder of the enemy enabling
> the left to rake them in flank, while the right, with a coolness unexampled, scarcely
> threw away a shot at their front. The enemy at last broke and fled in wild disorder"[16]
> [Report of Brigadier General James T. Holtzclaw, CSA, commanding Brigade of oper-
> ations November 20–December 27, 1864].

From the Union point of view it was equally heartbreaking. After the cheers
had faded and the battle smoke had cleared, the same painful sight met their
eyes. Men in blue lay strewn about the ground like piles of straw haphazardly
scattered over the landscape. Some mercifully were dead in an instant; others,
writhing in agony, awaited their turn. Although courageous in the extreme,
the impetuous charge had achieved little. "The [Union] assault was made,
and received by the enemy with a tremendous fire of grape and canister and
musketry; our men moved steadily onward up the hill until near the crest,
when the reserve of the enemy rose and poured into the assaulting column
a most destructive fire, causing the men first to waver and then to fall back,
leaving their dead and wounded—black and white indiscriminately mingled
lying amid the abatis, the gallant Colonel Post among the wounded"[17] (Report
of Maj. Gen. George H. Thomas, USA, commanding Department of the Cumberland).

The single most important objective of such reckless audacity was for
the purpose of distracting the Confederate artillery. If the advancing infantry
could "draw the fire of the enemy" upon themselves, it was hoped the remaining troops (those not immediately gunned down) would be of sufficient force
to scale the abatis and silence the guns. Without question, those in front
would die by the hundreds:

> The front of the assaulting force was covered with a cloud of skirmishers, who had
> been ordered to advance rapidly, for the purpose of drawing the fire of the enemy, as
> far as possible, and to annoy his artillerists, and to prevent, as much as it could be
> done, the working of his guns. The assaulting force was instructed to move steadily
> forward to within a short distance of the enemy's works, and then, by a "bold burst,"
> ascend the steep ascent, cross the abatis, dash over the rude but strong parapet, and
> secure the coveted goal.
> The troops were full of enthusiasm, and the splendid array in which the advance
> was made gave hopeful promise of success. Near the foot of the ascent the assaulting

force dashed forward for the last great effort. It was welcomed with a most terrific fire of grape and canister and musketry; but its course was onward. When near, however, the enemy's works (a few of our men, stouter of limb and steadier of movement, had already entered his line) his reserves on the slope of the hill rose and poured in a fire before which no troops could live. Unfortunately, the casualties had been particularly heavy among the officers, and more unfortunately still, when he had arrived almost at the abatis, while gallantly leading his brigade, the chivalric Post was struck down by a grape-shot and his horse killed under him. The brigade—its battalions bleeding, torn, and broken—first halted and then began to retire; but there was little disorder and nothing of panic. The troops promptly halted and were readily reformed by their officers. But for the unfortunate fall of Colonel Post, the commander of the assaulting brigade, I think the attack would have succeeded. I had watched the assault with a keen and anxious gaze. It was made by troops whom I had long commanded and whom I had learned to love and admire for their noble deeds on many a hard-fought field[18] [Report of Brig. Gen. T.J. Wood, USA, Commanding Fourth Army Corps].

Disregarding the futility of the initial charge, two hours later the order was reiterated and a second major infantry assault poured across Holtzclaw's front, all to no avail. As expected, the immediate Confederate response compelled the enemy to stay well protected for the interval, opting for a deafening artillery barrage and the exchange of small arms fire. "At 2 p.m. the enemy attempted a second charge, less determined than the first. Their brave officers could neither lead nor drive their men to such certain death.... The shelling of the enemy's batteries between 12 and 3 p.m. was the most furious I ever witnessed, while the range so precise that scarce a shell failed to explode in the line. The enemy seemed now to be satisfied that he could not carry my position, and contented himself by shelling and sharpshooting everything in sight"[19] (General James T. Holtzclaw, CSA).

As the sun began to set over the war-torn landscape, the 18th Alabama and those stationed nearby found themselves in a jubilant disposition. "All were rejoicing at the victory won," and "were in fine spirits and confident of success," Confederate General S.D. Lee subsequently reported, unaware of the fateful events then taking place along the left-center of the line. Turning their attention in that direction and peering into the heavy mist, the 18th observed puffs of smoke coming from distant Confederate batteries stationed on the far left. Strangely, the batteries were pointed in the wrong direction. Through the thick fog it was difficult to make out what had happened. Suddenly, the realization struck. The Federals had broken through, captured a battery, and were bombarding the Confederate left. Bate's Florida units had, without warning, collapsed and fallen in upon themselves, exposing the entire army to the advancing Federal troops of Generals John Schofield and A.J. Smith, who were in the process of quickly surrounding them. "All his [Federal] assaults were repulsed with heavy loss till 3:30 PM, when a portion of our line to the left of the center, occupied by Bate's Division, suddenly gave way. Up to this time, no battle ever progressed more favorably; the troops in excellent spirits, waving their colors and bidding defiance to the enemy"[20] (Reports of General John B. Hood, CSA, commanding the Army of Tennessee).

"[C]ontending against three to one [odds], and being flanked on both sides,"[21] the Confederate lines left of center were forced to yield. The War for Southern Independence hung precariously in the balance as the Confederate lines pitched, heaved, and wavered, finally giving in as the Yankees poured through like water through a bursting dam. "About 4:00 p.m. I saw the left suddenly give way three or four brigades distant from me. Almost instantaneously the line crumbled away till it reached me"[22] (Report of Brigadier General James T. Holtzclaw, CSA, commanding Brigade of Operations, November 20–December 27, 1864). Forced to retire "under the destructive fire of eighteen guns, 600 yards distant, sweeping almost an open plain," Holtzclaw, without the aid of his staff, gathered his dispersed command "about one mile from the field" along the pike, being "directed by the Major General [Clayton] commanding, to take position as rear guard of the army"[23] (Report of Brigadier General James T. Holtzclaw, CSA, commanding Brigade of operations, November 20–December 27, 1864).

In scarcely a moment, all was lost on the left Confederate line. "[S]uddenly all eyes were turned to the center of our line of battle near the Granny White pike," Lee later wrote in his official report. A sudden breakthrough had occurred, men "flying to the rear in the wildest confusion."[24] The enemy was on their heels and closing in fast, heading for his left. Reacting quickly, Major General Edward Johnson's division took up the task of repelling them, but in vain. All was irreplaceably lost. The onrushing movements of the Federal charge advanced swiftly, taking Lee's rear and threatening his left flank (Report of Lieutenant General Stephen D. Lee, CSA, commanding Army Corps of operations November 2–December 17, 1864).

The Confederate Army in Full Retreat

Because of a heavy mist and rain settling in around noon, the entire field was covered in a dark shroud, greatly limiting visibility. Stevenson, positioned "a short distance from the left of the Franklin pike," was unaware of what had happened. Soon enough he would learn that the Confederate lines on the far left had crumbled. With few exceptions the entire army was dispersing and taking flight. "Toward evening General Lee sent me information that things were going badly on the left"[25] (Report of Major General Carter L. Stevenson, CSA, commanding Division of operations September 29–

December 17, 1864). "The result [of the Federal breakthrough] was decisive. The whole Confederate left was crushed in like an eggshell, and the rout quickly spread to the rest of the line. In General Hood's own words, he 'beheld for the first and only time a Confederate army abandon the field in confusion.' The actual losses in killed and wounded had been very light on each side; General Hood admits that he lost fifty-four pieces of artillery; his loss of prisoners was numbered in thousands."[26] "I [Gen. Hood] was seated upon my horse not far in rear when the breach was effected, and soon discovered that all hope to rally the troops was vain. I did not, I might say, anticipate a break at that time, as our forces up to that moment had repulsed the Federals at every point, and were waving their colors in defiance, crying out to the enemy, 'Come on, come on.'"[27]

Having accomplished the initial breakthrough, Thomas's troops kept up the momentum, sweeping all before them. As Federal artillery rained iron and fire on the exposed Confederate left, the Yankee infantry charged ahead, rolling up the Confederate line and putting them on the run, including a drummer boy of the 46th Alabama, a dozen or so infantrymen, and their captain. "In the afternoon the enemy concentrated a number of guns on an exposed point, and massed a body of infantry against it. Under cover of artillery fire, this body charged and broke through the Confederate line, which soon after gave way at all points. At first, of course, there was more or less confusion; but order was soon restored."[28]

Late in the evening on the 16th Gen. Bates' division on the extreme left gave way. That caused the Federals to turn our left flank so they could form a line across our left and charge our line on the flank, which compelled the right to give up the ditches and fall back. The ground was so boggy we couldn't run. The stoutest soon got ahead. I [drummer] think I was among the hindmost with my drum on my back when a Federal not over fifty yards away called to me, saying: "Stop, you little devil, with that drum!" I jumped behind a tree, looked back, and saw that he was going in different direction. I went as fast as I could to a rock fence and clambored over it. I was then on the road and could travel faster. I did not go far until I met Gen. S.D. Lee on his horse with a battle flag in his hands appealing to the men to form a line there. He told me to beat the long roll. I did so and expected to receive a bullet, but to my surprise the Federals began to retreat. They thought it was our reserve being called into line of battle when they heard the drum. Our brigade and Cummings' Brigade rallied to General Lee and in a little while a battery of artillery joined us in a run. I never saw cannons discharge canister shot as fast during the war. Pettus' Brigade, Cummings Brigade and Colby's Battery saved our supply train from being captured. The two brigades and the battery covered Hood's retreat two days and nights. The Federal cavalry tried hard to capture us.[29]

I [Capt. George E. Brewer] was in charge of my regiment, the 46th Alabama, and know that we were not driven out, nor do I believe we could have been.... The enemy being in front, flank and rear, the retreat became a rout. It was the only rout of which I was ever a participant. The woods and pike were filled with stragglers making to the rear. I saw Generals Pettus, Stevenson, Lee, and other officers trying to rally the men, but without avail. I was among the very last, owing to the time lost in trying to get my men out.... By this time I had come up with a few of my own men that were known to be cool and determined. We reached the pike near the crest of a hill over-looking the battle ground. Two pieces of artillery were there, but seemed to have been abandoned. Looking back, the enemy pursuing seemed but little better organ-ized than the Confederates, but were simply straggling along, firing upon the Con-federates. I asked the handful of men with me to give the advance a few rounds. They did so readily, and others coming along joined us. Something like a dozen stood together shooting as fast as they could load. It resulted in a check to the enemy's advance, and we resumed marching to the rear. After going some distance, we found a line of some two or three hundred drawn up facing towards the foe. There were six-teen stands of colors in this short line. After waiting awhile, the enemy again came into view; but it only took a few rounds to make them drop back under cover of the hill. After waiting awhile, as they appeared no more, we continued our course back toward Franklin, our numbers constantly increasing. Several miles were put between us and the enemy, when about 10 or 11 p.m. we bivouacked. Lee, Stevenson and Pettus were there.[30]

Although shocked and overwhelmed over what had transpired, the Southerners held out to the last, then retired. "Late in the afternoon our lines were broken away to the left. We [Confederates] held our position until the last moment, and were the last to leave the field covering Hood's retreat."[31] "About dark Gibson's Louisiana Brigade formed the rear guard to protect our badly demoralized army."[32] By no means content to allow the enemy the advantage, S.D. Lee burst upon the scene, heading straight into the action on the Franklin pike, riding "until he reached the rear of Stevenson's Division … right into the midst of the fugitives and the face of the enemy, who by this time had reached the rear of Pettus's Brigade." Grasping a stand of colors, General Lee held them aloft. "Rally men, rally! For God's sake, rally! … This is the place for brave men to die!"[33] Lee's quick and courageous action momen-tarily halted the onrushing Federal tide as a number of regimental colors quickly gathered about him. With the Union advance briefly checked, the Confederates held, allowing sufficient time for Clayton's division to form a line of battle in Lee's rear.

From the Federal perspective, "all had caught the inspiration, and officers of all grades and the men, each and every one, seemed to vie with each other in a generous rivalry" as they rushed uncontrollably through the fog, sweep-ing the ground before them in a wide arc, breaking into the Confederate left and assaulting the works. "[T]he attack on all parts of the enemy's line was resistless"[34] (Report of Brig. Gen. T.J. Wood, USA, commanding Fourth Army Corps). "Pressed on all sides, and perceiving that further resistance was futile if not impossible, the Confederates broke and fled in confusion from the field, leaving nearly all their Artillery and many prisoners to fall into our hands"[35] (James Harrison Wilson, Major-General, USV, Brevet Major-

General, USA, "The Union Cavalry in the Hood Campaign"). "In a conflict of this nature I knew we would have greatly the advantage of him, as our supply of ammunition was inexhaustible and his limited"[36] (Report of Brig. Gen. T.J. Wood, USA, commanding Fourth Army Corps).

Earlier that morning, Brigadier General James Chalmers' Confederate Cavalry Division had been ordered to position itself on the Hillsborough Pike, a few miles west of Lee's position near the Franklin pike, presumably to hold the road open and keep it in possession should the need arise for the army to withdraw under fire. Chalmers responded by placing the brigade of Col. Edmund Rucker near the point where the road stretching from Brentwood connects with the Hillsborough Pike. Rucker had hardly gotten situated when the action began in earnest. Hoofbeats sounded in close proximity and drew even closer. In the semidarkness it was nearly impossible to know with certainty who was approaching. Before Rucker was aware of it, elements of the 9th Illinois and 12th Tennessee Federal cavalry units had surrounded him, bringing on a fierce saber and pistol duel, recalled by some as the worst they had encountered during the war. Overcome and unable to differentiate between the enemy and his own men, Rucker was soon captured but not before he had bought precious time for the Confederate army's unhindered withdrawal. Due in part to the dense darkness and in part to their earnestness to take on Chalmers' horsemen, the Federal cavalry had become temporarily disorganized. "He [Hatch] had not proceeded far before he encountered Chalmers' division of cavalry, and, although it was then almost dark, attacked it with the greatest promptitude and vigor, driving it from a strong position behind rail breast-works. Brigadier-General Rucker, commanding a brigade, a number of prisoners, and the division battle-flag were captured. The night was so dark and wet, and the men and horses so jaded, that it was not deemed practicable to push the pursuit farther"[37] (Reports of Bvt. Major General James H. Wilson, USA, commanding Cavalry Corps, Military Division of the Mississippi of operations, October 24, 1864–February 1, 1865).

The [Union] cavalrymen had, however, become separated from their horses by an unusual distance, and ... were hurried forward as rapidly as possible.... Croxton, who was most available, was ordered to mount and push without delay through Brentwood, to be followed by Hatch and Hammond as soon as they could mount.... [I]t had become so dark before they were well under way in pursuit that the men could scarcely see their horses' ears. It was a rainy and disagreeable night, but nevertheless Hatch, Knipe, Croxton, Hammond, Coon, and Spalding dashed forward, each vying with the other for the advance, and each doing his best to reach the Franklin turnpike that night so as to drive the now thoroughly disorganized enemy from his last line of retreat[38] [James Harrison Wilson, Major-General, USV, Brevet Major-General, USA, "The Union Cavalry in the Hood Campaign"].

Stevenson, still engaged with the enemy and unaware of the severity of

3A   21

HOOD'S RETREAT

DEC. 16, 1864

In this neighborhood, late in the evening of his decisive defeat at Nashville, Hood reorganized his army for withdrawal southward. Lt. Gen. Stephen D. Lee's Corps, supported by Chalmers' Cavalry Division, covered the withdrawal, fighting continuously until the army bivouacked near Spring Hill, 21 mi. S., the night of Dec. 17th.

TENNESSEE   HISTORICAL   COMMISSION

Tennessee State Marker: The Withdrawal Begins.

the situation, was soon forced to concede defeat. A dreaded sense of retreat hung in the air. With no other alternative, the remaining Confederate lines suddenly began to fold. "When the true situation of affairs became apparent, and it was evident that the whole army, with the exception of my division and Clayton's, had been broken and scattered, the order for their withdrawal was given..."[39] (Report of Major General Carter L. Stevenson, CSA, commanding Division of Operations, September 29–December 17, 1864).

"There was no fight left in them"

"From this point the whole of Hood's army crumbled right and left. Their backbone had been broken two weeks before at Franklin. There was no fight left in them."[40] Stunned at the sight, Pvt. Dozier and the 18th Alabama, posted near the center, observed dim outlines through the dense fog and battle smoke. The left of the line had crumbled and was giving way. Then the ominous order came—"Every man for himself!"—resulting in the ensuing mayhem of a sudden, rapid withdrawal, stampeding troops making their best efforts at an escape south alongside the pike through "fields, woods, and ... streams."[41] Scores of fleeing Confederates fell into enemy hands in the dash southward, captured by Federal cavalry before reaching the relative safety of Franklin. "I heard the command, Retreat! for the first time in battle. And for the first time I showed the enemy my heels."[42] "The enemy, hopelessly broken, fled in confusion through the Brentwood Pass, the [Union] Fourth Corps in a close pursuit, which was continued for several miles, when darkness closed the scene"[43] (Report of Maj. Gen. George H. Thomas, USA, commanding Department of the Cumberland). "Amid the indescribable confusion of other troops, and with the enemy pouring in their fire upon their flanks and from the front—having rushed toward the break and then forward when they perceived that the troops on my left had broken—it was impossible to withdraw the command in order, and it became considerably broken and confused. Many of them were unable to get out of the ditches in time and were captured"[44] (Report of Major General Carter L. Stevenson, CSA, commanding Division of operations, September 29–December 17, 1864). Many Confederates simply surrendered at the works. For them, four years of the worst struggle in the nation's young history had finally come to an end. An indefinite stay in a dreaded Federal prison must have seemed a partial relief compared to the present degree of misery.

For a brief moment, as the onrushing bluecoats swept across the lines as leaves before a strong wind, the fate of an army hung in mid-air. "The whole army, except this division, Pettus's brigade of Stevenson's division and the Thirty-ninth Georgia regiment of Cummings' brigade, also of Stevenson's division, which had a short time before been sent to me as a support and held in reserve, was then in complete rout."[45] Had the Union army, in the instant of its unanticipated victory, seized the opportunity and taken the occasion to use its considerable resources to its fullest, within a matter of hours the Army of Tennessee would have ceased to exist. "[T]he wonder is that Thomas, with a large and well-appointed army, more than treble the strength of Hood, did not press his right, seize the Franklin turnpike and capture the entire army."[46]

We [Confederates] retreated nearly two miles ... during which time quite a number gave down, already weak and worn. They sought protection in ditches, although it was raining and very muddy, while some were killed while retreating.... After having to run nearly two miles up hill in the rain, with our wet baggage holding us to the mud, we could not feel free. All was confusion among us and the enemy was pressing our flank. Their artillery was playing on each side of the Pike at long range.... We found the Pike worked up shoe-mouth deep. By this time it was not the question, "where is my regiment" but "where is a comrade or personal friend?" It was a sad and weary night as we marched to the rear with no human hope to encourage us. The Army was greatly reduced and what few men were left seemed incapable of any important service.[47]

Cavalry commander Major General James Harrison Wilson, USA, was nothing if not determined. On the afternoon of the 16th he was full swing into the pursuit. In a message to Brigadier General Johnson, who was commanding the Sixth Division Cavalry, Wilson laid out his intentions. By the next day his entire force would be brought to bear upon the fleeing Confederates. With a captured Confederate communique in his hands, Wilson could read more than what was written. Hood's army was in a bind. According to the message, General Hood was heavily relying on his cavalry to give his army time to escape. The immediate threat was Wilson's mounted troopers. At the moment, only they had the mobility and thrust to reach the Confederates with any degree of threatening power. The way things were quickly shaping up offered a solemn portent. The results of the ensuing struggle would greatly depend on the success or failure of the Union cavalry commander's elite divisions.

Eight miles south of Nashville on the Granny White pike, Wilson dictated a brief order: "[K]eep crowding the enemy and try to get into Franklin. Shove him as closely as possible; give him no peace. A dispatch from General Hood, captured with General Rucker, says the safety of his army depends upon the ability of Chalmers to keep us off; time is all he wants. Don't give him any. I will meet you somewhere on the Harpeth River tomorrow with the whole force." Ending his order, Wilson took a look at the surrounding set of circumstnces. So far, all had gone well, extremely well. With more than a hint of satisfaction, he added, "This has been a splendid day."[48]

In the early evening of the 16th of December, well into the sweeping Union charge over the Confederate trenches, General George Thomas received a telegraphed message. It was a personal note of congratulations from the president of the United States. Quite pleased with the army's successes the previous day, Mr. Lincoln evidently saw that an expression of national gratitude was in order: "Please accept for yourself, officers, and men the nation's thanks for your good work of yesterday." To receive a letter from the nation's president was no trifling matter; and one commending duty and performance on a major field of battle surely added to the weight of its importance. But the praise was brief. As Thomas read on, the tone of the message stiffened: "You made a magnificent beginning. A grand consummation is within your easy reach."

It is interesting to note that the president sent congratulations as well as his instructions directly to George Thomas, not through the regular channels of military protocol. The president was skipping over the heads of the

War Department as well as Thomas's superiors and communicating with him directly and personally. One can only surmise the awkward combination of elation and embarrassment that must have surrounded Thomas. As to the letter's contents, the previous day's work, however successful, was to be construed only as a beginning. Thomas was to bring it all to a "grand consummation." Mr. Lincoln's admonition left no doubt as to his intended meaning. Thomas needed to be reminded of his duty and of the critical reality of the situation he was confronted with. His job was far from over. And as is so true in the polical/military combination, Abraham Lincoln—sitting cozily in Washington, D.C.— was under the distinct impression that with the successes of the 15th the culmination of Union victories for the remainder of the battle (the field of which was literally covered in sheets of solid ice) would be "within easy reach." And finally, as if it were not clear enough, the president ended his note of thanks with a hammer blow: "Do not let it slip."[49]

What had begun with a word of congratulation and thanks for a hard-won day had ended with an order that must have chilled Thomas to the bone. As commander in chief, the president of the United States had given him a directive, personally. General Thomas was ordered to win the contest at Nashville. The president had concluded that it would be an easy task. There would be little, if any, room for failure. What General Thomas may have easily percieved was that this would not be the last time he would feel the heat from Washington. And he would have been right. Relatively soon he would be the recepient of additional letters of the same nature. Not only had he endured them during the siege of the previous two weeks, he was to deal with the goading impatience of the authorities for the rest of the month. Nevertheless, Thomas's immediate reply glowed with praise for the army's efforts on the 16th as he outlined the details of the day's events, leaving nothing unsaid as to the completeness of the Union victory.

Notable among the Confederate ranks of defenders holding in check the forward advance of Federal cavalry streaming down the turnpike was the stalwart Seventh Alabama. "Mere youths," as described by a participant, the Seventh was composed of young men from Alabama University whose "unconquerable tenacity" and "brilliant valor" had enabled them to fight through the overwhelming odds arrayed against them "until their ranks were cut to pieces," the sight of which "excited general notice and praise."[50] By the onset of late evening, the Confederate army, enveloped in an "inky black" darkness brought on by dense fog mixed with a ceaseless, soaking rain, attempted a general reorganization of its scattered command a "few hundred yards from the abandoned line of battle." Pulling themselves together, the dispersed remnants of Hood's command commenced its long and harried journey south, sheltered from numerous Federal cavalry charges by Chalmers' division.[51]

True to the now familiar concept that this war, however ferocious, was yet a "gentleman's war," Union cavalry commander General Wilson could not neglect an occasion to express his admiration for the enemy's military expertise when warranted. Chalmers' effort on the evening of the 16th of December 1864 was no exception.

A Rear Guard Operation

Hatch's [Union Cavalry] column had not gone more than two miles when its advance under Colonel Spalding encountered Chalmers's cavalry strongly posted across the road behind a fence-rail barricade.

It was a scene of pandemonium, in which every challenge was answered by a saber stroke or pistol shot, and the flash of the carbine was the only light by which the combatants could recognize each other's position. The gallant Confederates were driven in turn from every fresh position taken up by them, and the running fight was kept up till nearly midnight. Chalmers had, however, done the work cut out for him gallantly and well. He was overborne and driven back, it is true, but the delay which he forced upon the Federal cavalry by the stand he had made was sufficient to enable the fleeing Confederate infantry to sweep by the danger-point that night, to improvise a rear guard, and to make good their retreat the next day[52] [James Harrison Wilson, Major-General, USV, Brevet Major-General, USA, "The Union Cavalry in the Hood Campaign"].

This one incident, the bold stand of Chalmers' cavalry enforcing a postponement of Wilson's assaults subsequent to the Union breakthrough, may well have been the initial action that rescued Hood's army, enabling it to reform and then commence the retreat in full. According to one account Wilson's dismounted cavalry had made "the fatal mistake" of allowing themselves to get beyond the quick reach of their mounts, delaying any possibility of rapid pursuit until nightfall. "[W]ith night came a drenching rain. Two miles from the battle-field they [Wilson's cavalry] came upon Chalmers' cavalry division, which was covering the Confederate retreat."[53] Regardless of the appalling situation confronting the Confederates, eventually Chalmers was able to check Wilson's advance, providing a temporary buffer between the two armies.

Coming to grips with the severity of the situation as it developed, the exhausted, despondent Confederate infantry ranks still emerging from defensive positions along the hillsides unwound from the chaos and set themselves in motion, searching out their respective units and commands. Full retreat loomed—imminent and inescapable. Leaving behind on the ice-covered hills the last remnants of its final fight for national independence, the battered Army of Tennessee slowly began extricating itself from the disaster that had befallen it. It began to move. In the days that lay just ahead, when human brutality and the relentless cruelty of nature would unite in a furious effort to capture them wholesale, the Army of Tennessee would once again be called upon to gather its remaining strength and meet the ultimate test of its endurance. "On the summit we reformed with [the] other commands, but discovering the Federals flanking us, [we] moved on rapidly toward [the] Franklin Pike ... and emerged at Brentwood, exchanging a few shots with the Federals.... [T]he Army that night was almost in chaos. We bivouacked on the roadside."[54] "Hood's army was in a wretched state, the clothing of the men was scant, and the percent of the barefooted was distressing. On the retreat out of Tennessee the weather was very severe; rain, sleet and snow falling upon the army after the second day's march; but the spirit of endurance seemed to rise as difficulties multiplied."[55]

"Having been informed by an aide of the General commanding that the enemy was near Brentwood, and that it was necessary to get beyond that point at once, everything was hastened to the rear," S.D. Lee subsequently wrote. Commissioned with the duty of protecting the retreating army, Lee's corps took its position at the rear, groping its way in the thick darkness and remaining there through the crucial first phase of what was destined to become an excruciating, unforgettable period in the lives of those who witnessed it. "Order among the troops was in a measure restored at Brentwood, a few miles in rear of the scene of disaster, through the promptness and gallantry of Clayton's division, which speedily formed and confronted the enemy, with Gibson's brigade and McKenzie's battery, of Fenner's battalion, acting as rear guard of the rear guard."[56]

After standing its ground for hours while covering the withdrawal of Hood's army throughout the late afternoon and early evening of December 16, at 10:00 that night Lee's exhausted corps halted in the pelting rain, falling out all along the Franklin pike from Brentwood to the outskirts of Franklin, seven miles north from the town of ghastly memories, the unearthly little village of mass graves and eerie surroundings. Obviously morale in the Confederate army had collapsed in a downward spiral and would never be fully recovered. The crushing knowledge that all was now lost had caved in upon them like an irresistible landslide. No doubt the sight of Franklin, Tennessee, lying quietly on the near horizon had broken the strength of the stoutest among Hood's survivors. Even so, the will to fight remained intact. Defeat in battle is one thing, surrender of the will another. In Union commander George Thomas's view, both had suffered irreversible setbacks in Hood's battered army. "With the exception of his [Hood's] rear guard, his army had become a disheartened and disorganized rabble of half-armed and barefooted men, who sought every opportunity to fall out by the wayside and desert their cause to put an end to their suffering."[57]

Major General George Thomas's official report, stated in part above, regarding the Confederate army's disheartened morale and unwillingness to fight on at the onset of its retreat from the hills of Nashville lies in sharp contrast when viewed as the situation continued to develop over the next several days.

> It was evident that while we had large numbers of poorly-clad and barefooted men, the accusation that they "sought every opportunity to fall out by the wayside and desert their cause" was without foundation. Immediately after the break in our line the troops sought their own organizations, reformed under their officers.... The men, with an occasional exception, had arms in their hands. At Franklin there were several thousand stand of arms, a very large proportion captured from the enemy ... [and] the army retired with fifty-nine field pieces and an ample supply of ammunition. The successful resistance to the assault of the Federal cavalry near Franklin by the rear guard of Lee's corps, repeated at Spring Hill the next day by the rear guard of Cheatham's corps, does not sustain the Federal general's report that our army was a "disorganized rabble." While disasters had multiplied and the suffering was great, the spirit of the men was unbroken.[58]

Upon receiving word of "the disaster at Nashville" on the night of the 16th, Confederate cavalry commander General Nathan Bedford Forrest turned his attention to Hood's retreating army. With typical candor, Forrest's estimation of the day's events seemed to sum it all up: "The affair today [December 16] was most disgraceful."[59] Although previously ordered by General Hood to fall back by way of Shelbyville and Pulaski, Forrest realized what Hood, far from the scene, could not. It was entirely too impracticable to take the designated route. Compelled by his own discretion, Forrest was forced to act otherwise and abandon the order. Due to his wagons with the many sick and wounded still in the vicinity of Triune, "and the swollen condition of the creeks, caused by the heavy rain then falling," Forrest instead relocated his cavalry from Wilkerson Cross-Roads on the Wilkerson Pike outside Murfreesboro, moving them en route to Lillard's Mills on the Duck River. Concurrently, General Abraham Buford's Cavalry Division, moving out from a position on the Cumberland River toward the Nashville Pike, protected Forrest's rear as he set in motion his vital wagons and artillery pieces.

At Forrest's command, the Cavalry Brigades of Buford and Brigadier Gen. Frank C. Armstrong soon combined forces, covering the retreat of Hood's exhausted infantry trudging southward through the deep, ice-crusted mud along the Franklin pike. Destined on this long, unforgettable march to be of major significance in the defense of Hood's retreating columns, the additional momentum of Confederate cavalry under Chalmers swung rapidly into action. "The enemy's cavalry were annoying us [Confederates] at every point, and it took skillful management to hold them in check. General Chalmers' Division of Forrest's Cavalry held them back until after dark, allowing our main Army to retreat in order."[60] "It was a dreadful night, the mud about a foot deep was frozen, but not sufficiently to bear the weight of our horse."[61] Forrest's cavalry command (in no better condition than the main body of infantry), positioned outside Murfreesboro and removed from the scene of action south of Nashville, faced an equally difficult situation. Cut off from the bulk of its army, Forrest was now on his own. Many arduous miles over rough terrain would have to be hurriedly covered before he would finally connect with the main body of Hood's army somewhere along the Columbia Pike, assuming that the army would survive that long. "Most of the infantry under my command were barefooted and in a disabled condition ... along almost impassable roads"[62] (Report of Maj. Gen. Nathan B. Forrest, CSA, Commanding Cavalry).

Oddly, and to the relief of many in Hood's distraught army, no serious Federal pursuit took place on the ominous, frigid night of the 16th of December. Perhaps due to a combination of dense darkness, the surprising nature of the swiftness of Confederate retreat, and the possible presence of Forrest's fearsome cavalry brigades stalking the area, Union pursuit was unable to fully exploit the breakthrough. According to "common rumor" among Hood's straggling lines, the Southern army was waiting for them, regardless. But for some unknown reason the anticipated engagement never took place:

> The [Federal] enemy did not follow, and for some cause they did not fire any volleys into our retreating men, but seemed to have turned and gone back when they reached the position our infantry had abandoned. We all understood at the time, by common rumor, that Forrest had sent Gen. Armstrong with a body of cavalry to get between the enemy and Murfreesboro, and when the battle commenced, he was to attack them in the rear, and we would bag the whole command. So we understood Gen. Armstrong carried out his part of the plan, which caused the hasty reverse movement of the enemy. I did not see a dead or wounded man, as the result of that shameful affair. I never expected to see such a thing happen, even among the greenest Southern militia. There must be many of those men still living, and they ought to explain through the public press, the cause of their action. I have never seen a line from any one about that affair. I think it was the effect of the battle of Franklin.[63]

In light of the disastrous situation that had transpired, many Confederates plodding down the Franklin pike, keenly aware of the extreme danger they were in, must have shared the somber realization that in the days ahead the fight for survival was to be of the sternest character. They could hardly have found themselves in a more uncertain and highly dangerous set of circumstances. Around the Federal campfires however, things were of a vastly different disposition: "By the day's operations the enemy had been driven from a strongly entrenched position by assault and forced into an indiscriminate rout. In his flight he had strewn the ground with small-arms, bayonets, cartridge-boxes, blankets, and other material, all attesting the completeness of the disorder to which he had abandoned himself. The captures of the day were 14 pieces of artillery, 980 prisoners, 2 stand of colors, and thousands of small-arms. It may be truthfully remarked that military history scarcely affords a parallel of a more complete victory"[64] (Report of Brig. Gen. T.J. Wood, USA, commanding Fourth Army Corps).

As a result of the day's achievements, overconfidence abounded, an overbearing, misplaced conviction soon to become evident from the general command downward. In the euphoria of the day's initial success and the close proximity of complete and final victory the Federal command had carelessly laid aside a vital precept: Never underestimate your opponent. "Behold, the day, behold, it cometh: thy doom is gone forth; the rod hath blossomed, pride hath budded. Violence is risen up into a rod of wickedness...."[65]

Cavalry: Intelligence, Protection, and Swift, Sudden Movements

Unlike most of the larger and more important engagements that occurred between the Union and Confederate armies during the War Between the States, the Battle of Nashville was decisive. A section of Hood's threadbare ranks had suddenly collapsed from within, allowing a powerful frontal charge by Thomas's cavalry to begin sweeping the field. As the supporting Federal infantry realized what had happened and took up the movement forward, crowding the Confederate positions and turning them back, its emboldened regiments carried all before them. What followed was a matter of course. Distinct from previous encounters, the Battle of Nashville signaled finality. The one, last, all-out attempt for the Confederacy to gain independence through the battlefield was lost. Gathering its broken ranks to protect its remnants as it withdrew from the field, nothing was clearer to the South than this: the onrushing Federals had gained possession of the field. With the city of Nashville wrenched from Hood's grasp, all was lost, the campaign an utter failure. Although he had not sustained a tactical triumph nor yet been outfought in battle, Hood's army was beaten badly.

As with all victorious commanders, at this point Thomas, who was surely taken by complete surprise at the sudden and unexpected turn of events, was faced with an all-important decision. Now that victory (in his case, total victory) had been achieved, what would be the next move? Undoubtedly he was confronted with the inducement to rest, to reassemble and take stock of his forces, to take the necessary time to consider his options, even at the cost of letting the bulk of the enemy escape. Hood's army would be moving fast. Every moment to hasten its escape and widen the distance between them and the certainty of a reasonably cautious yet determined full-scale attack by the pursuing Federals would be used to the utmost. Although an easy target now running from the battleground, the South yet possessed the advantage of a ferocious survival skill. Terribly wounded though it was, it was certainly not dead.

The Union commander would have to determine the practical feasibility of a prolonged pursuit. At the end of a two-day battle, was his army prepared to sustain itself for an undetermined length of time in rigorous pursuit of a demoralized, infuriated enemy in the dead of winter? The wholesale victory at Nashville had been a major triumph for the Union and Thomas had engineered it, despite the interference and pressures from the Washington authorities. The temptation to take time out for a little reflection and self-acclaim would have been hard to resist. And even though the enemy forces were running for their lives, at the moment Thomas had no way of knowing their exact condition or their intentions. Perhaps the next bit of information to come his way might be in the form of an urgent message indicating that the Confederate army was re-forming and preparing a major counterassault. Would sending his army out in pursuit, moving for the most part on the excitement of victory rather than from a well-informed plan, be the wisest of moves? Was his cavalry caught up in the momentum of success, rushing heedlessly ahead, temporarily detached from its primary purpose, that of gathering intelligence? Was the enemy preparing to defend itself and fight it out to the last man rather than be driven out of the state? If Thomas should decide that pursuit was the best of options, how should it be organized? All of these considerations were the responsibility of the commanding general, and in the face of sudden victory the need for quick and decisive thinking was paramount. A delay of just a few short hours for resting, reequipping, or reorganizing could mean all the difference.

One thing must have been obvious to all: there would be no call for, or acknowledgment of, a truce—a lull in the fighting for each side to recover its wounded and dead and to benefit from a respite from the severity of combat. The full-scale nature of this battle would continue undiminished either in an unrelenting pursuit or in another engagement at another time and place. Today there would be no armistice, no ceasefire. The only settlement would be in surrender or annihilation. At the point of sudden victory, the Union commander was immediately laden with increased responsibilities. He had to be aware of the fact that, after two days of fighting, many in his army were physically exhausted, their weapons spent, their mouths dry, and their stomachs empty. With the onrush of the advance troops, exhilaration would be playing a major part in the successive phase rather than discipline and the carrying out of orders. Could he pull it all together in time for a successful, organized pursuit? It would take an effective, authoritative, and clear-minded commander to make it work, nothing less.

From the Confederate perspective, one word summed up the situation south of Nashville on the evening of December 16, 1864: Exposed. Retreating from the battlefield with units and commands scattered and missing, many soldiers were captured and lost to the enemy; many more were in the process of moving south down the pike or running fearfully through the fields without weapons or supplies. The Army of Tennessee was in the most dangerous and threatened position possible. Should their way be blocked either by the simple fact of a vast army funneling onto a narrow road or by an advanced segment of Federal cavalry cutting off further progress at its head, the result would inevitably be the same. Only the action of an effective rear guard could save them.

Theoretically, the principle of an aggressive, sustained pursuit was based upon the concept of trailing an enemy's path, harrying him as much as possible by nibbling at the scattered remnants of his army without exposing the pursuers to undue danger. Depending on the terrain and the general lay of the land, including the road conditions and availability of food and water, there frequently was little more that could be done than to follow as closely behind as possible, waiting for a sufficient lapse in morale, supply, endurance, or a combination of all three to disintegrate the retreating ranks sufficiently to induce surrender.

Another more enterprising and aggressive tactic of overtaking a retreating army—one that George Thomas's troops employed with tremendous drive in the particular use of his freshly mounted cavalry brigades during the winter of 1864—was to rapidly press forward along the flanks of the main body beyond the reach of the rear guard and move rapidly to the enemy's front. In this way the hunters could literally race past the head of the retreating columns and cut off the way of escape by placing vast numbers of mounted troopers in the path of the retreating enemy while the force of footsore infantry caught them in the vise by simultaneously attacking the army's rear. As a result of a successful maneuver of this kind the retreating army would be surrounded with no hope of escape while fighting on at least two fronts. At that point their only recourse would be to die in place with guns ablaze or to take the more humiliating option: to surrender.

Under the spirited leadership of an indomitable rear guard such a threat was greatly reduced. A seasoned rear guard was capable of screening the movements of its main body, keeping the pursuing army off balance in discerning the direction the army had chosen and therefore what its objective might be, as well as to forestall attempts to cut it off. An effective and unbeatable rear guard was the essential element of survival for an army in retreat, especially so in December of 1864 on the roads south of Nashville, Tennessee, and beyond.

2

Saturday, December 17, 1864

Battles and Skirmishes in Williamson County,
Tennessee, Including Confrontations
Along the Franklin-Columbia Pike
and Four Battles in One Day

"On the 17th we continued the retreat toward Columbia, encamping for the night at Spring Hill. During this day's march the enemy's Cavalry pressed with great boldness and activity, charging our infantry repeatedly with the saber, and at times penetrating our lines. The country being open was favorable to their operations"[1] (Report, General John B. Hood, CSA, commanding Army of Tennessee) "December 17. The march was continued toward Columbia–Stewart in front, Cheatham next, and Lee in the rear, with Chalmers' and Buford's cavalry. General Lee's rear harassed considerably by the enemy's cavalry near Spring Hill. Lieutenant-General Lee slightly wounded. The army camped between Franklin and Spring Hill in the order of march. Army headquarters at Spring Hill"[2] (Journal of the Army of Tennessee). "The cause so dear to us all, to all human appearances, was hopeless. Want and privation almost super-human awaited them...."[3] "The men were not panic stricken or frightened. The term does not apply to old soldiers that have seen years of hard active service. They looked sullen, sad and downcast. I think they had seen enough to convince them that there was not a ray of hope for the success of our cause and they were willing to quit and go home. Their conduct pointed that way."[4] "The retreat to the Tennessee River was not a rout. It was well conducted, and there was almost constant fighting between the rear guard and General Wilson's cavalry, which conducted a vigorous pursuit almost to the Tennessee River."[5]

Following the bitter fighting of December 16 and the collapse of the Confederate left, the Army of Tennessee began a desperate withdrawal southward. Retreating back over the same roads they had struggled up just two weeks previously, these ragged, ill-shod (if not totally barefooted) Southern soldiers found themselves in a ceaseless running battle spanning well over 100 miles in length. In full retreat, Hood's frayed army fought for its life, shielding itself against a well-fed, well-shod, and well-equipped persistent Federal cavalry in constant pursuit over the ice-covered roads of middle Tennessee. "The Winter of 1864–5 was the coldest that had been known for many years. The ground was frozen and rough, and our soldiers were poorly clad, while many, yes, very many, were entirely barefooted.... Even the keen, cutting air that whistled through our tattered clothes and over our poorly covered heads seemed to lash us in its fury."[6] "Hundreds of men were without shoes, and literally left trails of blood on the half-frozen ground over which they marched."[7]

It is remarkable how little appears in our published histories of the deeds of valor and endurance on the part of the Army of Tennessee. All eyes seem centered on the defenses of Richmond, and in history we of the Western Army receive the indifferent notice of neglected step children, as we largely shared that same fate in the campaigns of the war. I would not detract one iota from the praise given to the valor and deeds of the Army of Northern Virginia, for they deserve all the praise they can get. But that is no reason we should be neglected, for I am sure soldiers never carried themselves better or did their duty more nobly than did ours.... Valley Forge bore but little comparison to the patient endurance of hardships of the Confederate soldiers who worked their way from Nashville to Tupelo. Very many of them utterly barefooted and but few with shoes that would protect their feet, they left their tracks in blood cut from bare feet by frozen ground. Numbers had only the back of pant legs dangling behind, the front scorched off trying to dry and warm around the camp fires at night after plodding all day in rain and sleet and mud. The next morning the mud was frozen, gashing their feet, while their legs looked blue as the cold winds chaffed them. Without a blanket, many of them coiled up by the fire on the ground to forget in sleep all this bitterness and to dream of wife and babies.... Never was an army made of better stuff, and they ought to command the veneration of every lover of country.[8]

"The defeat at Nashville on that cold December day, and the retreat that followed, will never be effaced from the memory of the Army of Tennessee. Scattered, cold, the piercing north-west wind chilling them through and through; wet, hungry, ragged, and in a great many instances barefooted; retreating over the frozen ground before a well-organized and well-disciplined army, the remnant of the Army of Tennessee found its way across the swollen Tennessee [River]."[9]

During that harsh, unforgiving mid–December of 1864, at least four desperate clashes between the retreating Confederates and the relentlessly pursuing Federals occurred in Williamson County, Tennessee, along what is today the route of U.S. Highway 31. The first of these encounters took place at Hollow Tree Gap (aka Holly Tree Gap), along Highway 31 slightly north of the intersection with Moore's Lane. The second occurred between the present Mack Hatcher Bypass and the intersection of Old Liberty Pike and U.S. Highway 31, north of the town of Franklin along the northern bank of the Harpeth River. The third was near Winstead and Breezy Hills, where U.S. Highway 31 passes through the small gap between them, and the fourth near the tiny village of West Harpeth where U.S. Highway 31 crosses the West Harpeth River, slightly south of where it connects with Goose Creek By-Pass.

Where today long lines of traffic push through crowded intersections and people jabber on cell phones, conduct business, shop, and pick the kids up from school, in December 1864 rapidly advancing columns of rugged, frostbitten, veteran Federal cavalry swarmed down upon the tattered remnants of the Army of Tennessee retreating south through the ice-crusted mud of the Franklin pike. In that freezing, friendless winter of 1864 acts of outstanding courage were performed, lives again given in decisive engagements adding a progressive, dismal sense of finality to the harsh reality of Confederate defeat.

Hollow Tree Gap: Federal Cavalry "Undeceived"

The opening rounds of these bloody clashes would occur in the northern portion of Williamson County on December 17, 1864, in a narrow defile through which the Franklin pike (U.S. Highway 31 now) ran called Hollow Tree Gap. The Confederate rear guard at this point comprised mainly elements of Lieutenant General S.D. Lee's Corps (which formed the first phase of the army's rear guard action). The divisions of Major General Carter Stevenson and Major General Henry Clayton of Lee's Corps consisted primarily of men from Alabama, Georgia, and Louisiana. Their Federal counterparts in this encounter were cavalry commander Brigadier General Joseph F. Knipe's Seventh Division, in particular Brigadier General John Hammond's First Brigade, composed of men from Indiana, Pennsylvania, and East Tennessee.

On December 17, 1864, the Hunter was after the Prey: "By early dawn the [Hammond's Federal] First Brigade was in the saddle en route for the Franklin Pike, the 19th Pennsylvania [Cavalry] in advance, supported by the 10th Indiana [Cavalry]."[10] The temperature south of Nashville hovered just above freezing on the morning of the 17th. Thick fog greatly reduced visibility, and one Confederate recalled that the "rain was falling in torrents." Misery prevailed and conditions in the coming days would only worsen. "Probably in no part of the war have the men suffered more from inclement weather than in the month of December, 1864, when following Hood's retreating army from Nashville to the Tennessee River."[11]

The previous day's humiliating defeat on the Nashville hillsides had done its work. From Atlanta to the hills of Tennessee the Confederate army had endured the most trying months of the war. Yet Nashville, as well as the balance of Tennessee, still lay in the firm grip of Federal occupation. The campaign to liberate Tennessee, so full of high anticipation, had not only failed it had turned unexpectedly disastrous. Hood's army was hanging on by its fingernails. Yet, despite the loss of so many comrades, of cohesive morale, and possibly the war itself, somehow they held themselves together, clinging to the slightest hope, a faint mirage, the remnant of a faded dream. It wasn't the end of the Army of Tennessee. Although the Confederates had been overwhelmed and driven from the field, the Federal army was soon to encounter a major discovery: the old adversary was far from conquered.

Early on the morning of the 17th of December, Hood's army awoke with grim memories. The frightful disaster at Franklin, with its irretrievable losses only two weeks past, coupled with the disgraceful rout from the trenches of Nashville had crippled the army beyond repair. It would never be the same again. With the remaining commands hopelessly scattered, combined with the utter lack of desperately needed supplies, a sense of sullen, inevitable tragedy had swept over the survivors. The present position was indeed precarious. Sudden capture en masse or annihilation were for the first time dreaded possibilities. Pulling themselves to their swollen feet, the Confederate army tugged their frigid bodies from the icy mud and formed up, astonished that General George Thomas had not done more during the night to encircle them. By all accounts it should have happened. Assembling their scattered units, the army soon took to the road, commencing the march southward through the rain to Franklin and far-off Columbia. General Stewart was leading, Cheatham following, and S.D. Lee protecting the rear. As the army began to unwind, the divisions of Chalmers' and Buford's cavalry regiments promptly took the duty of defending the flanks. Turning northward up the pike on a quick reconnaissance assignment, Chalmers' cavalry plunged rearward as the army's main body hurried southward.

"[T]here is a ridge running across the countryside, and the pike ran through a low gap in this ridge. On the ridge on both sides of the pike Hood posted his army to check the enemy's advance."[12] Preparing for the inevitable Federal cavalry assault, Hood positioned his rear guard for defense at Hollow Tree Gap. Just south of the gap, Stovall's Georgia Brigade of Clayton's Division and a section of Bledsoe's Missouri Battery formed for battle east of the Franklin pike, priming themselves for the coming attack. The moment was critical, the enemy definitely on the move. Only a limited Confederate cavalry force guarded their highly vulnerable flanks. Hood's infantry, after weeks of battling man and nature, were exhausted beyond measure. Half-starved and certainly dealing with frostbite and overexposure, Clayton's Division took its grim stand at Hollow Tree Gap. Surely, Federal pursuit was imminent. "Daylight on the morning of the 17th found us in position at Hollow-Tree gap, five miles from Franklin-Stovall's brigade and a section of Bledsoe's' battery being upon the right and Pettus' brigade upon the left of the road, and the other two brigades in rear."[13]

With complete victory within his grasp, the Federal commander would undoubtedly hold nothing back, in particular his well-rested cavalry units, eager to enter the fray and pound the Army of Tennessee into submission. After the taste of victory the day before, every man in his army was itching for more. Awakening early, the Union host stirred from a chilly sleep, bracing and preparing itself to face the frigid weather and the certain trials that lay just ahead. The state of elation experienced by the rank and file of Thomas's army regarding the previous day's successes soon reached the Federal high command stationed in Virginia, the wires hot with heady congratulations of jubilation and "confidence being restored," of a "glorious victory" being achieved the previous day, and of a one-hundred–gun salute being given at sunrise in tribute to Thomas by the Union forces under the command of General George Meade, "in honor of this brilliant triumph." In the Shenandoah, upon hearing the news Major General Phillip Sheridan took a momentary break from his villainous depredations of the local citizenry to send "hearty congratulations" to Thomas and his army for their "brilliant victory," also arranging a two-hundred–gun salute amid "much cheering."[14] Rear Admiral S.P. Lee, USN, stationed not far from the scene of action, was particularly overjoyed, equating Thomas's generalship and other qualities to that of his fellow Virginian General Washington:

> Clarksville, December 17, 1864.
> Major General G.H. Thomas:
>
> I have the honor to acknowledge receiving, and to thank you for the early telegraphic copy, of your admirable official report to the President of your great and glorious victory over the enemy of our country and of mankind on the 15th and 16th instant. I am deeply impressed with the belief that our whole country will now or hereafter appreciate the generalship, statesmanship, and patriotism of your campaign, resulting in the signal defeat of General Hood's army, in which centered the strength and hopes of half the rebellion, with little loss, under great difficulties and with probably political consequences and more important than have followed the previous achievements of the war. Permit me on this occasion to express my humble admiration of your distinguished public services, which evince all the high qualities of virtue, patriotism, and ability, characteristic of our first great countryman.
> Respectfully and faithfully yours,
>
> S. P. Lee,
> Acting Rear Admiral, Commanding Mississippi Squadron.[15]

Thomas's reply, including a possible note of embarrassment at the reading of Admiral Lee's heady compliments and "flattering congratulations," contained a request for the admiral's assistance: to send up the Tennessee "one or two ironclads and a few gunboats, for the purpose of destroying Hood's pontoon bridge near Florence, [Alabama] and at the mouth of Duck River, [near Columbia] where it is reported he is now [through a prearranged plan] building a bridge."[16]

Within a week, that seemingly routine request would carry far-reaching implications as to the success of Thomas's mission. What they all must have surely known but neglected to acknowledge was the enduring quality of the Army of Tennessee's indomitable determination to fight it out to the last man. Against impossible odds for nearly four years the South's finest had given their all in the struggle for national independence. Despite the recent calamities, by the winter of 1864 they were still a major force to be reckoned with. Rather than superior strategy, tactics, and fighting ability, the Federal army's "brilliant victory" appears as little else than the sweep of fate that suddenly turned in their favor, demonstrated by Thomas's uncharacteristic reaction due to his surprise as he learned of the breakthrough on the Confederate left.

"During the hurrying night ride down the Granny White turnpike I was overtaken by General Thomas after it was so dark that men could recognize each other only by their voices. Thomas, riding up on my right, exclaimed in a tone of exultation never to be forgotten: 'Didn't I tell you we could lick 'em? Didn't I tell you we could lick 'em, if they [referring to the Washington authorities] would only let us alone?' After a few words of congratulation he turned about and leisurely rode back into camp"[17] (James Harrison Wilson, Major-General, USV, Brevet Major-General, USA, "The Union Cavalry in the Hood Campaign"). At 3:30 in the morning of December 17, 1864, Federal cavalry commander Brevet Major General James Harrison Wilson was wide awake. Having risen so early, although he was obviously clear-headed and alert at such an hour, it is highly unlikely that he had gotten any sleep at all. Located on the "Granny White pike, eight miles from Nashville," Wilson put into written orders what he had doubtless been occupied with for the last serveral hours: the placement of his cavalry divisions in their line of attack on Hood's retreating lines. He had not a moment to lose. John Croxton's brigade was to approach the Franklin pike "by the most direct road" and hem in the Confederates by exerting pressure on them from the road or roads running east of the pike. General Knipe's division was ordered directly south, toward Franklin, bearing down on the Confederate rear guard via the Franklin pike and any roads west of it. Following nearly on the heels of Knipe's brigades, Hatch's division would pursue the retreating army to Brentwood, covering the road west of the pike. General Richard Johnson's division would make his way south over the Hillsborough pike, swinging a wide arc further west.

This raging flood of Union cavalry streaming south over the roads heading toward Franklin resembled a massive tidal wave of military might. With the enemy so close and in such evident disarray, Wilson was holding nothing in reserve. His forces, composed of some of the toughest fighters in Thomas's army, were borne over the roads as if shot from a giant sling. The entire landscape seemed to heave and buckle under the onslaught. The ground rolled with the endless sight of line upon line of blue-clad horsemen hefting long sabers in the overhanging mist. The noise much have been deafening.[18]

James Harrison Wilson was a busy man in the fall of 1864. Successive to his position as commander of the Third Cavalry Division under General Philip Sheridan then operating in Virginia's Shenandoah Valley, the following October General Grant had reassigned him (with his brigades) to Sherman's command, who had turned off from pursuing Hood's army and had pitched camp at Gaylesville, Alabama.

Born in 1837 near Shawneetown, Illinois, Wilson graduated from the United States Military Academy at West Point twenty-three years later in 1860 with an aptitude for topographical engineering. As the war evolved, Wilson's career progressed, moving him through the ranks and bringing him to his most challenging work, commanding Federal cavalry. Characteristically tenacious, Wilson learned the toughness of war through participation with George B. McClellan as his aide-de-camp during the Peninsula Campaign. He was also on hand during the invasion of the Army of Northern Virginia into Maryland later that same year. Having achieved a better than average successful career thus far, Wilson had shown much to commend himself to his superiors. Much more would be expected of him in the latter days of 1864.[19]

> Cavalry is a most difficult force to organize, arm, equip, and instruct at the outbreak of war. Not only must men be found who have some knowledge of the use and handling of horses, but the horses themselves must be selected, inspected, purchased, and assembled. Then, after all the delays usually attending the organizing, arming, and equipping of a mounted force, many months of patient training, dismounted and mounted, are necessary before cavalry is qualified to take the field as an efficient arm. It is an invariable rule in militant Europe to keep cavalry at all times at war strength, for it is the first force needed to invade or to repel invasion, and, except perhaps the light artillery, the slowest to "lick into shape" after war has begun. In the regular cavalry service, it was a common statement that a cavalryman was of little real value until he had had two years of service.
>
> It is therefore, small wonder that during the first two years of the great struggle, the Federal cavalry made only a poor showing.[20]

Under Sherman's personal authority Wilson eventually received a promotion. He was now in the position of chief of cavalry, "placed in absolute command of all the mounted forces of the three armies," as he put it, the "three armies" presumably being the Army of the Cumberland commanded by George Henry Thomas, the Army of the Ohio led by John M. Schofield, and Wilson's own cavalry corps. By order of Sherman, this newly created cavalry command, the "Cavalry Corps of the Military Division of the Mississippi," was free to move, acting in coordination with but entirely independent of the army chain of command. Although a step up for Wison and a credit to his industriousness, it was not an easy task to begin the work. As the majority of the Union cavalry in the Western theatre were spread out "from east Tennessee to south-western Missouri," Wilson had inherited more than his share of organizational responsibilities.

In the anticipated execution of his assignment to oversee the observation of the movements of Hood's army then moving northwest (in addition to the responsibility of protecting the vulnerable, comparatively slow-moving Federal infantry) Wilson's part in the coming drama would be paramount. Unknown to anyone as the seasons began to change from the pleasant, invigorating days of late fall to the bone-chilling winter of 1864, the Federal "Cavalry Corps of the Military Division of the Mississippi" was destined to play the overriding role at Nashville and the subsequent pursuit of Hood's army. Much work, however, lay ahead in seeing to the creation and development of his new assignment. "Do the best you can with it," Sherman had advised. With "12, 000 men, mounted, armed, and equipped," not including 3,000 more who operated as dismounted infantry, James Harrison Wilson would soon demonstrate that he was fully determined to do so.[21]

Early on the shadowy morning of December 17, 1864, in preparation for commencing a major movement of Federal infantry down the Franklin pike in the wake of Hood's retreating army, General Thomas J. Wood's Fourth Infantry Corps moved out, Wilson's Federal cavalry preceding them by several hours.

Headquarters Fourth Army Corps,
Near Nashville, December 17, 1864 6 a.m.

Orders of the day for the Fourth Army Corps for today, December 17, 1864:
The advance against the enemy will continue this morning ... [and] the enemy pressed with all vigor possible. Attacks will [not] be made upon his solid works except under special orders.[22]

By order of Brigadier General Wood

"At 12.30 a.m. of the 17th instructions were received from the commanding general of the [Federal] forces to move the Fourth [Infantry] Corps as early as practicable down the Franklin pike in pursuit of the enemy. At 6 a.m. of the 17th I directed division commanders to advance as early as practicable, move rapidly, and if the enemy should be overtaken to press him vigorously. The night had been rainy and the morning broke dark and cloudy. It was, hence, nearly 8 a.m. before the column was well in motion, but it then advanced rapidly"[23] (Report of Brig. Gen. T.J. Wood, USA, commanding Fourth Army Corps). "The [Federal cavalry] pursuit was resumed at the earliest dawn next morning [the 17th] and was kept up throughout the day, with a succession of sharp engagements, in which the Union cavalry was always victorious"[24] (James Harrison Wilson, Major-General, USV, Brevet Major-General, USA, "The Union Cavalry in the Hood Campaign"). "I shall be able to do the enemy more damage by crowding him now, by the shortest roads.... I have already ordered Johnson to move very early by the Hillsborough pike for Franklin, and will do the best I possibly can with the balance of the force"[25] (Maj. General James Wilson, U.S. Cavalry Hdqrs., Cavalry Corp, Mil. Div. of the Mississippi, Granny White Pike, Eight Miles from Nashville, December 17, 1864, 3 a.m.).

Around sunup on that dismal morning, impetuous cavalry commander General Wilson, after receiving directives from Thomas to commence the chase, got moving, making preparations to send Knipe's Division (Hammond's Brigade) accompanied by General John Croxton's First Brigade, directly down the Franklin pike within the first few hours, "the 19th Pennsylvania in advance, supported by the 10th Indiana Cavalry." The Fifth Division led by General Edward Hatch would intersect the pike at Brentwood. Wilson was leaving nothing to chance in the desperate effort to "get into Franklin with the whole force," if possible. A special emphasis was noted: do whatever is necessary to thwart any joining of forces with Forrest's cavalry, then located in the area of Murfreesboro. "The infantry ought, therefore, to crowd the enemy vigorously on the Franklin pike, and, if possible, prevent a junction of Hood and the forces now in the direction of Murfreesborough"[26] (Maj. General James Wilson, U.S. Cavalry Hdqrs., Cavalry Corp, Mil. Div. of the Mississippi, Granny White Pike, Eight Miles from Nashville, December 17, 1864, 3 a.m.).

A few miles distant, on the west side of Hollow Tree Gap, Pettus's Alabama Brigade of Stevenson's Division prepared themselves as well. An attack was looming. The hardened veterans of Lee's corps situated along the crest of Hollow Tree Gap set themselves like stones, readying to receive the enemy. Gibson's Louisiana and Holtzclaw's Alabama Brigade, both of Clayton's division, moved quickly into reserve, positioning themselves some 600 yards in the rear, and waited. "On the hilltop we could overlook the country to the north of us and easily observe the approach of the enemy."[27]

Given the sight of the Confederates on this campaign, so ragged and unkempt, and the trail of discarded accoutrements, many Federal cavalrymen considered the notion of a Confederate defense as one of pointless futility. Was it not just a simple matter of overtaking the retreating Confederate columns and beating them into submission? To many it seemed so, although Union Fourth Corps commander Thomas Wood's forward infantry units were powerless to begin the march, having been bogged down in the heavy rain and deep mud of the Franklin pike since before dawn. As a result, the

Federal infantry was not in progress until 8:00 a.m. As soon as it had begun to move it marched in rapid motion, with Wilson's cavalry in the lead pressing the enemy on all sides, straining at the bit for an opportunity to take on the fleeing Confederates one last time.[28]

No doubt most of the Union rank and file were of the opinion that, following the overthrow at Nashville, there was no fight left in these living skeletons, thinly clad in filthy, ragged, grey and butternut tatters. But they were wrong. As one Federal cavalryman later wrote, "The guns and other equipment strewn along the road, the apparent abandonment of everything that impeded their flight, every door yard filled with illy-clad shivering prisoners, had led us to the conclusion that we had a 'walk over.' Hollow Tree Gap undeceived us."[29]

As the morning of the 17th slowly crept on, the Federal army kept up its efforts to stay ahead of the game on all fronts. Hood's army was on the move southward, possibly evacuating the state. As a consequence, the Union leadership would see that all available pressure was exerted to take full advantage of every situation that presented itself. A brief directive from the Department of the Cumberland, probably delivered early in the day, set the stage for serious trouble within the Confederate ranks. The Federal army under Brigadier General R.S. Granger was to "immediately reoccupy the railroad as far as Decatur, throwing supplies into Decatur by means of steam-boats." With the Nashville-Decatur Raliroad (running paralell to Hood's receding columns) under complete Federal control, the use of the railroad as a provider for much-needed Confederate supplies and equipment was ruled out. On the other hand, should the Union army decide to use it as such, nothing could stop them.

By the following day the work had begun in earnest. In a message by Col. W.W. Wright, chief engineer of the U.S. Military Railroad, written to his superior, the superinendent of Military Railroads, things were moving along as scheduled. By nightfall of the 18th, the rail lines from Nashville to Franklin would be servicable. The rest would follow quickly. "Everything is working well," noted Wright.[30] Meanwhile, on the same day in the same city, another department of the U.S. army was busying itself in its own particular role in the drama of pursuing Hood's troops. Although not placed in field service, the Quartermaster Department stationed in Nashville was nonetheless of primary importance to the task at hand. Without the constant flow of supplies and equipment necessary for a prolonged operation extending over many miles of a deserted and ravaged countryside, there could be no reasonable hope for success. On the 18th, Brigadier General J.L. Donaldson, the chief quartermaster, would have encouraging news for the U.S. quartmaster general: "We open the Cumberland [River] today. Transports here have left under convoy of the gun-boats … [and] the department is doing all it can to sustain the army in pursuing the enemy, giving up most of the transportation of the department for that purpose."[31] With weather conditions soon to turn into one of its worst winters, the U.S. army in pursuit of General John Bell Hood and his Army of Tennessee would need every scrap of food that could be sent.

Around 8:00 a.m., as units of Wilson's cavalry divisions had taken to the road in earnest, Confederate cavalrymen of Chalmers' division (who had been picketing the northern side of the gap) came galloping quickly southward, back toward the safety of the Confederate lines. Close behind them and with carbines blazing rode the Federal cavalry advance of the 19th Pennsylvania, supported by the 10th Indiana, in "a most vigorous pursuit, his cavalry charging at every opportunity and in the most daring manner ... determined to make the retreat a rout if possible." A fierce, violent exchange of gunfire ensued, Clayton's brigades opening a devastating fire into Hammond's oncoming Federal cavalry regiments, leaving 22 killed and wounded and more than 60 taken as prisoners as the Federals quickly withdrew. "Their boldness was soon checked by many of them being killed and captured by Pettus' (Alabama) and Stovall's (Georgia) brigades and Bledsoe's battery, under General Clayton. Several guidons were captured in one of their charges"[32] (Report of Lieutenant General Stephen D. Lee, CSA, commanding Army Corps of operations, November 2–December 17, 1864). The following quotes are from various reporters of the events above:

> At Hollow Tree Gap, a considerable body of infantry were strongly posted, who repulsed the two regiments in front with the loss of 22 killed and wounded and 63 prisoners, principally from the 10th Indiana.[33] About 8 a.m. the enemy's cavalry made their appearance, driving in our own cavalry in a most shameful manner, a few pursuing them even through the line of infantry and cutting with their sabers right and left. A few shots from the infantry, however, drove them back, with the loss of a stand of colors. About 9 a.m. they again advanced upon this position, when we succeeded in capturing about 100 men, with their horses, and another stand of colors"[34] [Report of Major General Henry D. Clayton, CSA, commanding Division of operations November 20–December 27, 1864].

"On the 17th the brigade advanced to the Franklin pike, the 19th Pa. in advance. They soon came upon the enemy and engaging them drove them in confusion to Hollow Tree Gap, six miles from Franklin, where a considerable fight ensued."[35] "Starting south before day, we were passed before night by a number of our cavalry, who twitted us about running away, stating that they were going back to show us how to whip Yankees, so we need not be afraid anymore. A good many soldiers had come in through the night and early hours of the 17th, so that it looked more like an army again."[36] "At a point a mile beyond Brentwood, on the Franklin Pike, [Confederate] cavalry was found in line of battle across the road. The Nineteenth was ordered by

General Knipe to charge with saber. Without waiting to form lines, the command dashed forward in columns of fours, and scarcely had the rebels delivered a single volley, when it was upon them. Unable to withstand the impetuosity of the onset, the rebel line broke … for two miles, and until it reached the infantry column at Hollow Tree Gap, it was closely pressed."[37]

As day dawned Pettus's Brigade was formed in line with the curving of the hill to the left of the pike as we faced Hollow Tree Gap, Stovall to the right, and Bledsoe's Battery at the pike. After we had been in position something like an hour, firing was heard in the direction our cavalry had gone. The firing was not very heavy nor did it last long, and was followed by only an occasional shot coming nearer. In a short time a deafening clatter of galloping horses rung out on the morning air, and overcoats of blue were flying over the backs of horses as the cavalcade rushed down the pike, filling it as far back as we could see. It was our cavalry, who were going to show us how to fight Yankees. Immediately upon their heels and even mixed with the rear were the pursuing cavalry of the enemy; but one could not be told from the other, as the Confederates under Forrest had on blue overcoats recently captured.[38]

"Hammond, pushing on in vigorous pursuit, came up with the enemy just beyond Brentwood, drove him [Chalmers] back to Hollow Tree Gap, four miles north of Franklin, where he made a stand. General Knipe attacked with the main part of the brigade, while General Hammond, with the balance, turned the position and attacked the rebels in flank."[39] "Here the enemy's infantry and artillery was concealed from view and before its position was known the regiment was charging upon it. Suddenly saluted by canister at short range, and showers of bullets … [and] being unsupported, it was unable to stand, and fell back upon the rest of the brigade."[40]

Some of the Federal cavalry had run behind our lines in the pursuit, and all might have done so and we none the wiser, for all the apparel looked alike. The Federals who passed in, seeing our colors and the ragged grays around them, halted, and would have turned back, but General Pettus gave orders to fire, and from both sides of the hills a volley was poured in at close range. They were ordered to surrender, and began to speedily to dismount. A large number had dismounted, when some gallant officer rode rapidly up the line, ordering the men to remount and fall back. The larger part did so, receiving our fire as they left. Those who had entered our lines nearest the gap surrendered.[41]

"About 9 a.m. they again advanced upon this position, when we [Confederates] succeeded in capturing about 100 men, with their horses, and another stand of colors."[42] "About 250 prisoners and 5 battle flags were taken."[43] "At about 10 a.m., we [the acting rear guard] were withdrawn from this position."[44]

Farther down the pike, the rain-soaked Confederates observed the sight of the Federal charge with keen interest. "[W]e saw across the valley from us, and coming down the slope, many Yankees and several stands of Yankee colors. In the distance and fog they were taken by Col. Hunley to be an advance by the enemy, when in reality they were a number of prisoners captured on the ridge in the charge made on our line by the incautious foe."[45] Taken by complete surprise as a result of the enemy's audacity, Hammond's cavalry charge was brutally halted in its tracks as it dashed headlong into the Confederate infantry line of Stovall and Pettus and the destructive fire of Bledsoe's Missouri battery. Hurriedly recovering and withdrawing, the ongoing Federal momentum turned to a flanking maneuver, moving around the Confederate line in the rear of Lee's guard, suddenly turning the tide of battle in favor of the bluecoats. "I was soon compelled to withdraw rapidly toward Franklin, as the enemy was throwing a force in my rear from both the right and the left of the pike, near Franklin and five miles in my rear. This force was checked by Brigadier General Gibson with his brigade and a regiment of Buford's cavalry under Colonel Shacklett. The resistance which the enemy had met with early in the morning, and which materially checked his movement, enabled us to reach Franklin"[46] (Report of Lieutenant General Stephen D. Lee, CSA, commanding Army Corps of Operations, November 2–December 17, 1864). "Gen. Knipe engaging the enemy with the 10th Ind. and 19th Pa., while Gen. Hammond passed around the right of the enemy and gained the rear, when the position was handsomely carried. Gen. Knipe had been repulsed, however."[47] "Hammond, pushing on in vigorous pursuit, came up with the enemy just beyond Brentwood, drove him back to Hollow Tree Gap, four miles north of Franklin, where he made a stand. General Knipe attacked with the main part of the brigade, while General Hammond, with the balance, turned the position and attacked the rebels in flank. About 250 prisoners and 5 battle flags were taken"[48] (Report of Brevet Major General James H. Wilson, USA, commanding Cavalry Corps, Military Division of the Mississippi of Operations, October 24, 1864–February 1, 1865).

By battle's end, more than an hour later, over 250 Confederates had been captured and certainly dozens killed or wounded. The colors of the Fourth and Thirtieth Louisiana Infantry regiments had been captured among those of at least three other Confederate regiments. Wilson's cavalry had, for the moment, gained the rear of Lee's corps before withdrawing.

Gen. James F. Knipe, of the Seventh Cavalry Division, made a lucky hit on Saturday afternoon, near Brentwood, capturing two flags, belonging to the Fourth and Thirtieth Louisiana Cavalry, together with about two hundred and fifty prisoners, including twenty commissioned officers, two brigade musicians, and two sets of musical instruments one of silver an the other of brass. The flag of the Thirtieth Louisiana was faded and torn, red cotton ground, with blue cross, and twelve silver bullion stars on the cross. That of the Fourth Louisiana (commanded by Colonel Hunter, who was also captured) is a magnificent one. The ground is of red bunting, with a cross made of heavy blue silk, the border of yellow twilled silk, twelve gold stars being upon the cross. This flag bears the following inscription: "Jackson, Port Hudson, Baton Rouge, and Shiloh."[49]

"[W[hile being posted there [at the Gap], I moved the balance of my brigade to attack the enemy, who was approaching the road between us and Franklin. I drove him back very easily, and was moving to the road again, when I was informed by a staff officer of Lieutenant General Lee (Lieutenant Farish) that Colonel Hunter and his detachment had been captured"[50] (Report of Brig. Gen. Randall L. Gibson, CSA, commanding Brigade of operations December 15–17, 1864).

Although substantial losses were suffered on both sides, fortunately for the Confederates another costly couple of hours were secured, allowing the retreating army to safely make its way southward. Much commendation is due Clayton's division for effectively defending the army's rear from the first of many fearful Union cavalry assaults. "In a short time the battery and infantry renewed the retreat, and after going a mile or more to the rear they passed behind a part of Clayton's division formed across the pike. This division, much depleted, met and drove back the next attack of the enemy, and fell back behind the line of Stovall and Pettus again formed across the pike, and who met and repelled the next attack. Thus by alternate lines these two commands covered the retreat of the fleeing armies."[51] Clayton's division, "much depleted," continued its defense of the main body throughout the morning hours of the 17th until the army's arrival at Spring Hill, where Clayton was relieved by Stevenson's division.

> 9 a.m. they [Union Cavalry] again advanced upon this position, when we succeeded in capturing about one hundred men with their horses and another stand of colors. At about 10 a.m. we were withdrawn from this position and crossed Harpeth river. A few miles from this place, after some slight skirmishing, we were relieved by Major General Stevenson's division."[52] "General Clayton displayed admirable coolness and courage that afternoon [the 16th] and the next morning in the discharge of his duties. Gibson, who evinced conspicuous gallantry and ability in the handling of his troops, succeeded, in concert with Clayton, in checking and staying the first and most dangerous shock which always follows immediately after a rout. The result was that even after the army passed the Big Harpeth, at Franklin, the brigades and divisions were marching in regular order"[53] [Gen. J.B. Hood].

The sudden, dramatic repulse of the Federal cavalry charge at Hollow Tree Gap, achieved by the brigades of Pettus, Stovall, with Holtzclaw in reserve and the aid of Bledsoe's battery, drove the point home with unmistakable clarity. As long as there remained a man with a musket in the Army of Tennessee, that amy would be a serious force to reckon with. The sudden, disastrous Confederate defeat at Nashville had become insufficient evidence that the Confederate army had lost heart and capitulated. Doubtless, Hollow Tree Gap spoke loud and clear to Union commander George Thomas and his bold subordinates. No longer were they under the illusion they were pursuing a beaten, dejected, dysfunctional army. The facts relayed quite the opposite message. George Thomas was faced with the stern reality of an infuriated, deadly foe to contend with. At Hollow Tree Gap, Hood's army, regardless of its ragged condition, demonstrated its enduring capability to inflict severe harm on not only the Union army itself but also on the Union's ultimate goal of cutting off the Confederates and capturing them outright. The Army of Tennessee, although broken and struggling for life, was still dangerously formidable. It would never, even in this the darkest of hours, be an easy prey for an overconfident Union Army.

A Running Battle through Franklin, Tennessee

A running battle took place from near modern-day Mack Hatcher Bypass to the Harpeth River, along both sides of Franklin Road, north of

Tennessee State Marker at the Harpeth River.

town on Saturday, December 17, 1864. For the veteran soldier of the Army of Tennessee, the mention of this date would forever conjure up vivid memories, beginning with the agonizing withdrawal of the Confederates over the fog-enshrouded hills south of Nashville beneath a merciless downpour and passing through Hollow Tree Gap to the brutal confrontation at the Harpeth River, just north of the town of Franklin. "Many [Confederates] were ill-clad and unshod—some with their feet wrapped with pieces of blanket—some actually bleeding tramping on the frozen ground. On this retreat came the sternest trials of the war"[54] (Essay by Luke W. Finlay, formerly of the 4th Tennessee Infantry, CSA).

The stubborn stand taken by the Army of Tennessee at Hollow Tree Gap had temporarily blunted Wilson's attempts to run them over by sheer force, giving the retreating Confederates breathing room and undoubtedly instilling a surge of the old confidence, now so desperately needed. Although Wilson had for the time being been beaten back, it was no occasion for him to slack off. From the moment the Confederates had withdrawn from the gap and taken up the line of march southward the Federal cavalry was in the saddle, preparing for another round of assaults, planning to "throw a force in Lee's rear" by attacking down "the different roads that led into the pike between him and Franklin."[55] Long before sunup the cavalry under Wilson's command had been in swift motion. Knipe's 7th Division had taken the advance, cross-

Remains of a stone bridge at the Harpeth River.

Remains of a stone wall along the Franklin pike.

ing over country roads and merging with the Franklin pike while bearing
down on the Confederate rear guard, with John Croxton's Brigade of
McCook's Division on his left. Hatch's 5th Division had merged onto the
Franklin pike via the Granny White "and a country road," eventually coming
up in Knipe's rear.

After encountering the stubborn resistance of Lee's rear guard at Hollow
Tree Gap, Richard Johnson's 6th Division (Harrison's Brigade in the advance)
had moved out quickly. Although much delayed, Johnson would push hard
throughout the morning hours down the Hillsboro pike, in time crossing the
Harpeth River and moving "rapidly to Franklin" on the heels of the fleeing
Confederates, striking them in the flank and forcing them in due course "to
retreat to a new position, south of the town."[56] "Orders were also sent to Johnson [after the Union breakthrough of the Confederate lines at Nashville] to
move rapidly by the Hillsborough turnpike, and after crossing the Harpeth
to turn up its south bank and fall upon the enemy at or near Franklin. Every
one obeyed orders with alacrity, but darkness and distance were against
them"[57] (James Harrison Wilson, Major-General, USV, Brevet Major-General,
USA, "The Union Cavalry in the Hood Campaign"). "Upon the morning of
the 17th I moved at 4 o'clock in the morning down the Hillsborough pike,
driving the enemy's pickets, whom we found in barricades on the ridges
beyond Brown's Creek; forded the Harpeth where I struck the flank of the
rebel rear guard of cavalry, who were there posted to prevent the passage of

the river by General Knipe's division, which had advanced down the Franklin turnpike"[58] (Report of Brigadier General Richard W. Johnson, USA, commanding Sixth Division). The Federal cavalry units of Hatch, Johnson, and Knipe were cutting through the approaches to Franklin like water pouring through a sieve. With orders from Wilson, General Croxton's cavalry was to "push along as fast as possible by the road you fell back on when Hood advanced on Nashville. Cross the Harpeth River and endeavor to strike the enemy's flank on the Lewisburg pike." With Croxton moving on the Confederates, this additional charge would put practically the entire cavalry force Wilson had on hand into the streets of Franklin, surrounding the enemy on three sides while gobbling up any scattered remnants that had fallen behind during the fighting. "Watch well your left," Wilson advised him. Confederate cavalry could appear as suddenly as lightning.[59]

Lee's Corps, protecting the army's rear and facing the high probability of shortly becoming surrounded by Federal cavalry, withdrew rapidly toward Franklin as Wilson's divisions advanced on both flanks in a bold attempt to take him in one sweeping movement. Regardless of their wretched condition there was no rest for the overwrought Confederate army. Constantly moving, fighting on the run and fending off vicious attacks of Union cavalry who obstructed their every step, the army held together its broken ranks and sustained their retrograde movement toward the outskirts of Franklin.

Tennessee State Marker near the Lewisburg railroad.

Remains of a stone wall along the Franklin pike.

Following the Confederate withdrawal from Hollow Tree Gap down the Franklin pike, a pitiful sight caught the eye of many a Yankee cavalryman, perhaps a portent of the suffering that lay ahead for every brave soul that held a rifle or brandished a blood-spattered sword. "After repulsing our advance [at Hollow Tree Gap] the enemy fell back. The 9th Indiana was ordered up and took the advance. As we moved through the Gap we saw the saddest sight of the campaign. A trooper lay beside the road gasping his life away, and near him with a ghastly wound in his breast, lay dead the little curly-headed boy, Duane A. Lewis, Co. B, sixteen years old, the General's Orderly, whose bright and joyous face and fearless innocence had endeared him to the heart of every soldier in the brigade. The pitiless rain fell upon his upturned childish face; his eyes were open, but their light had gone out forever."[60]

North of the Harpeth River on the edge of the village of Franklin, another aggressive stand would be taken by the Confederate rear guard of S.D. Lee's Corps in anticipation of putting yet more distance between themselves and the rapidly approaching Federals.

The Confederate Stand at the Harpeth River

The weather had again turned against the retreating Confederates. A chilling rain began to fall, swelling the river beyond its muddy banks. Knowing that there were but moments to spare, the rear guard, assigned the task of keeping the enemy at bay, dug in on the northern bank of the Harpeth and prepared to fight.

The Action at the Railroad Underpass

In what has been described as part of "perhaps the largest cavalry engagement on American soil," at around 10:00 on the morning of December 17, 1864, Wilson's intrepid horse soldiers swept over the open fields south of Hollow Tree Gap in a furious, headlong charge, the main body of troopers forging straight ahead into the confrontation that awaited them at the river's edge, while elements of Knipe's Division, veering off to the Union left, bore down on the Confederate rear guard, then defending the eastern flank of the Harpeth between the Franklin pike and the Nashville & Decatur railroad, not far from the Liberty pike. Advancing through the pouring rain toward Franklin, Brig. Gen. John Hammond's 1st Brigade of Knipe's 7th Division quickly came under a galling fire near the railroad underpass, where a segment of Randall Gibson's Louisianans were posted. The 9th Indiana, in the forefront of the charge, returned fire, gradually displacing the fleeing Confederates, who fell back "in good order." Some of the participants described the action:

> When we reached Franklin, the Louisiana Brigade formed line from pike to railroad and kept the enemy in check until all of our wounded and ammunition train safely crossed the Harpeth River, then the brigade turned in good order.[61]
>
> On our arrival at Franklin, my shoes had fallen from my feet, and I was now barefooted in the deep snow, with a hostile army pressing. I do not think now that I regarded it with any degree of great misfortune at that time, but I did not get a pair of shoes until we reached Tupelo, Miss., having marched all the way from Franklin, Tenn., to that place in my bare feet, a distance of two hundred and fifty miles. I certainly came near to freezing to death. I had no blanket, nothing but my sword and pistol. This part of my life as a soldier is so sad that I do not care to describe the retreat of the army from Nashville to Tupelo[62] [Capt. R.N. Rea, CSA].

> After waiting some time and the attack was not renewed, we continued our march toward Franklin. Some distance to the rear Clayton's Division was formed across the pike. After passing his line, we again formed and halted. It was not long till Clayton's line was charged; but the enemy was driven back, and Clayton then formed in our rear. The retreat was continued thus in alternate lines until Pettus took position on the banks of the Harpeth River at Franklin. The rest of the army passed over the river. We were here again heavily assailed, but drove back the foe. The Federal report says they drove us across the river. This is not correct, nor could it be, for the river was much to swollen to allow crossing except by bridge. As soon as the enemy were driven off we fell back to the Franklin side as rapidly as could be done over the temporary bridge. While crossing a poor fellow who had fallen on the bridge was strug-

gling to regain his footing and begging piteously; but every fellow was so anxious to get across that the last I saw of him he was still wallowing in the mud and the men were running over him. After crossing the river, which was near midday, we had a short, much needed breathing spell. The night of the 15th had been spent in moving to the new line and intrenching, the day following in fighting, most of the night in marching and reorganizing, and on the 17th we had been fighting and marching; so we were much worn with loss of sleep and active work. If it could be called rest, it was brief; for as soon as affairs could be put in shape Pettus' and Cummings' Brigades were again chosen for the rear guard, as we had been all morning.[63]

We were formed across the pike about one mile north of Franklin to await the arrival of the enemy, and we had not long to wait until three regiments of (Hammond's) Brigade of Indianians came in sight. As we were so inferior in point of numbers, they did not deem it necessary to form line of battle; but came at us with drawn sabers by fours and sections of eight, one column keeping the pike and one regiment on either side, about fifty yards apart. Our artillery between us and Franklin were firing very rapidly at the advancing foe, and from the number of shells that exploded immediately over our heads we concluded that our gunners were cutting their fuses very short. We fought them until they were within about forty yards of us, with our gallant colonel riding up and down the line imploring us to stand and whip them. Our line then broke, as nearly all the men had fired their last cartridge. About twenty-five loose horses, whose riders had been shot as they advanced on our line, continued the charge after their owners had been unhorsed, and they remained with us in the stampede to Franklin. As we filed into the pike we passed Colonel [William F.] Taylor [7th Tennessee Cavalry, C.S.A.], who was fighting, still looking after the rear, though all alone, and it was thought that he killed three of the enemy before they were repulsed near the river by infantry and artillery.[64]

Shortly after the Confederate withdrawal upon the same hilltop from which Bledsoe's cannon had fired off a few earlier parting shots, the Federal advance of Hammond's First Brigade of Knipe's Seventh Division formed in line of battle. As the concealed Confederates of the rear guard waited with freezing, trembling fingers tightening on the triggers of their muskets, Knipe's Federal cavalry troopers swept southward in a powerful rush, carbines firing and sabers unsheathed. With its left flank on the tracks of the Nashville & Decatur Railroad and its right flank several hundred yards west of the Franklin pike, Hammond's Brigade swiftly descended upon what was left of S.D. Lee's battered Confederate corps. But before the Federal cavalry realized what lay hidden in their immediate front, the defensive lines of General Randall Gibson's Louisiana infantry brigade, with Pettus's Alabamians of Stevenson's division combined with elements of Buford's cavalry in support, had formed for battle and were engaging the enemy. Repelling the Federals outright, Gibson's brigade brought the attempted flanking movement to a temporary standstill and halted the momentum of their threatening advance. "The enemy was very bold, and did all they could to make Hood's retreat a perfect rout."[65] "Rain was falling in torrents. As soon as the enemy found we had abandoned the line on the ridge they crossed it and swept down the valley on us. Being held in check to some extent by our cavalry and some artillery, Col. [Peter F.] Hunley had moved over to the north side of the ridge and passed along until he struck a road coming to Franklin and crossed back and struck the pike a short distance above Little Harpeth River, which skirted Franklin on the east."[66]

As the Federals, barely discernable through the thick, overhanging fog, closed in on the Confederate positions posted on the banks of the Harpeth, Confederate artillery (believed to be of Bledsoe's Missouri Battery) again opened on them with a fierce barrage of double-shot canister, beheading horses and virtually vaporizing their riders. In an instant, Confederate cavalrymen burst forth from concealment with sabers slashing, firing pistols at near point-blank range. Nearby, a ragged line of shivering Southern infantrymen took careful aim, firing repeatedly as column after column of blue-clad cavalrymen advanced, perceived through the dense mist only as vague forms—unearthly outlines of heavily bearded men on horseback waving silver sabers, the lurid flash of gunfire stabbing the darkness, blinded warhorses emerging from the haze in wild pandemonium, the shouts of command of their riders melding with the horses' own thundering hoofbeats, all coming within range of the Confederates' rain-drenched rifles. "Here the enemy appeared in considerable force and exhibited great boldness, but he was repulsed and the crossing of the Harpeth River effected"[67] (Report of Lieutenant General Stephen D. Lee, CSA, commanding Army Corps of Operations, November 2–December 17, 1864).

I [Gibson] was again placed in position in an earthwork 1,000 yards from Harpeth River [north], and before any instructions reached me our cavalry stampeded. The enemy, 5,000 strong, charged in three columns, with squadrons covering the intervening ground and connecting them—one in front, one in rear upon the left flank, and one in rear upon the right flank. I found a section of artillery [Bledsoe's Missouri Battery] upon the road and a part of a regiment of infantry under Colonel [Peter F.] Hunley. I had the section to open upon the enemy, but it had no effect except to increase the speed of his flanking columns, and made no impression upon that one advancing directly upon our front. After firing ten rounds, with no better effect, I ordered the officer (I do not know his name) to move his pieces to the rear. I also directed Lieutenant Colonel [Robert H.] Lindsey, commanding Sixteenth Louisiana Volunteers, upon my extreme right, to deploy his regiment as skirmishers in retreat, and Colonel [Francis L.] Campbell [13th Louisiana Infantry] and Major [Camp] Flournoy [19th Louisiana Infantry], with the First, Thirteenth, Nineteenth, and Twentieth (in all, about 250 muskets) to move to the rear and to fight as they went. I also directed Col. Hunley to deploy his men as skirmishers. Colonel Campbell broke up, by a well-delivered fire, the column charging down the road, and thus gave the section of artillery time to cross the river. The enemy came up to within 100 yards of this section and fired his revolvers at those about it. My command fought its way to the river, entirely surrounded, with a loss of 10 killed, 25 wounded and 5 captured[68] [Brig. Gen. Randall Gibson, CSA].

"I [Holtzclaw] moved in rear of the brigade in line of battle to within one mile of Franklin, where I passed the brigade of General Gibson, drawn up to support a section of artillery."[69]

General Knipe's orders to Hammond had been clear. With no pretext of caution he sent them forward into the fray, pressing his division into a hasty, impulsive charge, slamming them into a well-fortified Confederate position entrenched on the riverbank. For many in Hammond's Brigade, it would be their last charge.

[General Knipe ordered,] "Take your command and go to Franklin; don't skirmish with the enemy three minutes, but attack him where found and drive him through the town." The rain was gently falling, the heavy fog of early morning was somewhat dissipated, yet so dense that objects could not be distinctly seen at a distance. With a long trot we swept down the pike against a shadowy foe—ourselves but shadows. The depressing weather and the sad scene just passed ["the little curly-headed boy"] made the lightest heart grow heavier as we swept along. Suddenly from the woods on the left a body of Confederate horse sprang into the road in front of us, and in a ghostly gallop led the way into their lines. Debouching into the open near Franklin, the cannon from the fort opened on us with shell. The head of the column turned to the right a short distance and wheeled into line—the center and left coming on "front into line." Hammond being at the head of the column gave the command to charge before the line was barely formed. The right sprang forward at the command and was rapidly followed by the center. The left under Capt. Hobson was not yet in line and did not hear the command. Hammond again shouted "Charge!" Hobson was looking after the alignment and did not hear the command. Hammond galloped to him and said: "You cowardly son of a bitch! Why don't you charge?" Hobson raised himself in the stirrups and said; "Boys, we will show who are cowards! Forward! March! Charge!!" and lead the boys right up to the fort, where he was shot through the heart. A stone wall on the left caused them to crowd on the center and against the fort. The right also was forced to press in on the center by reason of a nursery, which, for horses, was practically impenetrable. The center charged right down the open grounds on the left of the pike.[70]

Another soldier wrote as follows:

Some five hundred yards, over undulating grounds, made miry by recent rains, from the advance (9th Indiana Cavalry, Colonel George Jackson commanding), of Hammond's brigade, and upon the north side of Big Harpeth River was a section of a battery, supported by two regiments of infantry, strongly intrenched behind abattis and rifle pits; in front of them a regiment of cavalry drawn up to receive a charge. On the south side of the river four guns were so planted as to enfilade the road. Filing and forming to the right and left of the road, with a coolness, which seemed utterly regardless of the terrible accuracy with which the rebel guns were aimed, while their shells were mangling horses and their riders, the men seated themselves more firmly in their saddles, tightened their reins, and "looked on sky and tree and plain" as sights they might never see again. Led in person by Col. Jackson, in a line which would have awakened the admiration of old Hardee himself, the 9th, at a walk, advanced to victory—many of them, alas, to death.[71]

Without the slightest intention to slacken the pace, Knipe's division pushed ahead, regardless of the losses they had incurred or the stout opposition of S.D. Lee's rear guard, a line of musketry that evidently could not be overwhelmed regardless of the intensity of the attack that confronted them. "The enemy having retreated [from Holly Tree Gap] we followed rapidly, the Ninth Indiana in advance, to near Franklin, and drove the enemy across the river and through the town, capturing, it is reported, 2 stand of colors and 200 prisoners. In this charge we lost three fine officers, among whom was Captain Hobson, Ninth Indiana Cavalry, a man remarkable for the prompt discharge of his duties and his bravery. He is a great loss to the service. The Ninth Indiana was supported by the Tenth Indiana and Fourth Tennessee, but the first regiment deserves the principle credit of the charge and the success."[72]

The 7th Tennessee [Confederate] had been ordered to Franklin for escort duty, except Col. W.F. Taylor, who, with a portion of his command, remained north of the Harpeth River until later for the purpose of watching the movements of the enemy, who were already advancing in three columns. Colonel Taylor, accompanied by his sergeant, Major John Somerville, and the writer, proceeded to the Franklin Pike, just north of Franklin, where a strong Federal force, led by General Wilson, commanding cavalry, was pushing ahead with determination. Remarkable as it was, this trio of Confederates threw themselves between the enemy and the pontoon bridge across the Harpeth above Franklin, and there held the entire Federal force at bay for some ten or fifteen minutes, firing their pistols while moving to and fro to make show of numbers. Of course the Federals did not know the situation. Having expended all the loads from his pistol, Col. W.F. Taylor called to the writer, having two pistols, who loaned him one, and they all kept shooting. In the meantime several of the enemy charged below these men, but returned to their command, seemingly afraid to remain. As soon as we knew that the other two columns of Federals had crossed the river we marched deliberately over and passed through Franklin, hurrying some infantrymen before us, and passed beyond the breastworks south of town. Immediately a solid line of cavalry was in our rear, and in front of us was the Confederate corps of Gen. Stephen D. Lee, at the time in command of the rear of the army. All this time the Federals had been at these three men, probably expending more than one thousand shots, but not one touched a man. We moved deliberately to the left of our army and took position with our regiment.[73]

Holtzclaw's Stand at the Harpeth

As Holtzclaw's Alabama brigade of Clayton's division approached the Harpeth, Yankee cavalry passing through the rising water with hurricane ferocity swooped down on them in an infuriated charge. Muskets leveled, Holtzclaw's brigade formed into a staggered line of solid resistance, covering the withdrawal of General Gibson's artillery, then in quick abandonment of its position. But the damp weapons of Clayton's division proved useless, having been soaked in the pouring rain. Defense was futile as Federal cavalry charged in among them with pointed sabers and flashing pistols, emptying their carbines into the horrified faces of the enemy.

Several hours before the clash then raging at the water's edge, Holtzclaw had sent a small detachment of 75 men on a five-mile foot race from Hollow Tree Gap to the banks of the Harpeth River. Detouring Wilson's cavalry brigades, the assumed objective for the maneuver was to arrive at the river in advance of as much of the enemy force as possible and to prepare for the army's defense. As it turned out, the unit, drained of much of its stamina due to the long run, arrived on the Franklin pike near the banks of the Harpeth at the point where Gibson's Louisiana brigade, with his battery, was positioned. Aware of the perilous situation that confronted him, Gibson assumed command of the exhausted detachment, ordering it to remain in position at the riverbank and cover his retreat and that of the artillery. With no time for discussion, the small detachment of Holtzclaw's men fell into line, facing the massive onrush of some 2,500 Federal cavalry bent on his destruction. It was a death trap. Without question each one must have known he had come to his last remaining moments on earth. If by a miracle the men would somehow escape the onrush of death, their only hope was a dismal prospect of capture and an undetermined length of stay in a miserable Federal prison.

Holtzclaw's ragged men held their place, hearts pounding. The furious charge of Wilson's cavalry thundered down upon them in a surging mass of ferocity and lit into them. Pistols, carbines, and muskets flashing, gun butts and sabers slashing, artillery shells whistling and shrieking overhead: all were put to bloody use in a most frightful display of savagery as terrified horses trampled down to the ground those opposing them. Following a few brief moments of brutal fighting, Holtzclaw's unit was quickly overwhelmed and surrounded, cut off from the main body stampeding over the bridge north of the river. Those Confederates not trampled down, bludgeoned, or shot soon fell captive. For a few fortunate souls, escape came by either fleeing on horseback or leaping into the freezing river while warding off savage saber blows, keeping mere steps ahead of Wilson's cavalry wildly splashing into the icy water at their backs. Fleeing for their lives, a handful of Confederates somehow outdistanced their pursuers and reached the opposite bank.

Notable among the acts performed that day at the water's edge were the efforts of one Colonel Falconnet, as recorded in Clayton's official report: "Colonel Falconnet, commanding a brigade, who, when about to cross the Harpeth River, seeing the enemy charging upon Gibson's brigade, drew his revolver, and gathering less than 100 brave followers, dashed upon the enemy, more than twenty times his number"[74] (Report of Major General Henry D. Clayton, CSA, commanding division, of operations November 20–December 27, 1864. But for the segment of Holtzclaw's brigade surrounded at the river's edge with no way of escape, nothing could avail but an exasperated surrender. Nonetheless, due to these remarkable efforts, another precious few minutes were bought for the Confederate army as it continued on, hastening its wagons into Franklin over the rapidly swelling river. Moving in the heat of desperation bordering on panic, Hood's remnants quickly clattered over the bridge, scarcely slipping past the encircling Yankee cavalry pushing relentlessly forward on both flanks and in their center, squeezing them in a vise-like grip and searching for the quickest route of access over the flooded waters of the Harpeth leading into the battle-scarred town of Franklin.[75]

> I [Holtzclaw] moved in rear of the brigade in line of battle [from Hollow Tree Gap] to within one mile of Franklin, where I passed the brigade of General Gibson, drawn up to support a section of artillery. I hurried across the river and formed on the southern bank, in Franklin. By the time I had formed, the enemy's cavalry pursued Buford's cavalry division, driving it in confusion into the river. They were repulsed by Pettus' brigade, in the works north of the river, and the section of Bledsoe's battery, in my line on the south, not getting in musket range of my command. The portion of the regiment I had detached in the morning and could not communicate with passed around the hills to the left of the pike, running five miles to get there. They came into the pike just at the position taken by General Gibson, exhausted with running around the enemy's cavalry. Without notice to myself or authority from the major general, Brigadier General Gibson ordered this detachment of about seventy five men to remain and cover the battery. Then withdrawing with the battery he withdrew his brigade, while my small detachment, in obedience to his orders, held the position, covered the retreat of himself and the section. As a matter of course they were overwhelmed by the enemy's cavalry, 2,000 or 3,000 of whom had surrounded them, three officers and five men only escaping[76] [Report of Brig. Gen. James T. Holtzclaw, CSA, commanding Brigade of operations November 20—December 27, 1864].The enemy retreated rapidly toward Franklin, with General Hammond in close pursuit, the 9th Ind. advanced to near Franklin, driving them across the river into town. Here the enemy planted a battery of artillery on a high point, and was annoying Gen. Hammond's advance. He directed Maj. Stephens to take his regiment and cross the river and charge into the town, and try to gain the rear of the battery. Maj. Stephens did as directed. He ordered Captain Bishop to take his company C and lead the charge, while he and Captain White, who was the officer of the day, that day, accompanied him. As soon as they crossed the river the artillery withdrew at a gallop.[77]

Nearly overtaken, the remainder of the Confederate line north of the Harpeth held to the last moment, to the last cartridge, and then retired, making a dash through the bone-chilling water for the other side, using what strength they still possessed to reach the southern bank before the Yankees could cut them off.

> We were formed across the pike about one mile north of Franklin to await the arrival of the enemy, and we had not long to wait until three regiments of (Hammond's) Brigade of Indianans came in sight. As we were so inferior in point of numbers, they did not deem it necessary to form line of battle; but came at us with drawn sabers by

fours and sections of eight, one column keeping the pike and one regiment on either side, about fifty yards apart. Our artillery between us and Franklin were firing very rapidly at the advancing foe, and from the number of shells that exploded immediately over our heads we concluded that our gunners were cutting their fuses very short. We fought them until they were within about forty yards of us, with our gallant colonel riding up and down the line imploring us to stand and whip them. Our line then broke, as nearly all the men had fired their last cartridge. About twenty-five loose horses, whose riders had been shot as they advanced on our line, continued the charge after their owners had been unhorsed, and they remained with us in the stampede to Franklin. As we filed into the pike we passed Colonel [W.F.] Taylor [7th Tennessee Cavalry, CSA], who was fighting, still looking after the rear, though all alone, and it was thought that he killed three of the enemy before they were repulsed near the river by infantry and artillery.[78]

Events on the north bank of the Harpeth were transpiring at a furious pace. Bursting into the fray, with the capture of Holtzclaw's detachment within their grasp, the Federal cavalry smelled blood and pushed the pursuit to the fullest measure, sweeping everything in their path. Gibson's brigade, posted on the far side of the river, immediately assumed the charge of holding them off as the trailing elements of Hood's wagons, loaded with the wounded of Nashville and what supplies and munitions were still available, rumbled hurriedly over the bridge into Franklin.

> I [Gibson] was again placed in position in an earthwork 1,000 yards from Harpeth River.... The enemy, 5,000 strong, charged in three columns.... I found a section of artillery upon the road and a part of a regiment of infantry under Colonel [Peter F.] Hunley. I had the section to open upon the enemy.... I also directed Lieutenant Colonel [Robert H.] Lindsey, commanding Sixteenth Louisiana Volunteers, upon my extreme right to deploy his regiment as skirmishers in retreat, and Colonel [Francis L.] Campbell [13th Louisiana Infantry] and Major [Camp] Flournoy [19th Louisiana Infantry], with the First, Thirteenth, Nineteenth, and Twentieth (in all, about 250 muskets), to move to the rear and to fight as they went.... The cavalry of the enemy charged all around us. Colonel Campbell broke up, by a well-delivered fire, the column charging down the road, and thus gave time to the section of artillery to cross the river. The enemy came up within less than 100 yards of the section and fired his revolvers at those about it. My command fought its way to the river, entirely surrounded[79] [Report of Brig. Gen. Randall L. Gibson, CSA, commanding brigade, of operations December 15–17, 1864].

As Gibson's regiments speedily withdrew under what covering fire the "section of artillery" and Holtzclaw's small detachment could offer, Confederate engineers under the command of Captain David Coleman of the 29th NC, under "a heavy fire from Yankee sharpshooters," burned the rail trestle bridge, forever sealing the fate of the remaining 75 Confederates from Holtzclaw's brigade stranded on the northern bank of the river. Compelled to flee through the rising Harpeth, most of those still trapped on the riverbank were either killed or captured during the dash for the other side. Some, too weak to continue, were literally trampled in the muddy embankment by the pursuing Federal cavalry. The tragedy is marked, as many of these boys, crushed under the hooves of Yankee cavalry, simply disappeared from sight. It may be that many still lie there, their remains embedded in unmarked cracks in the earth, buried by roads and thoroughfares.

Descending like a sweeping scythe, the Federal cavalry simply overwhelmed the outnumbered remaining Confederate defenders left behind on the riverbank. After gathering their shivering prisoners, Wilson's forces crossed over at fords located "above town," pouring into Franklin from all sides, racing with the rising waters of the Harpeth. The battle with all its savagery was over in probably less than thirty minutes. Pushing ahead, the Federals quickly re-formed, continuing their dogged pursuit. Crossing at some shallower points on the river, both above and below Franklin, Wilson's cavalry immediately formed by brigade and charged through town, rushing forward in a frenzied attempt to overtake Hood's rapidly retreating army.

Regardless of the tremendous force of Wilson's charges the Southerners held valiantly before offering up their lives or surrendering as the vanguard of the army gained yet more valuable time and distance ahead of the pounding hoofs of Wilson's horse soldiers. "When we reached Franklin, the Louisiana Brigade formed line from pike to railroad and kept the enemy in check until all of our wounded and ammunition train safely crossed the Harpeth River, then the brigade turned in good order."[80] "At about 10:00 a.m. we were withdrawn from this position and crossed Harpeth River."[81] (No. 240, Report of Major General Henry D. Clayton, CSA, commanding division, of operations November 20–December 27, 1864). "The Federal cavalry soon reached the north bank of the river and began shelling our line. The fire was responded to with great spirit by Lee's batteries, and we could see the Federal cavalry scatter. General Lee, riding along a stone fence encouraging his men, was wounded by a fragment of a shell."[82]

Crossing the river into town, Wilson's dauntless cavalry drove themselves forward in a frantic, desperate attempt to envelop Hood's army before the possibility of an escape became a reality. The timing of Knipe's crossing over the railroad bridge and entry into town proved fortuitous, coinciding with Harrison's advance under General Johnson's command, arriving from the Hillsboro pike and crossing the Harpeth's south bank in his wake, where he "struck the flank of the rebel rear guard of cavalry who were there posted to prevent the passage of the river." The Seventh Ohio Cavalry captured some 50 prisoners of the Confederate rear guard, while Hatch and Croxton crossed over soon after at the fords above town. In a matter of moments the bulk of Wilson's forward cavalry units had filled the streets of Franklin like a rushing torrent. Scarcely had the citizens of Franklin put behind them the horrendous battering the town had endured just weeks before. Yet, here again Franklin was engulfed in ferocious war. The whole town seemed to be submerged in it. Wilson's cavalry, measured in the thousands, advanced like a crashing wave, pressing the Confederates at every turn and covering every possible route of escape[83] (Report of Brigadier General Richard W. Johnson, USA, commanding Sixth Division, of operations November 24–December 19, 1864). "On the 18th [17th] we [Croxton's Brigade] crossed the [Granny White] pike, passed around Brentwood, down the Wilson pike to Matthews' house, swimming the Harpeth at McGavorck's Ford"[84] (Report of Brigadier General John T. Croxton, USA, commanding First Brigade, First Division, of operations October 24, 1864–January 14, 1865). Wilson's charges, in the manner of all genuine cavalry attacks, must have been awesome to behold. Rarely, if ever, does such a fearsome sight present itself.

> To describe a real cavalry charge, however, where sabers are crossed and skulls are cleaved, as was the case at Franklin on the 17th inst., and do it justice, is impossible. One may tell how hundreds of well-drilled, well mounted men, with clean blades, seen through the clear morning air, moving like machinery, is a sight not often seen, and a splendid embodiment or representation of power, and in the rush of a charge may liken it to the tornado, that must sweep the earth unless averted. This may be said, but a hundred instances of individual prowess must necessarily be overlooked. In fifteen minutes the battle was won. Two stands of colors, two guns and 250 prisoners were the spoils of victory. The remainder of the enemy, in confusion, fled through Franklin, leaving it to be taken with near 2,000 of their wounded, without further fighting.[85]

Upon the arrival of Federal cavalry within the town and as S.D. Lee was in the process of evacuating, the Confederate wounded still languishing within Franklin since that memorable night of November 30 suddenly came under the heavy hand of Union capture. What their fate was to be, no one knew. But one thing was certain. There would be no letup to the chase. "At Franklin the enemy's hospital with about 2,000 wounded fell into our [Union] hands: 200 of our own wounded, left there on the retreat to Nashville, were also recovered.... The pursuit was immediately continued"[86] (Reports of Bvt. Major General James H. Wilson, USA, commanding Cavalry Corps, Military Division of the Mississippi of operations October 24, 1864–February 1, 1865).

Earlier that morning, after a "brief delay" in allowing the cavalry to pass, the Federal infantry of Wood's Fourth Corps had resumed the march, slogging through "very heavy" roads, making comparatively meager advancement and altogether missing the furious hand-to-hand clash at the Harpeth River, arriving at the outskirts of Franklin by early afternoon. "8:00 AM, started in accordance with orders. Wilson's Cavalry started ahead of us, on the Franklin Pike, and drove the enemy's skirmishers before them. Our advance and movement was rapid. 1:20 PM we arrived at Franklin, on the north bank of the river, with the head of the column. General Wilson's Cavalry has just crossed. The stream is too much swollen to admit of the passage of infantry, and there are no bridges"[87] (Journal of the Fourth Army Corps). Most notable to the trailing Union infantrymen was the abundance of discarded Confederate "small-arms, accouterments, and blankets," strewn along the muddy road, denoting to them the "unmistakable evidence" of complete victory and Confederate demoralization. "The whole line of march of the day bore unmistakable evidence of the singleness of the victory our arms had achieved and the completeness of the rout"[88] (Report of Brigadier General Thomas J. Wood, USA, commanding Fourth Army Corps, of operations October 26, 1864–January 5, 1865).

Fortunately for the Confederates, the initial stand at Hollow Tree Gap coupled with Lee's invaluable rear guard, General Gibson's effective resistance of numerous Federal cavalry charges on the Franklin pike soon afterward and at the banks of the Harpeth had paved the way for the bulk of the Confederate army to cross the Harpeth's bloodstained waters in relative safety and make its way into Franklin without major loss. But surely in the forefront of the minds of most was the uneasy sensation that spoke of the nearness of Federal cavalry, which was just a step away. Glancing warily over its shoulder, Hood's army quickened its pace.

As the Army of Tennessee weaved through Franklin with Wilson's indefatigable cavalry nipping at its heels, this was certainly the most trying of moments. A mere two weeks previously, while charging the works at Franklin, Hood's army had undergone what is considered to be the most fearsome and terrifying five hours of battle men have ever had to countenance. The fate of Tennessee, the fate of the western army, and possibly the fate of the Confederacy had hung there in the balance as the fighting raged incessantly in all its passionate fury, encompassing the most ferocious, inhuman levels of this war, and perhaps of any war. Now, with defeat at their backs only hours before, the soldiers of Hood's army were forced to retrace their steps through town, to revisit the horror, to pass through that awful scene of carnage, where if victory had been won on that fateful November night the War for Southern Independence would surely have taken a vastly different course in its immediate development. How many of those who had fought that battle still lay where they had fallen, partially buried in those deep, deadly trenches, some covered only by fallen comrades, others still sprawled upon the open field? Union and Confederate wounded lay in the homes, churches, streets, and yards of Franklin weeks after the battle's rage had finally ended, filling the town to its limits—every house a hospital, every building with a roof sheltering the wounded and dying, Union and Confederate, from the bitter cold that had invaded Middle Tennessee. Edgar Jones of the 18th Alabama remembered it all too well:

The struggling army made its way through Franklin. The Eighteenth (Alabama Infantry), what was left of it, with the brigade passing through the famous locust thicket. We passed along where many of the dead had been buried, ditches having been dug and the dead having been placed in them side by side. We marched along over these ditches, our feet sinking down in the soft, wet dirt. I saw more than one hand or foot exposed and I distinctly felt my foot rest on a dead body as it sunk into the mud. It was a gruesome sight. And then the stench arising from these dead bodies was something fearful. Some troops held the bridge and the river line for some time, and then we abandoned Franklin for good. Then commenced the most memorable retreat it was ever my misfortune to witness during the great struggle the South so heroically carried on in the interest of States Rights and Constitutional liberty.[89]

After overseeing the army's crossing, S.D. Lee upon his approach into Franklin lost no time in urging the host forward, ever guarding the army's vulnerable rear as he went. Soon realizing the presence of thousands of Confederate wounded, as well as Union, still held up in the town, Lee pushed ahead, not wanting to "subject them and the town to the fire of the enemy's artillery." With a certain degree of reluctance, he yielded Franklin without a fight:

It must have been a strange, heart-sickening sight to the bewildered women and children lining the gates and porches and windows, as we passed by, to see us so soon retracing our steps, in such a plight. Gazing silently at us, a jostling herd of haggard men, equally silent ourselves, they stood, as column after column went by. What were their thoughts, their feelings? The rain still poured in torrents upon us, more dogged in its pitiless pursuit than the enemy. It still beat us down, as it had been doing day and night, day and night, ever since the day of our defeat, until the drops felt like heavy shot upon our heads. No sound save its merciless pour, and the slushy tramp of that miserable multitude hurriedly wading with bent forms and straining eyes through the freezing mud, and the demonical howl of the ferocious wind.[90]

South Franklin: Holtzclaw's Stand in the Trenches

The Confederate army's advance regiments had hardly reached the outskirts on the south of town when Wilson's cavalry "entered Franklin in triumph, from which it had been driven only a few days before in disorder and confusion" after the Battle of Franklin. In response, elements of Clayton's division instantly formed and "covered the retreat on the left of the [Columbia] Pike," skirmishing with the enemy on the run while fighting off brutal Federal assaults approaching them on all sides. Under Clayton's firm protection the army withdrew, continuing southward, the fighting lasting into the darkness of night. "From the time we left Franklin until nightfall we were constantly engaged with the enemy. We formed a line of battle and held the enemy in check until the other Brigade would form in our rear some 100 yards; then we would fall back, sometimes under fire, and form in the rear of the other Brigade again, and that Brigade would file back behind us and thus we did all the afternoon."[91]

Passing through town on the defensive and reaching its southern perimeter, Holtzclaw's brigade soon came upon what must have been a macabre, solemn sight: the former breastworks of November 30, where the grim battle had raged so furiously about them throughout that long night. Some "friend or comrade" still lay in the shallow, frozen ground, only partially buried. Holtzclaw himself recalled, "I went into line next [after the stand at the north bank of the Harpeth], just outside the trenches of Franklin." Immediately, the converging forces of Union cavalry were on him, dashing "up to within 300 yards of my line, firing carbines and pistols." How surreal it must have been for the frayed men of Holtzclaw's Brigade, fighting again alongside their departed comrades in the same unforgettable trenches of mere weeks ago. Rising from behind the breastworks, Holtzclaw engaged the enemy, repelling them with several deadly volleys. After scattering the Federals, Holtzclaw warily resumed the march. "I then marched back in line, halting every few yards until I passed through the gap south of Franklin"[92] (Report of Brigadier General James T. Holtzclaw, CSA, commanding brigade, of operations November 20–December 27, 1864).

Upon the arrival of Wood's infantry at the edge of the Harpeth early that afternoon, the dominant sight that greeted them was the destruction of "all the bridges over the Big Harpeth" and the fact that "the rains of the previous night and that morning had so swollen the stream as to make it impossible by infantry [to cross] without a bridge, [so] it was necessary to halt to build one, the pontoon train not having come up"[93] (Report of Brigadier General Thomas J. Wood, USA, commanding Fourth Army Corps, of operations October 26, 1864–January 5, 1865).

With all the bridges down, a new one had to be constructed, and quickly. The developing situation was slowly taking a grim turn. Despite all human ingenuity and a tremendous amount of effort, Thomas was soon to learn that more difficulty lay in store for the main body of Union infantry, which, combined with Wilson's cavalry, had the manpower to capture and subdue Hood. In a mood of exasperation, Wood related the unfortunate setback in a pressing communiqué: "It will be impossible to accomplish the work, owing to the rapid rise in the river, the swiftness of the current, and the amount of driftwood coming down the stream.... I see no other way than to wait for the pontoon train. This should be hurried forward for I am confident that we cannot cross until it comes up ... [so] hurry that forward [and] we will put it down and cross [the Harpeth] immediately"[94] (Th. J. Wood, Brigadier-General, U.S. Volunteers, Commanding). "The stream is too much swollen to admit of the passage of infantry, and there are no bridges ... 2 p.m., Colonel

Suman, Ninth Indiana, with his regiment, is directed to bridge the river[.] It is doubtful whether he will succeed in putting one up, as the river is rising rapidly"[95] (Journal of the Fourth Army Corps).

In addition to the present distress and much to their dismay that afternoon, due to the rapidly rising waters of the Harpeth the probability of building an adequate bridge within a reasonable amount of time was remote at best, which by early evening had become clear. Despite the extraordinary efforts of his engineers to create a safe crossing, Wood had to concede a measure of defeat, even if only temporarily. Wiring to his staff, he admitted the failure:

> Headquarters Fourth Army Corps, Franklin, Tenn., December 17, 1864–8 p.m.
>
> General [Kimball]; The prospect is that we will not have the bridge finished before a late hour tonight. Let your troops rest as well as they can. We will not move before 3:00 AM.[96]
>
> By order of Brigadier General Wood

Although the Federal cavalry had forded the river earlier in the day and was "sharply engaged with the enemy's rear guard several miles in front," much to his chagrin Wood would have to simmer, building and repairing bridges before crossing and, regrettably, losing more precious time. For his plodding infantry brigades the pursuit was beginning to take on the appearance of a prolonged, excessively strenuous effort with an uncertain outcome.

"Burning with impatience to get forward and join in the conflict," Wood's infantry eventually (on the morning of the 18th) "pushed rapidly across the Harpeth, pressed forward and marched eighteen miles that day, though the road was very heavy and many crossings had to be made over the streams." Although seriously repulsed on several occasions to that point, with the passing of each critical engagement Union victory seemed almost within reach, only to be snatched from them at the last moment. Clearly, there was little the highly motivated Union army would not undergo to secure its objective. In addition to the increasing difficulties, Wood noted in his account that "the weather was very inclement"[97] (Report of Brigadier General Thomas J. Wood, USA, commanding Fourth Army Corps, of operations October 26, 1864–January 5, 1865).

Among the nagging setbacks one bright glimmer of hope emerged, although in the end it amounted to nothing but fanciful rumor. According to information supplied by General John Schofield, Confederate cavalry commander Nathan B. Forrest had "certainly" been killed in the vicinity of Murfreesboro, during a major defeat of his Confederate cavalry. (Schofield's 23rd Army Infantry Corps, also in pursuit, was bogged down that afternoon near Brentwood not far from Granny White pike. General A.J. Smith's infantry, clogging the pike in his front, had made it all but impossible for him to proceed any farther.)

Headquarters Army Of The Ohio, In the Field, December 17, 1864.
Major General George H. Thomas,
Commanding, &c.:

General: I have the honor to inform you that citizens on the road in rear of where we fought yesterday report that the universal testimony of rebels, officers and men, is that Forrest was killed certainly at Murfreesborough, where they admit their cavalry was badly whipped.

Very respectfully, your obedient servant,
J.M. Schofield,
Major General[98]

Within a day or so, Thomas would know how unreliable that report was.

With no other option available, Hood's weary army—stretched out along the Columbia pike south of town and depleted of everything but honor—tramped on, keeping as much distance as possible between them and the opposing forces. Regardless of the cost, there would be no straggling. Any idle, careless maneuvering or laxity in will power would undoubtedly end in disaster.

By 1:30 that afternoon, Major General Wilson, assured of victory close at hand, wired his superior from war-torn Franklin:

Hdqrs. Cavalry Corps, Mil. Div. of the Mississippi.
Franklin, Tenn., December 17, 1864–1 p.m.

Brig. Gen. W.D. Whipple,
Chief of Staff, Department of the Cumberland

General: The rebels are on a great skedaddle; the last of them, closely pressed by Knipe, passed through this place two hours and a half ago. I have directed Johnson to try and strike them at Spring Hill. Knipe is pressing down the Columbia Pike; Hatch close on their left; Croxton I shall direct down the Lewisburg Pike. The prisoners report the rebel army in a complete rout, and all the Tennesseans are deserting. Colonel Alexander, my chief of staff, is just in from Johnson, who is well down on the Columbia Pike, having struck here about the same time that Knipe did. The rebel rear guard is in position on the hills just south of here. I have everything in hand except Croxton, and will drive them without delay. The Harpeth is rising rapidly; all bridges down. Shove up your infantry and get up the pontoons.

Very respectfully, your obedient servant,
J.H. Wilson, Brevet Major General

Knipe has 5 battle-flags and 300 prisoners. The rebel army seems to be down on Hood.

J.H.W[99] [Major General James Harrison Wilson correspondence].

From Wilson's perspective the "rebels" were a demoralized mob. With his numerous brigades covering all routes leading south, bearing down hard on the fleeing Confederates, his moment was at hand. The mention of a complete rout in progress, the "certain death" of Forrest, and the fact that Confederate desertions were many doubtless boosted Union morale and spurred the men to even greater efforts. But in the hours ahead, Thomas and his eager troopers would need more than an increase in morale to whip the Army of Tennessee.

The Confrontation at Winstead and Breezy Hills

"About 1:30 p.m., some two miles from Franklin, the Yankee Cavalry made a bold assault on our rear guard. A more determined effort was never made to rout a rear guard than this one, and it continued into the night."[100]

The Confederate Stand at Winstead Hill Gap

Appoximately two miles from south Franklin, "many of the [CSA] infantry were without shoes, staggering on the frozen ground with bleeding feet."[101] Stopping in Franklin for a brief moment, yet still keyed up and pushing on in a fiercely determined pursuit of Hood's fleeing columns, Federal cavalry commander James Wilson sent a succinct communication to headquarters:

> Hdqrs. Cavalry Corps, Mil. Div. Of the Mississippi,
> Franklin, December 17, 1864–1:20 P.M
>
> General [Whipple]: The rebels began passing through here early yesterday morning, cavalry, artillery, and infantry. One of our surgeons here says he never saw a worse rabble; they are completely demoralized. I'll do what I can for the rear guard. Can't hear definitely of Forrest, though it is reported that he withdrew from Murfreesboro yesterday.[102]
>
> J. H. Wilson
> Brevet Major General

Soon enough, James Wilson would hear definitely of Forrest.

Early Afternoon

Throughout the morning hours Wilson's troopers had pressed on without the slightest letup. Knipe and Hatch, having merged forces since crossing over and entering Franklin, bore down the Columbia pike as the brigades of Johnson and Croxton moved quickly for the enemy's flanks on the Carter's Creek and Lewisburg pikes. The orders were to "push rapidly forward and endeavor to pass around the flanks of the enemy's rear guard; and to press it continually" in an all-out effort to "break up their last organized force and disperse the disorganized and flying mass they were covering"[103] (Report of Bvt. Major General James H. Wilson, USA, commanding Cavalry Corps, Military Division of the Mississippi, of operations October 24, 1864–February 1,

1865). "He [Knipe] crossed the Harpeth near the railroad bridge. Johnson's division, with Harrison's brigade, having pushed out at 4 a.m. on the Hillsborough road and crossed, came up the south bank of the Harpeth and entered Franklin about the same time. Hatch, having struck the Franklin pike two miles south of Brentwood, pushed to the left and crossed at the ford on the Murfreesborough road. Croxton crossed at his old crossing two miles above the town. The rebels, finding Johnson on their flank, fell back to a strong position on the Columbia Pike two miles south of Franklin"[104] (Report of Bvt. Major General James H. Wilson, USA, commanding Cavalry Corps, Military Division of the Mississippi, of operations October 24, 1864–February 1, 1865).

Completely exhausted and numbed by the harsh weather, Hood's army pushed themselves on, a dispirited, broken-down mixture of men wounded to the heart, an army nearly paralyzed from pain and astonishment. Passing over the grisly battleground of November 30 with its numberless scars and gravesites, the Confederate rear guard made its way through the ravaged town of Franklin, having burned behind them, in the face of Wilson's oncoming cavalry, the bridges spanning the Harpeth River. With little more than moments to spare, the greater part of the army had crossed the swollen Harpeth and passed through town. In the dash for safety, and certainly with no small measure of anguish, Hood's fleeing army was forced to leave their wounded from the battle of Franklin behind them, in enemy hands. Scarcely eluding Wilson's attacks, the frontal lines of Hood's forces had made their way into the open on the Columbia pike, south of town. Soon they would be facing yet another series of ferocious charges that would last into the dark hours of the night. There would be no reprieve from Thomas. "[After departing Franklin] [t]he rebels, finding Johnson on their flank, fell back to a strong position on the Columbia pike two miles south of Franklin, leaving his hospitals, about 2,000 wounded, and 10,000 rations in our hands"[105] (Report of Bvt. Major General James H. Wilson, USA, commanding Cavalry Corps, Military Division of the Mississippi, of operations October 24, 1864–February 1, 1865).

Around 1:30 p.m., in a soaking rain, as S.D. Lee's rear guard held in check the aggressive Union cavalry striking incessantly at its rear and flank, the van of the Confederate army, also under Federal fire, approached the vicinity of Winstead and Breezy Hill Gap, some two miles distant from Franklin on the Columbia Pike. From the moment of Confederate defeat outside Nashville and the initial withdrawal and through the bludgeoning of the lead elements of Wilson's cavalry at Hollow Tree Gap, the stern conflict at the Harpeth River and the retreat through Franklin, Lee's corps had performed admirably. Due to the strenuous efforts of his rear guard action, and despite the horrific conditions, the army was yet intact. "Some four or five hours were gained by checking the enemy one mile and a half south of Franklin and by the destruction of the trestle bridge over the Harpeth, which was effected by Captain Coleman, the engineer officer on my staff, and a party of pioneers, under a heavy fire of the enemy's sharpshooters"[106] (Report of Lieutenant General Stephen D. Lee, CSA, commanding Army Corps, of operations November 2—December 17, 1864).

The Fedral cavalry ever persistent, the unmistakable sounds of its approach were soon distinctly discerned as the Confederate rear guard strained for a glimpse of the enemy through the thick, grey fog and prepared for battle. The measure of visibility must have been gauged in yards, even in feet, but certainly not in miles. As the light slowly began to fade over the misty landscape and the shadows began to stretch themselves out under the thick covering of haze, the rank and file of blue and grey were distinguished only by the familiarity of their voices. The dim, shadowy fog all but covered their eyes, as if a thick veil had fallen over their faces, leaving them nearly blind to one another and to the world around them. Nondescript forms darting in and out of the shadows vanished as quickly as they appeared. "General Wilson's Cavalry is skirmishing heavily with the enemy, who is drawn up in line of battle about three miles beyond Franklin"[107] (Journal of the Fourth Army Corps).

The fighting here must have been substantial, as the whole of Wilson's cavalry force was now out on open ground, the only considerable obstacle being the rain-soaked fields lying deep in mud. Here the fighting grew to extreme intensity, as the entire cavalry corps was involved in charging one segment of Hood's army. As with the other clashes of the day, hand-to-hand combat characterized the encounter at Winstead Hill as well.

The 4th Tennessee [Cavalry, U.S., of Hammond's Brigade, Knipe's Division] took the advance and pushed over the [Harpeth] river, through the town and out on Lewisburg Pike, followed by the brigade. Flanking the enemy out of a position between this and the Columbia Pike, we moved across to this latter road, and leisurely moved down towards Columbia. On either side of us great columns of cavalry were moving through the fields in parallel lines. The entire cavalry corps was in sight. The whole face of the country seemed covered with the mighty host. A mile to the front, a range of heavily wooded hills at right angles to the pike, rose abruptly from the plain. On the brow of the hill a battery in the road opened on us with shell. The first shell, passing over, bursted beyond our rear; another and another followed. The stragglers felt an impulse of valor unfelt before, and made vigorous efforts to get to the front. The pace of the command visibly quickened—broke into a trot, and soon were galloping, while still above us shrieked the shells. Alas! Not all! Those in the rear could see the column, opening and closing at frequent intervals, as the horsemen passed on either side of the dead and wounded men and horses who had fallen. Reaching a break in the wall which fenced in the right side of the road, the head of the column, turning, dashed into the field on the right. Dismounting at the edge of the woods, which was also the base of the hill, we advanced upon the enemy, and drove him from his position. It was said that in this action the 4th [U.S. Cavalry] Regulars, lead by Knipe in person, went into line, without dismounting, charged the enemy, and, after a sharp hand to hand fight, drove him in confusion from the field. The whole corps was engaged in this action, and in thirty minutes from the discharge of the first gun, the entire rebel force, who were [not] killed or [taken as] prisoners, were in full retreat.[108]

"Hatch moved out between the Lewisburg and Columbia pikes; Knipe on the Columbia pike; and Johnson on the Carter's Creek pike. General Knipe attacked by the front, while Hatch and Johnson moved upon the enemy's flanks, and although the rebel rear guard was composed of Stevenson's division of infantry [and] Buford's division of cavalry, it was pressed rapidly back, with heavy skirmishing, to a position just north of the West Harpeth River"[109] (Report of Bvt. Major General James H. Wilson, USA, commanding Cavalry Corps, Military Division of the Mississippi, of operations October 24, 1864–February 1, 1865).

Shortly after the leading elements of Hood's army had crossed the Harpeth and had become engaged near Winstead Hill, Lieutenant General Lee, commanding the rear guard, was wounded in the heel by a shell fragment, probably fired by Battery I, First Illinois Light Artillery. "Soon after crossing the Harpeth, Lieutenant General Lee was wounded" (Report of Major General Carter L. Stevenson, CSA, commanding division, of operations September 29—December 17, 1864). "A shell fragment had taken off his spur and shat-

Stone wall at the Little Harpeth River.

Stone wall at the West Harpeth River.

tered a few bones in his heel" (*Medical Histories of Confederate Generals*, Jack D. Welsh, M.D., p.137). Unaffected by his injury, Lee afterward ordered Stevenson's division to the relief of Clayton's as replacement brigades in the rear guard. Putting Chalmers' cavalry on both flanks to blunt the Federal cavalry offensive, Lee prepared for what was surely in the making. Soon the massive onslaught of Federal cavalry would cover the fields on all sides, endeavoring to overwhelm them. Regardless of his injury, Lee retained command of his corps until nightfall.

Subsequent to providing a successful defense against Wilson's enormous cavalry charge, the Army of Tennessee continued their march southward as a dense darkness slowly began to envelope them. As night fell, the rear guard took up a position "in open fields," just north of the village of West Harpeth, situated on the banks of the river. "When about three miles from Franklin General Lee ... directed me to take command of the cavalry commanded by Brigadier General Chalmers, which, with the rest of my division was to constitute the rear guard."[110] (No. 329, Report of Major General Carter L. Stevenson, CSA, commanding division, of operations September 29–December 17, 1864).

The Battle at West Harpeth

Near the crossing of the West Harpeth River by the Franklin/Columbia Turnpike, extending westward toward the railroad tracks: "Late in the evening, apparently exhausted with rapid marching, the rebels took a strong position in open fields about a mile north of the West Harpeth. It was then almost dark from fog and approaching night"[111] (Reports of Bvt. Major General James H. Wilson, USA, commanding Cavalry Corps, Military Division of the Mississippi, of operations October 24, 1864–February 1, 1865). "The weather, still wet, was very cold, the roads desperately muddy, horses and men so hungry and jaded that despondency was now stamped upon the somber features of the hardiest."[112]

Upon reaching the West Harpeth River, another 3 miles southward, some of the fiercest fighting of the retreat took place. Flanked by the Johnson house ("Laurel Hill") on the Columbia pike and the West Harpeth River, the last battle fought in Williamson County, Tennessee, in the War Between the States was fearfully played out. The Federal cavalry lost no time in seeking the upper hand.

The time approaching 4:00 p.m. and nearing night, with the dim visibility further reduced by dense fog and rain, the rear of Hood's army peered into the darkening haze, hard on the lookout for the slightest movement in their direction. Emerging out of a dismal, unearthly mist, Wilson's cavalry advance suddenly broke upon the Confederate rear guard, now mostly comprising infantry from Stevenson's division, as the Confederate cavalry was

West Harpeth River.

West Harpeth Battleground.

largely out of ammunition. The results, although with some minimal success for the Union army, were in the end dreadfully predictable. "Late in the evening the enemy was found in open fields, one mile north of the west Harpeth. Wilson at once ordered Hatch and Knipe to charge the flanks of this force, and Lieutenant Hedges, with a detachment of the Fourth U. S. cavalry to attack its centre on the road. The enemy opened with artillery, but Wilson's forces, undeterred by this fire charged his centre and flanks, drove him from position and captured his guns. Darkness prevented further pursuit."[113]

> The enemy did not press us again until we arrived near Johnson's house, five or six miles north of Spring Hill. Here I formed my line, having about 700 infantry, with the cavalry on my flanks. The enemy advanced rapidly upon me, attacking me in front. I found it impossible to control the cavalry and, with the exception of a small force on the left, for a short time, to get them into action. I may as well state that at this point, as soon as the enemy engaged us heavily, the cavalry retired in disorder, leaving my small command to their fate. The enemy perceiving the shortness of my line, at once threw a force around my left flank and opened fire upon it and its rear. This was a critical moment, and I felt great anxiety as to its effect upon my men, who, few in numbers, had just had the shameful example of the cavalry added to the trial of the day before [Maj. General Stevenson].

The shivering Confederates, though heavily pressed by fatigue and overexposure, remained disciplined. Under the sabers of Federal cavalry (and to avoid being taken in the rear), Stevenson's division engaged in an unusual Napoleonic tactic: the "Hollow Square," a defensive maneuver, formed by creating three sides of a square, bayonets forward. Thus formed, the Federals were initially repulsed. Several participants described the action as follows:

I at once ordered Colonel Watkins to prepare to retire fighting by the flank, and General Pettus to move in line of battle to the rear, with a regiment thrown at right angles to his flank, thus forming three sides of a square. Watkins drove the enemy in his front in confusion, moved, at the order which was given in the instant of success, by the flank, and charged those on his flank, drove them also. I halted again in about half a mile, formed a line upon each side of the pike—Pettus on the right, Watkins on the left, each with a regiment formed on his flank perpendicularly to his line to the rear—and having made these dispositions moved again to the rear. The enemy soon enveloped us in front, flank and rear, but my gallant men under all their charges never faltered, never suffered their formation to be broken for an instant, and thus we moved, driving our way through them, fighting constantly, until within a short distance of Spring Hill, where we found that Major General Clayton, hearing of our situation, had turned and moved back to our assistance. Here I halted for a time, and Holtzclaw's brigade, of Clayton's division, was formed upon Watkins' left flank in the manner which I have described. While here the enemy made several attacks and opened upon us with artillery but were readily repulsed. This was sometime after dark[114] [No. 239, Report of Maj. Gen. Carter L. Stevenson, CSA, commanding Division, of operations September 29–December 17, 1864].

Within about two miles of Franklin on the Columbia Pike we formed line—Pettus on the right facing toward the enemy and Cummings on the left with two pieces of artillery on the pike. It had been raining before, and that day a slow rain was falling, so that the fields where the infantry was stationed was very muddy. Clayton's Division was moving slowly towards Columbia, so as to be in reach of support to Stevenson, if needed, but not supposed to be, as it was believed the swollen river would divide the opposing forces. Some of the same cavalry that were to show us how to fight Yankees were upon our flanks. About two o'clock or later in the afternoon a large force of cavalry quietly formed in our front, to which numbers were being added until the line far overlapped our flanks. It was a question as to who they were, since Federal and Confederate cavalry could not be designated by apparel. Soon they revealed themselves by a bold and vigorous charge upon us. This was the first time we had encountered cavalry, and it must be confessed that they awakened admiration by their gallant and brave bearing. They swooped down upon us with pistols, carbines, and sabers, hewing, whacking and shooting. Our cavalry flankers, desiring safety for themselves, left us to our fate. It was the most trying experience I had during the war. The enemy were so numerous as to envelop us, and withal they were brave fighters. Our infantry lines, seeing themselves abandoned by the cavalry and the enemy in close vigorous personal attack in both front and flank, after a few rounds, showed signs of wavering. This was manifest in both ours and Cummings' Brigades. I knew there was no chance of escape but by fighting; so I ran along my line entreating the men to stand as our only chance, for we would never get away in the large, open grounds around us, for there were enough of them to give three or four mounted men to chase down each fellow afoot. I suppose the commanders of the other regiments did likewise, for in a little while the lines were steady, with a grim determination on every face, using shot or bayonet as needed. On looking around it

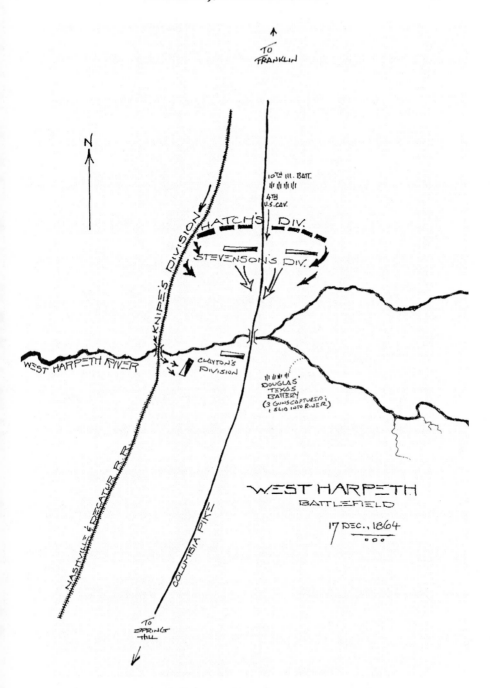

Map of West Harpeth Battlefield, December 17, 1864 (courtesy David Fraley).

was the same as far as could be seen on both sides of the pike. From the time the panicky feeling was quelled; never were soldiers, nor can they ever be, more determined, more fearless, or more effective, and withal they were cheerful throughout the remainder of the day. It must have been the outcome of the desperate situation. My heart swells to this day with a justifiable pride in such a soldiery.

When at last after desperate fighting we had driven them off, we about faced and marched till we saw them approaching again, when we about faced and met them with renewed punishment; this was repeated several times. When the day was closing and they made their last advance, they halted when within close range without firing a gun or other hostile demonstration. The inquiry in our minds was: "Who are they? If friends, why do they not come to us? If foes, why this waiting to attack?" Generals Stevenson and Pettus with their staffs were quite near me, and some one of their staff asked who they were. Nobody knew. Major Reeves, of Stevenson's staff, said, "I will find out," and rode down the pike about half way between the two lines, and soon after he started two or three from the other line came, meeting him. When they neared each other, Reeves wheeled his horse and rode back rapidly. He hardly commenced his return when a few men from the other line broke down the pike with speed, and, reaching our two pieces of artillery, cut down the wheels rendering them useless. As they dashed down upon the pieces we opened upon them with our whole force, and they replied spiritedly, but did not charge. While the engagement was on we heard heavy firing in our rear which continued for some time. When night had fully set in those in our front withdrew. In due time, we marched back a few miles and laid our weary bodies down for much needed rest. But little preparation was made for a comfortable bed, as three days had passed with but little sleep, rest, or food, but a good deal of fighting, with much mental anxiety, much plodding through mud, and our clothing cold, weighted with rain. It was known before we halted, however, why the enemy in their last approach had waited to bring on the action. A heavy detachment had been sent around the precipitous range of hills bordering the Columbia pike westward, so as to pass to our rear through a gap in the range, coming upon our rear and so enclose us on both sides and force a surrender, securing thus a victory for less cost than by fighting. Clayton had heard our constant fighting through the evening, and had halted his division between us and the gap through which the flanking party came, so as to render assistance, assured that we must need it after such strenuous fighting. It was our salvation, for the flanking force had passed through the gap and were passing to our rear when they met Clayton's men, who at once assailed and beat them off. There was a peculiar feature to this retreat. The retreating party bore off the spoils—clothing, shoes, arms, horses, saddles, blankets and other things.[115]

[When] I [Clayton] learned that the enemy were moving around General Stevenson I immediately placed my command across the road, Stovall's brigade, Colonel R.J. Henderson commanding, on the right, Gibson's in the center, and Holtzclaw's, Colonel Bushrod Jones commanding, upon the left[116]

Six miles south of Franklin, the division being at a halt in the road, I [Clayton] learned that the enemy were moving around General Stevenson. I immediately placed my command across the road, Stovall's brigade, Col. R.J. Henderson commanding, on the right, Gibson's in the center, and Holtzclaw's, Col. Bushrod Jones commanding, upon the left. Hearing considerable firing in the rear I ordered Colonel

Jones to move Holtzclaw's brigade forward in line of battle, keeping his right resting on the pike, so as to render any assistance that might be necessary to General Stevenson. Having given some general instructions to General Gibson as to keeping out skirmishers and scouts, I directed him to take command of the two brigades, and with my staff rode up the pike to communicate with General Stevenson[117] [No. 240, Report of Major General Henry D. Clayton, CSA, commanding Division, of operations November 20—December 27, 1864].

Regardless of Stevenson's staunch defense, with characteristic eagerness Wilson's intrepid cavalry charged repeatedly with vicious assaults, endeavoring to penetrate the unyielding Confederate rear guard's lines. "About 4:00 p.m. the enemy, having crossed a considerable force, commenced a bold and vigorous attack, charging with his Cavalry upon our flanks and pushing forward his lines on our front"[118] (Report of Lieut. Gen. Stephen D. Lee, CSA, commanding Army Corps, of operations November 2—December 17, 1864).

Late in the evening, the enemy took another strong position in the open fields, about a mile north of West Harpeth River, apparently with the intention to make a strong resistance to Gen. Wilson's future pursuit. Gen. Wilson ordered Gen. Hatch to form across the pike, and to the left, and Gen. Hammond to form on the right, and parallel to the Pike, while the 4th U.S. [Cavalry] was to form in columns of fours, on the Pike.

The battery was placed in the rear of the 4th U.S., on an eminence. The orders were for Hatch and Hammond to press their flanks, while the 4th U.S. was to charge down the Pike and break their center.... [T]he order "forward" was given, as soon as the 4th U.S. appeared on the Pike and out of range of the guns, while Gen. Hatch's artillery replied vigorously.[119]

[L]ate in the evening, a cold rain was falling. General Pettus called his brigade to attention and told us that we were surrounded. "What must we do?" Someone in the ranks told him we would try to do what he commanded us to do, as we had always done. He gave the command to fix bayonets and form a hollow square with guns loaded and go in position to guard against cavalry. We had not formed the square but a few moments before they charged us. Our men did not fire until they got close up to us, as the breech of our guns was on the ground and the men's right knees also on the ground with fingers on the triggers and bayonets raised to a level with their heads. The remainder of that cavalry did not bother our rear anymore. We made fires not far from there. I put on a new Federal suit of clothes and slept under two blankets. I got off of a Federal horse I captured when the rider was shot off in forty feet of me. I also got his rations and made coffee in his coffee pot and drank it out of his cup. I hope he was prepared to die and is in heaven now.[120]

For Wilson, with his total combined force on hand, traveling unencumbered in the open and literally spanning the countryside as well as covering the roads, it was now only a matter of time and opportunity. This starving, threadbare "rebel" rear guard couldn't fight on in such a stubborn, defiant manner indefinitely. Within moments, running heedlessly into the unbendable

Confederate line as darkness covered the scene, Wilson's cavalry slammed into a wall of lead that sent them reeling in all directions, entirely breaking the force of their charge and turning them out. Escaping with what was left of their regiments the only thought that made any sense was that of immediate survival, whatever it took to get it.

> Passing the enemy's flank, and reaching the pike in his rear, we moved forward to the attack. The 10th Indiana cavalry passed the enemy, who were ambushed behind a stone fence on the left, and who permitted us to likewise get well in the trap before springing it. Suddenly, from out of the darkness, "Halt! Who comes there?" sharply questioned a voice. "Federal cavalry," replied (Colonel) Jackson. "Fire!!" rang out the command, and immediately from a thousand muskets in our faces, gushed a sheet of flame. Down went man and horse. Another volley and the frightened horses reared and plunged, many falling in a ditch along side the road, crippling the riders.[121]

> Company L [9th Indiana Cavalry] was in advance. Moorhouse went down with a ghastly wound; Bristow fell dead; Jackson's horse went into the ditch, falling upon him, and inflicting permanent injuries to his breast. Acting Adjutant Comstock and another, whose name I cannot give, saved the Colonel from capture, by mounting him upon another horse and holding him in the saddle until a place of safety could be reached. Color Sergeant Ricks, of Company E, a noble boy, was killed and, in the darkness, the colors were lost. The rebels, protected by the wall, were safe from saber or bullet. The plunging of horses, the cries of the wounded, the shouting of the officers, the lurid flashing of guns, fitfully lighting the scene, made a situation inadequately described by the modified term of the "new version." The surprise, the darkness and disorder, the impossibility of returning the fire, left but one thing to do. A united rush was made to the right. The rail fence, bounding the road, went down with a crash—officer and man, with equal zeal, seeking safety in flight. The enemy pursued with shout and yell and hissing bullet. It was not a panic. It was good, hard sense. To get out of that hopeless hell was strictly business.[122]

As night overtook the scene, the fighting became terribly disorganized and mostly hand-to-hand. Due to the intense darkness, the rapidly escalating violence, and the closeness of the opposing forces, the charging Federals of Wilson's cavalry could hardly discern their own men from the Confederates.

With Hatch and Hammond bearing down on opposite roadsides off the pike, the 4th U.S. Cavalry (Wilson's escort commanded by Lt. Hedges) "formed in columns of fours on the pike" and pressed forward in a bold charge, aiming directly for Stevenson's center, smashing the line and scattering his infantry in "great confusion." Crossing the river, Hammond's brigade of Knipe's Seventh Division approached the pike, attacking its flank as Coon's Second Brigade pressed from the opposite side, the 4th U.S. Cavalry continuing its frontal assault. According to Wilson, only the darkness of night "saved the enemy's rear guard from complete destruction."[123] Yet Stevenson held firm, bringing on a terrible, fierce clash in the darkness, the fighting continuing until nightfall.

Hatch on the left and Knipe on the right were at once ordered to charge the enemy's flanks, while the Fourth regular cavalry, under Lieutenant Hedges, was directed straight against his center. Seeing what was about to burst upon him, the [Confederate] battery commander opened with canister at short range, but had hardly emptied his guns before the storm broke upon him as well as upon the entire rebel line.... Hedges rode headlong over the battery and captured a part of his guns, while Hatch's horsemen, under a counter-fire from their own guns, with irresistible fury swept everything before them[124] [James Harrison Wilson, Major-General, USV, Brevet Major-General, USA, "The Union Cavalry in the Hood Campaign"].

As Hatch's swift advance approached the enemy lines, he found himself instantly engulfed in a swirling mob, an indistinguishable mass of fighting men raging in the darkness. Confused, he halted, doubting that the force in his front were in fact those of the rebel rear guard. Seizing the opportunity, Stevenson re-formed and posted a battery in position. Undaunted, Wilson ordered a charge on all sides and was soon met by "a rapid fire from their [Confederate] battery, not over 300 yards from us. Hatch's battery promptly replied."

I [Clayton] saw a column of cavalry moving obliquely and just entering the road a few paces in my front. An infantry soldier of my command, recognizing me (it being then quite dark), ran up to me and whispered, "They are Yankees." Turning my horse to the left, so as to avoid them, I moved rapidly to the right of General Gibson's line, and after narrowly escaping being killed by several shots fired at me through mistake, I communicated the information to General Gibson, who promptly wheeled his brigade to the left and delivered a volley which scattered the enemy, killing many of them. I then, at the suggestion of General Gibson, moved back these two brigades behind a fence, in order to better resist a charge and also for greater security against firing into our own men. This position was scarcely taken when the enemy again began to move from the left upon the pike in our immediate front. Demanding to know who they were, I was promptly answered, "Federal troops," which was replied to by a volley, killing several and again driving them off, leaving a stand of colors, which was secured[125] [Report of Major General Henry D. Clayton, CSA, commanding division, of operations November 20–December 27, 1864].

Soon the enemy, in column and in line on both flanks, charged against our position. When they were about two hundred yards distant our guns opened with canister and grape. They reeled, thrown back in disorder, leaving the pike filled with dead and wounded men and horses. They evidently had not noticed our guns in their front. We did not pursue, but awaited another attack, which was also defeated, and Chalmers fell back to the line formed by Stevenson. During the two charges made by the enemy, men on both sides mingled in hand-to-hand conflicts. General Chalmers himself killed two Federal officers, and his accomplished adjutant general, W.H. Goodman, one time surrounded by several of the enemy, fought himself clear of all of them. General Buford had a desperate encounter with a Federal, both using sabers; Buford was wounded, but killed his antagonist.[126]

At Wilson's command, Lt. Hedges, urging his men ahead, "dashed forward at a gallop with sabers drawn," cutting into the Confederate battery, himself narrowly escaping capture on three separate occasions as Hatch and

Hammond's infuriated brigades dismounted and rushed forward into the dark struggle. "The [Confederate] enemy, broken in the center and pressed back on both flanks, fled rapidly from the field, withdrawing his guns at a gallop." As the tremendous force of their charge gained increased momentum, Wilson's troopers, regardless of the dense visibility, "pressed rapidly forward ... down the pike and on either side ... and struck the rebels in the flank. Pressed in all directions the [Confederate] artillerymen left their guns and saved themselves as best they could; the infantry scattered in all directions; darkness alone enabled the entire command to escape"[127] (Reports of Bvt. Major General James H. Wilson, USA, commanding Cavalry Corps, Military Division of the Mississippi, of operations October 24, 1864–February 1, 1865). "Generals Buford and Chalmers were sustaining the infantry on the two flanks. Meanwhile the enemy was becoming troublesome, though not following with that vigor which might have been expected. At this particular time Capt. W.A. Goodman, adjutant general for Gen. James R. Chalmers, narrowly escaped capture."[128]

In the end, the four guns of Douglas's Confederate Texas Battery were lost to the audacious Federals of Hatch's division, three being captured and one allegedly disabled and sliding into the West Harpeth River. The Federals had pressed hard, inflicting definite damage to the Confederates. For some who in four long years had seen it all, the hard-fought battle at the West Harpeth was by far the most bitter confrontation of the war:

Hammond's Brigade was deployed on the extreme right, Hatch's Division across the pike and through the fields to the left. The Fourth U.S. cavalry, my escort, Lieutenant Hedges commanding, formed in columns of fours on the pike. General's Hatch and Hammond advanced rapidly and the Fourth Cavalry at the charge. The enemy's line, broken and driven back, fled in great confusion; the flanks of our lines pressed on rapidly. General Hammond's brigade, crossing West Harpeth, struck the enemy on the pike again in flank, while Coon's Brigade, on the right of the road, the Fourth Cavalry on the Pike, pressed close upon their rear. The enemy abandoned three 12-pounders and carriage of a fourth. These guns can scarcely be called the capture of any particular division or regiment, though they were actually withdrawn from the field by the Fourth cavalry, my staff, and General Hatch in person. One of them has been credited to the Fourth Cavalry and the other two to Hatch's Division, though the charge of General Hammond, with the Tenth Indiana, upon the enemy's flanks, a quarter of a mile beyond, had probably a greater influence in causing their abandonment than the operations of General Hatch's command[129] [No. 194, Report of Brevet Major General James H. Wilson, USA, commanding Cavalry Corps, Military Division of the Mississippi, of operations October 24, 1864—February 1, 1865].

We had a long ride over a very rough country before we reached the rebel lines. The Little Harpeth also had to be crossed, which, together with the volleys of the enemy from a strong and well covered position, completely broke our line before we reached them. As we neared the fence behind which the rebels lay, we were greeted by a galling fire which carried death to many a noble heart. The enemy was dismounted and well covered, which gave them so great an advantage that they could not at first be dislodged. The Federals broke through the fence and joined in a hand to hand struggle with the enemy. Most of them were dressed in Federal uniforms, and as it was quite dark and foggy, it was with great difficulty we discerned friend from foe. Many of our boys, mistaking the enemy for friends, rode into their lines, and either obeyed the summons to surrender, usually pronounced over a dozen leveled muskets, or by desperate fighting cut their way out with fearful loss. Fierce hand to hand encounters and scenes of personal daring, where clubbed muskets, sabers and pistols were freely used, became the order of the hour. Now some poor fellow so overpowered by numbers as to make further resistance madness, would surrender; the next instant a ball from a friend's carbine would lay the captor dead at the prisoner's feet, and thus liberated he would rejoin his comrades in the fight. In this struggle, which for fierceness exceeded any the regiment ever engaged in, Company "L," Lieut. Crawford commanding, and Company "K," Serg't. Coulter commanding, were the principle actors in a conflict over the colors of Ross' (rebel) brigade. As the contending forces came together, Private Dominic Black, of company "K," ordered the rebel color bearer to surrender; he refused, when Black, followed by others rushed upon him. Just as he was in the act of striking the color bearer down with his saber, one of the color guard shot him through the heart. Serg't. Coulter then seized the flag, wrenching it from the hands of the bearer; the moment Coulter got possession of the flag, he was shot through the shoulder by a rebel not three steps distant; through severely wounded he succeeded in escaping with the prize.[130]

On reaching and driving in the rebels' left the Second Iowa pressed its way around to their rear, when a hand to hand fight ensued, resulting in the capture of one stand of colors and several prisoners. In this engagement Sergt. John Coulter, Corporal A. [Alexander] R. Heck, and Private [Dominic] Black, of Company K, captured and brought off a stand of division colors, after which Private Black and Corpl. A[lexander]. R. Heck were killed and Sergt. John Coulter was severely wounded. The sergeant, however, succeeded in bringing away the rebel standard. Sergeant [Herman] Margaretz, of Company F, same regiment, the second color sergeant was killed at the same place, but not until he had killed the rebel who demanded his colors. On burying the dead three Federals and five Confederates were found dead within three paces of each other. The firing in the rear, in conjunction with the brisk engagement in front, caused the enemy to fall back, and with detached portions of the brigade I continued to press his flank until dark, when I dismounted the Ninth Illinois, formed in range, and fired upon him by volleys, driving him from another position, and, in cooperation with other troops, capturing three more pieces of artillery. One of these pieces was brought off by the Ninth Illinois[131] [Report of Col. Datus Coon, 2nd Iowa Cavalry, Commanding Second Brigade, of operations from September 30, 1864, to January 15, 1865].

(The full names of those listed above were discerned via the following source: *The Roster of Union Soldiers, 1861—Iowa*, M541-1 – M541-29, edited by Janet B. Hewitt, Broadfoot, Wilmington, NC, 2000.)

I never saw the enemy so persistent at any other time in all my experience. They gave us absolutely no rest at all.... Darkness was coming on. We had reached a place on the pike on one side of which was a stone fence and on the other side, a woods. The enemy were making demonstrations as if they intended to charge us. So in order to better protect ourselves, we formed a "hollow square," the stone fence forming one side of the square. In this position we waited, but not long. It had become quite dark, but we could tell from the noise and confusion and commands being given that they were preparing for a charge.... We kept quiet and held our fire until they were almost upon us before we fired on them.... Quite a number of the enemy were killed and wounded. No damage was done us, other than a good scare, for we had never been charged in the darkness by cavalry. The horsemen coming through the woods with sabers clanking and horse's hooves breaking the sticks and men and horses tearing through the timbers, and in addition to all of that there were the voices of many officers, and altogether it made a time of anxiety not soon to be forgotten.[132]

On the afternoon of December 17th the rebels made a stand on a ridge on the Franklin pike, and toward evening our whole brigade charged, mounted, and drove the enemy, while they fell back a short distance and made another more desperate and determined stand. This was just before dark; here we charged and drove them back again. In both these engagements the Ninth did a good deal of hard fighting, the rebels having contested every foot of ground; our brigade was barely able to hold its own. Colonel Coon and Captain Avery, A.A.G., rallied the men, when they again advanced, this time with their horses at a slow walk, firing rapidly, drove the rebels so fast as to compel them to leave their three-gun battery unsupported, which General Hatch observing, with but a handful of followers, rushed forward, capturing three twelve-pound brass pieces. The rebels soon re-formed, and made a desperate attempt to recapture this battery; but Captain Mock, with the Ninth Illinois Cavalry, stubbornly and successfully resisted every advance of the enemy. The Ninth here fired by volleys at the word of command. In this way, it being after dark, they prevented the enemy from taking advantage from the flash of our guns to return our fire. After repeated attempts to break through our lines, the Confederates withdrew, and the day was ours; the field, with the enemy's killed and wounded, as also their cannon, being in our possession.[133]

By 9:00 p.m. the fighting, for the most part, was over. The sound of gunfire was soon replaced by the all-too-familiar moans and wails of the wounded. A pelting, freezing rain covered the country.

A more persistent effort was never made to rout the rear guard of a retiring column. This desperate attack was kept up till long after dark, but gallantly did the rear guard—consisting of Pettus' [Alabama] and Cummings' [Georgia] brigades, the latter commanded by Colonel Watkins, of Stevenson's division, and under that gallant and meritorious officer Maj. Gen. C.L. Stevenson—repulse every attack. Brigadier General Chalmers with his division of cavalry covered our flanks. The cavalry of the enemy succeeded in getting in Stevenson's rear, and attacked Major General Clayton's division about dark, but they were handsomely repulsed, Gibson's and Stovall's brigades being principally engaged. Some four or five guidons were captured from the enemy during the evening[134] [Report of Lieut. Gen. Stephen D. Lee, CSA, commanding Army Corps, of operations November 2–December 17, 1864].

Before the fight was over night closed in and covered the field with a pall of impenetrable darkness. The scene, like that of the night before, was one of great confusion, but every musket-flash and every defiant shout was a guide to the gallant and unrelenting pursuers. Hammond, passing around the enemy's left, forded the West Harpeth, and with the Tenth Indiana Cavalry, Lieutenant Colonel Ben. Gresham commanding, struck a new line, formed a short distance south of the river, and in a desperate hand-to-hand fight, mounted men against footmen, saber and pistol against stout hearts and clubbed muskets, with the pall of darkness still over all, again scattered the enemy, capturing their remaining guns, and spreading confusion and terror throughout the retreating mass of now completely disorganized Confederates. It was 10 o'clock before the National cavalry ceased the pursuit, and an hour later before order could be restored to its ranks. Men and horses were ravenously hungry and almost worn out with three days of continuous marching and fighting, and there was nothing left them but to bivouac on the field[135] [James Harrison Wilson, Major-General, USV, Brevet Major-General, USA, "The Union Cavalry in the Hood Campaign"].

After his clash with Wilson's cavalry, and "finding that the enemy had evidently become disheartened and abandoned his attacks," General Stevenson resumed the line of march, placing his entire command on the pike. "Never did a command [Holtzclaw's] in so perilous position extricate itself by the force of more admirable coolness, determination, and unflinching gallantry." Stevenson then assumed command of Lee's Corps due to Lee's wounding near the Harpeth crossing earlier in the day[136] (Report of Major General Carter L. Stevenson, CSA, commanding division, of operations September 29–December 17, 1864). "The fight lasted until about nine o'clock. The 4th Tennessee [Cavalry] bivouacked in the field in line of battle. The weather was intensely cold."[137]

Two Federal cavalrymen would receive the Congressional Medal of Honor for actions in this vicious fight. In the end, more precious time was gained for the remainder of the retreating Confederate army, making their way southward to Columbia and on to the Alabama line. The war, or at least the fighting in Williamson County, Tennessee, had come to a standstill, if not to a bloody, bitterly contested end.

"The conduct of the [Federal] troops in this affair was most admirable, particularly that of the Fourth U.S. Cavalry, the Second Iowa, and Tenth Indiana"[138] (Major General James H. Wilson, USA, Commanding Cavalry Corps). Ever buoyant (but somewhat prematurely), Wilson didn't waste a minute to report the outcome:

Hdqrs. Cavalry Corps, Mil. Div. of the Mississippi.
Three miles north of Thompson's Station, on West Harpeth
December 17, 1864–6 p.m.

Brig. Gen. W.D. Whipple,
Chief of Staff, Department of the Cumberland

General: We have "bust up" Stevenson's division of infantry, a brigade of cavalry, and taken three guns. The Fourth Cavalry and Hatch's Division, supported by Knipe, made several beautiful charges, breaking the rebel infantry in all directions. There has been a great deal of night firing, volleys and cannonading from our guns—the rebels have none. It is very dark, and our men are considerably scattered, but I'll collect them on this bank of the stream—West Harpeth.

Hatch is a brick!

Very respectfully, your obedient servant,

J.H. Wilson, Brevet Major General, Commanding[139]

Another message, received by Wilson later in the evening, confirmed what many must have already guessed. The belated progress of Wood's infantry was no better situated that night than it had been in the morning. Complaining that the river had risen much quicker than he could cope with and the current flowed at such a dangerous pace, Wood was unable to construct a bridge. A crossing would not be possible without the use of pontoons, which he hoped would arrive soon. "The river rose so rapidly, the driftwood was so heavy, and the current so swift, that I have been unable to make a bridge, and do not expect to get over until the pontoons come. I have notified General Thomas, and asked him to hurry up the pontoons.... If the pontoons get up tonight, I hope to get off early in the morning, and will use all possible dispatch in getting up to you.... I will push forward"[140] (Th. J. Wood, Brigadier General of Volunteers).

By late evening Wilson had already begun preparing himself for the following day. Writing General Whipple from the Johnson House, the ever-lively Union cavalry commander extended praise and commendation to his troops, noting particularly Knipe's division, how it had "participated most handsomely in the affair of this evening," and the "brilliant behavior of the troops." Had there been enough daylight, he asserted, his cavalry "would certainly have destroyed their entire rear guard." In preparation for the first light, Wilson committed himself to "assemble everything ... along the line of the West Harpeth tonight.... As soon as it is light in the morning, and everything fed, I will push forward."[141]

Later that night the anticipated reply was received from Whipple, who commented on "the high appreciation of the conduct of yourself, officers, and men" and advised Wilson to "push on in the morning as early as possible."[142] No one would have expected anything different. Regardless of the setbacks, there would be no pause in the pursuit. Hood's army was nearly in the grip of Wilson's vise. Another day of hard, persistent fighting might just end it all. Wilson would "push forward" with everything under his command.

But the brutal engagement at West Harpeth had decided nothing. Although the balance had fallen in favor of the Confederates (having once again escaped capture), the outcome only strengthened greater resolve on both fronts. Due to the necessity of a brief transferral of command and a departure from the scene of action, the following day General S.D. Lee bade a temporary farewell to the men of his corps, noting particularly their performance of duty during the past several days:

General Orders, No. 67—Headquarters Lee's Corps, In the field, December 18, 1864

Before taking temporary leave of this corps, I desire to express to the officers and men of my command my high appreciation of the good conduct and gallantry displayed by them at Nashville in the engagement of the 16th instant, and to assure them that they can be held in no manner responsible for the disaster that day. I extend to them all my thanks for the manner in which they preserved their organization in the midst of temporary panic, rallying to their colors and presenting a determined front to the enemy, thus protecting the retreat of the army.

I would also respectfully thank the officers and men of Holtzclaw's and Gibson's brigades, of Clayton's division, and of Pettus' brigade, of Stevenson's division, for the gallantry and courage with which they met and repulsed repeated charges of the enemy upon their line, killing and wounding large numbers of the assailants and causing them to retreat in confusion.

I desire also to tender my thanks to Major General Stevenson and the officers and men of Pettus' and Cumming's brigades, of his division, for their skillful, brave and determined conduct while protecting the retreat of the army from Franklin yesterday; constantly attacked in front and on either flank, these brave troops maintained an unshaken line, repulsed incessant attacks, and inflicted heavy loss upon the enemy.

In conclusion, my brave comrades, I beg to assure you that I am not only satisfied with your conduct in the recent campaign, but that I shall repose unalterable confidence in you in the future—a future which, despite the clouds which seem to lower around us, will yet be rendered bright by the patriotic deeds of our gallant army, in which none will gain prouder laurels or do more gallant deeds than the veterans whom I have the honor to command.

S.D. Lee, Lieutenant General[143] [Lieut. General Stephen Dill Lee correspondence].

Enveloped in the deep covering of darkness on the Franklin pike, Hood's battered army retired, putting the day's fighting behind them. "The infantry rear guard bivouacked about Thompson's Station while the cavalry rested southward at Spring Hill."[144] From having laid siege to Nashville in the middle of a blizzard for nearly two weeks only to suffer the disgrace of an unnecessary defeat, Hood's men had fallen back in a fight for their lives, followed by a full day's march of 25 miles in a ceaseless running battle with Federal cavalry that ended in a fierce hand-to-hand encounter in pitch-black darkness. Their level of physical and mental endurance had been drained to the lowest ebb. They had taken enough. The time had come to ease off.

As unlikely as it seems, for a few stolen hours the weary Army of Tennessee took a moment's rest and lay down in the mire and the cold rain. Although food was scarce, if available at all, a brief reprieve from the intense fighting had finally arrived. There was little to eat, true enough; the pressing, gnawing hunger was engraved on their faces. But at least, for a short while, their lives were not in the sights of Federal rifles. All of them must have known instinctively that it wouldn't last. Soon they would be on their bleeding feet again, their bloodshot eyes straining through the mist for movement of blue-clad troopers—Hood's army fighting the dark horsemen and pushing on for the Tennessee River. Once across, they could unwind, refit, and regroup. But that was days away.

We [the 18th Alabama] remained near this spot almost the entire night, wet, tired, and hungry. It had been the most strenuous day we had ever experienced. Marching, fighting, and maneuvering all day long without even time to eat, and if you had an appetite, you did not have the rations. So we struggled on and trudged on and fought on until overcome by weariness, fatigue and hunger, we lay down in the mud and dampness and fell asleep.[145]

In this affair, so trying to both officers and men, all behaved in the best possible manner. While I cheerfully concede all that is due to General Stevenson's Division in checking the advance of the enemy and thus helping to save the Army ... I believe it is not claiming too much to say that this Division, by preventing the enemy from massing in his rear, saved that Division.... After moving back a few miles the Division bivouacked for the night and resumed the march on the following day for the Tennessee River which it reached at Bainbridge on the 27th of December, after a most painful march, characterized by more suffering that it had ever before been my misfortune to witness[146] [Report of Major General Henry D. Clayton, CSA, commanding division, of operations November 20–December 27, 1864].

During the day we were almost constantly engaged with the enemy, who followed us vigorously with a strong force, often in close encounters, and held them in check until nearly night-fall, when by a series of bold charges they broke the lines of our infantry and cavalry, but were severely punished and driven back by the second line of infantry[147] [Report of Brigadier General James R. Chalmers, CSA, commanding Cavalry Division, of operations November 17–December 27, 1864].

General George Thomas, wiring to Lt. General U.S. Grant later that evening, was evidently satisfied with the day's outcome. His ferocious cavalry corps had launched itself into the fight of its life, mercilessly attacking Hood's retreating army at every turn. The enemy had been forced out of Nashville through Franklin and farther southward. Nashville and the regions surrounding it were finally cleared of Confederate military presence. Thomas would spare no effort to complete the victory obtained at Nashville.

Lieutenant General U.S. Grant:

We have pressed the enemy today beyond Franklin, capturing his hospitals, containing over 1,500 wounded, and about 150 of our wounded. In addition to the above, General Knipe, commanding a division of cavalry, drove the enemy's rear guard through Franklin today, capturing about 250 prisoners and 5 battle-flags, with very little loss on our side. Citizens of Franklin represent Hood's army as completely demoralized.... The enemy has been pressed today both in front and on both flanks. Brigadier General Johnson succeeded in striking him on the flank just beyond

Franklin, capturing quite a number of prisoners, number not yet reported. My cavalry is pressing him closely tonight, and I am very much in hopes of getting many more prisoners tomorrow....

I now consider the Cumberland perfectly safe from Nashville down, and have directed the chief quartermaster to commence shipping stores up it immediately. As there is also a fair prospect for another rise in the Tennessee River, I have requested Admiral Lee to send some ironclads and gun-boats up that river, to destroy Hood's pontoon bridge, if possible, and cut off his retreat.[148]

Geo. H. Thomas,
Major General, Commanding

Although time off was certainly an absolute necessity for the Union Cavalry, having been in the saddle since sunup, Major General Wilson had other thoughts on his mind that dreary night. "General Thomas directs that the Army will move in pursuit of the enemy, in the present order of the different commands, at as early an hour after daylight as possible tomorrow morning, December, 18th"[149] (Journal of the Fourth Army Corps). After receiving Thomas's order, Wilson relayed the message to his subordinates:

Special Field Orders   Headquarters Cavalry Corps No. 4
Military Division of the Mississippi,
Johnson's House, December 17th, 1864

I. Commanding officers will be very active tonight and early tomorrow in obtaining forage, and will see that every horse is well fed.

II. The Corps will be assembled in the following order tomorrow; Johnson's Division, with one regiment on Carter's Creek, the balance connecting with the Seventh Division, General Knipe, on the West Harpeth River. The Seventh Division will be on the right side of the Columbia Pike. The Fifth Division will be on the left of the Columbia Pike, its right resting on the left of the Seventh Division. General Croxton's Brigade will be on the Lewisburg Pike. When this disposition is effected, at 6:30 a.m. tomorrow the command will move forward in that order.[150]

The Army of Tennessee, sprawled out in the open fields around the West Harpeth, surrounded by a darkness that sent shivers through their bones, would need all the rest they could get.

3

Sunday, December 18, 1864

The Arrival of Nathan Bedford Forrest

December 18, 1864—Stewart's corps marched in front today, camping in line of battle on Duck River. Cheatham camped on Rutherford's Creek, and General Lee between the creek and Franklin. Army headquarters at Mr. Vaught's, Columbia.[1]—Journal of the Army of Tennessee

In a steady, heavy rain that was to last the entire day, the Union infantry corps of Brigadier General T.J. Wood, blocked on the far side of the Harpeth by its rising waters, must have burned with indignation. Time was slipping away. Every hour that passed without granting Wood's troops forward motion put more distance between them and Hood's army. The day before, having ruined all the bridges over the Harpeth at Franklin, the fleeing Confederates had left Wood's troopers stranded on the opposite bank, cut off from any further immediate pursuit. The ceaseless rains of the night of the 17th had further impeded any forward movement. The river had risen so dangerously high that any attempt at crossing without the aid of a pontoon bridge was out of the question. And to further aggravate the situation, the pontoons were nowhere in sight.

Wood's Federal Infantry Crosses the Harpeth

Although the stream was rising rapidly and the pontoons had not arrived, General Wood's engineers moved ahead with bridge construction throughout the rainy night of the 17th, his infantry finally making the crossing at daylight the following morning.

"Colonel Suman, Ninth Indiana, nobly volunteered to build the bridge, and thanks to his energy and ingenuity and the industry of his gallant regiment, it was ready—though he had few conveniences in the way of tools, the scantiest materials, and the stream was rising rapidly for the corps at daylight the morning of the 18th"[2] (Report of Brigadier General Thomas J. Wood,

USA, commanding Fourth Army Corps, of operations October 26, 1864–January 5, 1865).

Having bridged the rising waters of the Harpeth, Wood moved out rapidly. Forming up well before daylight on the morning of the 18th, the Fourth Corps passed over the swollen river into Franklin, working their way through the deep mud of the pike, throwing themselves forward as quickly as possible. Complete with "a battery of artillery to follow each division," including ammunition, headquarters, and hospital trains (followed by regimental baggage), Wood's troops forged ahead, marching through town southward down the Franklin pike by 8:00 a.m. "December 18; 7:30 AM, Colonel Suman reports that he has been working all night, and just finished the bridge; the [Harpeth] river rose so fast that he could scarcely work, and his bridge was once washed out. 7:30 AM orders at once sent to Division commanders to move at once "[3] (Journal of the Fourth Army Corps).

By the end of the day (as nightfall would arrive early), despite the harsh weather Wood's infantry had arrived in Spring Hill, all but closing the distance with the retreating Confederates as well as the Federal cavalry posted along the pike, "about two miles beyond Spring Hill." By that time the Federals were well into the fray with Hood's rear guard. "3:00 PM, head of [the infantry] column reaches Spring Hill. The mud is very deep, and it has been raining hard up to this hour since 8:00 AM; rain now ceasing. General Wilson's Cavalry has met the enemy's rear guard about two miles beyond Spring Hill and is now skirmishing with him"[4] (Journal of the Fourth Army Corps). "[M]oved at daylight, continuing the pursuit to Spring Hill, where we [Federals] found a considerable force of the enemy, and fired but a few shots, when they fell back in confusion"[5] (Report of Col. Datus Coon, 2nd Iowa Cavalry, Commanding Second Brigade, of operations from September 30, 1864, to January 15, 1865). "On the 18th at daylight [the cavalry] moved through Spring Hill, skirmishing continuously"[6] (Report of Brigadier General Edward Hatch, USA, commanding Fifth Division, of operations October 29—December 25, 1864).

Hdqrs Cavalry Corps, Mil. Div. of the Mississippi, December 18, 1864; 8 a.m.

General Whipple: Dispatch received. I have seventy or eighty wounded, scattered along the road, in houses. Please send ambulances for them at once.

J.H. Wilson, Brevet Major General

Some of our men captured last night have just come in, and report the enemy's rear guard strongly reinforced.

J.H.W.[7]

Cheatham's Corps Replaces Lee as Rear Guard

"On the 18th, Brigadier General Armstrong having come up with his brigade, and General Cheatham's corps having taken the place of General

Lee's as rear guard of the army, we moved down the turnpike from Spring Hill towards Columbia and crossed Rutherford's Creek, the infantry being on the pike and the cavalry in the rear and on the flanks. The enemy did not press us, and we had no fighting beyond a little skirmishing"[8](Report of Brigadier General James R. Chalmers, CSA, Commanding Cavalry Division, for Operations November 17 to December 12, 1864). "The [Federal infantry] corps was pushed rapidly across the Harpeth … and pressed forward," trudging over thick, impassable roads and streams. At last, after marching all day, it came to a weary rest. "Near nightfall it passed in front of the [Union] cavalry and encamped about a mile in advance of it. The weather was very inclement"[9] (Report of Brigadier General Thomas J. Wood, USA, commanding Fourth Army Corps, of operations October 26, 1864–January 5, 1865).

Wood was back in the game. Whatever amount of time he had lost in the last couple of days was now immaterial. He hoped his impatient troops, so keen on having their part to play in this unusual drama, would soon get their chance.

Wilson's Charge Thwarted Near Spring Hill

"On the road from Spring Hill to Columbia the rain poured incessantly, drenching us [Confederates] to the skin. The mud was liquid and had easy access to our dilapidated footgear."[10]

Early on the morning of the 18th the Federal cavalry saddled up, wasting no time, the Brigades of Johnson, Hatch, and Knipe covering Carter's Creek and Columbia Pikes, Croxton forming on the Lewisburg. With Johnson and Croxton streaming down the flanks, Wilson aimed for the Confederate line just beyond the vicinity of Spring Hill.

The sun, although surely only a dim outline through the fog, had hardly risen before the Union cavalry found themselves colliding with the indomitable Confederate rear guard lined on the Franklin pike, their paper-thin, ragged forms slowly emerging from the thick haze. Taking a stand near Spring Hill, Cheatham's Corps (having replaced Lee's shattered ranks), temporarily in command of the infantry rear guard, came under vicious attack. Nearly overwhelmed, Cheatham gave them "quite a check," sending the Federals staggering rearward.[11]

Despite the suddenness of their appearance and "the most strenuous efforts on the part of [their] troops," the collective forces of Wilson's brigades, "skirmishing continually" with the enemy, were unable to bring them in, due in large part to Hood's swift movement toward Columbia and the "densely wooded country, muddy roads, and plowed fields, rendered almost impassable by the constant rain." The cumulative effect of these forces pressed hard on the

Federal cavalry, creating a near impossibility for Wilson's troopers on the flanks "to get forward fast enough to overtake the enemy marching on the pike."

Approaching to within a few miles of Rutherford Creek, the Federal cavalry slowly ground to a halt. Owing to the inability of the supply trains to keep pace with Wilson, the chase was broken off with regret. With food and ammunition nearly gone, Wilson's only option was to pull back, recuperate, and reorganize. Around 1:00 p.m., revealing more than a hint of displeasure, he fired off another message describing the apparent futility of his current situation: "General [Whipple]: All our efforts to bring the enemy to a standstill this morning have failed.... I have halted to issue rations and ammunition."[12] Around 2:00 p.m., fatigued and certainly dissatisfied with the day's outcome, Wilson pulled off, setting up camp near Spring Hill and anxiously waiting for the trains to come forward.

As Wilson wrestled with the continual, mounting pressure, Confederate General B.F. Cheatham's rear guard halted a mere two miles distant below Spring Hill, guarding the crossing of the army's trains over the swollen waters of Rutherford Creek.[13] "[A]t 2 p.m., went into camp"[14] (Report of Brigadier General Edward Hatch, USA, commanding Fifth Division, of operations October 29–December 25, 1864). "Camped for the night three miles south of Spring Hill"[15] (Report of Col. Datus Coon, 2nd Iowa Cavalry, Commanding Second Brigade, of operations from September 30, 1864, to January 15, 1865). "Cheatham and Chalmers held their position six miles north of Columbia during the night of December 18."[16]

Ill at ease, Wilson contacted General Wood with a tense message. Hood's forward echelons were by now crossing the Duck River at Columbia, gaining more ground on the Federal advance. Surely he could not bridge the Tennessee in time! " ... General: I [Wilson] have halted my command ... about two miles from Spring Hill, to feed and issue rations.... I am informed that the enemy has two pontoon bridges across the Duck River.... Prisoners say that Hood cannot get across the Tennessee River, as our forces at Memphis had repaired the railroad ... and were marching out to attack him in flank"[17] (Journal of the Fourth Army Corps). Wood's reply was immediate and direct. The head of his column now in Spring Hill would "move up at once" and appear at Wilson's headquarters by late afternoon. Halting briefly on arrival shortly after 3:00 p.m. as Wilson's cavalry moved off the turnpike, Wood determined to "move on about one mile further," not far from Rutherford Creek, and afterward set up camp for the night in line of battle on the pike[18] (Journal of the Fourth Army Corps).

Regardless of his successful progress in bringing the infantry forward, and being keenly aware of the gravity of the situation, Wood noted that in all likelihood Rutherford Creek, just a few miles ahead, would be at flood stage and impossible to cross without the use of pontoons or a bridge. The creek presented another setback; also, "by all means the pontoon train should be hurried for the crossing of Duck River." Assured by his superiors that the necessary pontoons would arrive that evening, Wood's concluding orders that night included instructions to "continue the pursuit of the enemy tomorrow morning, marching at about 8 o'clock."[19]

By the afternoon of the 18th, Thomas's plan was becoming coordinated on three fronts. The swiftly moving force of Wilson's cavalry corps in the advance had been tormenting the Confederates from the beginning and were by far their most serious and constant threat. The fearsome Union cavalry brigades carried the full weight of the pursuit and remained the commanding general's most trusted means for a concluding victory. Thomas was under no blinding delusion. It was Wilson and his dauntless cavalry brigades that he was ultimtely relying on to do the most damage and to provide him with the most immediate and effective results.

The infantry corps of T.J. Wood, although much impeded by the terrible road conditions and the flooded Harpeth River, was dangerously close to contacting the enemy. Hour by hour Wood seemed just a step away. Should he ever close the gap, a major confrontation would immediately erupt, with devastating losses on both sides occuring as a result. On the third front now coming into play was the ominous spectre of the U.S. Navy under the command of Admiral S.P. Lee.

Thomas Calls on the U.S. Navy

As a consequence of a former written dialogue between Thomas and Admiral Lee, if all went well the admiral was to play a decisve role in the capturing or destruction of Hood's army. The navy would launch its gunboats at two points—on the Duck River, which Hood was soon to encounter (and had actually begun crossing), and at Florence, Alabama, on the Tennessee River. The transfer of Lee's gunboats down the Tennessee was designed to destroy the Confederate pontoon bridges, thereby cutting off Hood's retreat. Should the admiral succeed at either point there was little, if any, hope left for the Army of Tennessee.

Six hours later, after Admiral Lee had sent his communique to Thomas, the Union commander replied with his hearty approval of Lee's intentions. Included in his message was another request, one that the Army of Tennessee would have loathed to hear: "I shall be much obliged if, in addition to the movement on the Tennessee River mentioned above, you will be as well prepared as possible to convoy either from Johnsonville or Clifton a fleet of transports with troops up the Tennessee River to Florence."[20] Thomas was taking no unecessary chances, even at this early stage of the game. The prospect that more Federal troops might be needed to confront Hood at Florence was not being ruled out. It seemed that the Union commander would use any and every necessary means to bag the Confederates, even if it took every man in his army to do it.

In a brief message to chief of staff Major General Halleck a few days later, Thomas outlined the extent of his preparations, which would include the use of both land and naval forces:

> On the 17th I requested Admiral Lee, by telegraph, to proceed up the Tennessee River with as many ironclads as he could secure, in order that he might prevent the enemy throwing a pontoon bridge over the river, or to destroy the bridge, if they had thrown one over. He was to have started the next day. I have also made arrangements to throw a force across the river at Decatur, and move on Tuscumbia, to seize the bridge at Florence, if possible. That force started three days ago, and, if General Granger has acted vigorously, Decatur should be in our possession today. If the expedition against Tuscumbia be successful, I am confident that we shall be able to capture the greater part of Hood's army.[21]

> Geo. H. Thomas,
> Major General, U.S. Volunteers, Commanding.

For the Confederates there had been unrelenting, brutal cavalry assaults, the ever-present threat of Union infantry closing the gap in their rear, and now Federal gunboats poised to block the army's crossing at two points, before and behind. A grim picture was emerging for Hood's exhausted army, which for the most part was being held together by sheer determination.

Aware of the proximity of Wood's Fourth Corps, the Confederate rear guard, like a cornered, wounded animal, positioned itself not far up the road at the ready. The damage inflicted on Wilson's cavalry over the last couple of days had been considerable. A rash move on Wood's part now could prove disastrous. Wisely, Wood decided to stand down, rest, and wait for a better opportunity.

> Headquarters Fourth Army Corps,
> Spring Hill, December 18, 1864; 3:00 PM

> Major General Wilson:
> General: Your very satisfactory note of 2 p.m. has just been received. The head of my column is now in Spring Hill, and I will push on as far as I can tonight to keep well closed up.... On account of the extreme heaviness of the road the men are very much jaded and are straggling some....

> Very respectfully, your obedient servant,
> TH. J. Wood
> Brigadier General, Commanding[22]

Completing his correspondence, at 11:45 p.m., just a few miles north of Rutherford Creek (where Cheatam's rear guard was posted), Wood gave a final order. His plans for the next day would include no significant changes. The pace would remain in place: "Orders of the day for the Fourth Corps for tomorrow, December 19, 1864: The Corps will march in pursuit of the enemy, starting at 8 a.m...."[23]

On the night of the 17th, as the Confederate Army encamped along the road near Spring Hill in the order of march, General Hood chose to set up headquarters in town. Wiring James A. Seddon, the secretary of war, in Richmond, Hood gave a brief account of the army's defeat on the 16th, noting particularly the loss of "fifty pieces of artillery with several ordnance wagons" and a slight description of the losses in killed, wounded, and generals taken prisoner. "Early on the 16th [December] they made a general attack on our entire line, and all their assaults, were handsomely repulsed, with heavy loss, till 3.30 p.m. when a portion of our line to the left of the center suddenly gave way, causing, in a few minutes, our line to give way at all points, our troops retreating rapidly down the Franklin pike."

Hood's Army Begins Passage of the Duck River; HQ in Columbia

Confident in spite of the crushing blow the army had suffered, Hood did not change his plans to cross the Duck River at Columbia. Surrender, or the admission of defeat, from commander on down was clearly out of the question. "I still have artillery enough with the army, and am moving [from Spring Hill] to the south of Duck River"[24] (General Hood). The failure of Hood's army to hold its line on the afternoon of the 16th must have been the most bitter of memories, and the march southward in retreat gave them plenty of time to think it through. Col. Andrew Kellar of Cheatham's Division verbalized what many in the rank and file would have readily agreed to:

Hdqrs. Strahl's Brigade, Cheatham's Division, Amy of Tennessee,
In the field, December, 18, 1864
Maj. A.P. Mason, Assistant Adjutant-General, Army of Tennessee:

Sir: It is a duty I owe myself, brigade, division, to the commanding general, and to the country to state facts in regard to the panic of the army on the afternoon of the 16th. The lines were broken about 3:00 p.m. on a high hill west of the Granny [White] pike about half a mile, which hill was occupied by Tyler's brigade, Bate's division, and given up to the enemy without a struggle. My command was on Tyler's left, and the right of Cheatham's division. This hill, occupied by the enemy, over-looked the right of the army, and the troops seeing it in the hands of the enemy, and seeing the left wing of the army running without making a stand, fled also. It was not by fighting, nor the force of arms, nor even numbers, which drove us from the field. As far as I can now learn, I did not lose more than thirty men and about thirty-five small arms, already replaced. For the first time in this war we lost our cannon. Give us the chance and we will retake them.

Respectfully, your obedient servant, Andrew J. Kellar, Colonel, Commanding.[25]

But, contrary to the colonel's bold plea, the bulk of the army had recently experienced more death and destruction than they had been initially (or justly) called upon to bear. Regardless of Colonel Kellar's faith in the army's ability and resolve to continue the struggle, the grim reality pointed for the time being to the remainder of what had once been a proud, highly competent fighting force, despite the lack of military training or expertise. No level of proficiency could compensate for the ghastly sight of their emaciated, gaunt, skeletal bodies, hatless and shivering under the brute force of an ice-coated wind that seemed to cut right through them. For those who were inclined to engage in retrospect, the outcome of all their tremendous exertions had, in the final days of the war, proven fruitless. They had exhausted all their combined might and every opportunity to recover their land, homes, and liberties and had come up short. It was all but hopelessly lost.

Even so, despite the bloody footprints of the retreat from Tennessee, the torn and shattered Army of Tennessee would give the Yankees one more series of encounters, a shellacking that they would never forget. There would be no attempt at regaining what was lost. But the punishment that the audacious Yankee army would suffer during these frightful days would be seared in memory for the rest of their lives. For Hood and his army there would be no turning back in compromise or surrender of honor. Although crippled in soul and body, in the minds of the Southerners they would never excuse or tolerate betrayal at the hands of greedy Northern politicians. The retreat from Tennessee would continue, and with it the inevitable bloody engagements and the satisfaction of duty done. The furious, heavy hand of Confederate chastisement, meted out in measure consistent with the crime, would be returned upon the Federal army, upon whose heads it would fall.

Late in the day, after securing the crossing of the supply trains and the main body of Hood's army over Rutherford Creek, Cheatham's corps (with Walthall's brigade of Stewart's corps), guarded by cavalry, marched over. Surely much to Wilson's embarrassment, the van of Hood's army was definitely fording the Duck River.

Walthall Entrenches on the North Bank of the Duck River as Rear Guard

Passing over Rutherford Creek in the footsteps of Hood's leading columns, the Confederate rear guard slogged through what had once been known as a road, approached the Duck River, and dug in on the northern bank, holding the line well into the night of the following day. "The night of the 17th we encamped near Spring Hill, and about 2:00 PM the next day the Corps [Stewart's] took position north of Duck River, to cover the crossing of the Army on pontoon bridge at Columbia. Here we [Walthall's Division] entrenched, Major General Loring's Division on the right and mine of the left, and remained 'till 11 o'clock on the night of the 19th, when we moved across the river and encamped a short distance from Columbia, on the Pulaski Pike"[26] (Report of Major General Edward C. Walthall, CSA, commanding Division and Rear Guard of Infantry, of operations November 20, 1864–January 8, 1865).

Adding to the mounting difficulties facing Wilson and Wood, a more serious threat than blizzard-like weather, flooded rivers, and unbeatable Confederate rear guard tenacity had come to their attention. Nathan Bedford Forrest was reported in the vicinity. Early on the morning of the 18th Wilson had forwarded this unwelcome news to his superiors. Citing the testimony of a recently captured Confederate prisoner, the Union commander related the ominous details. Forrest, "with Jackson's division of cavalry and two brigades of infantry" (mostly barefooted) having left their former positions outside Murfreesboro two days before, might well be in the vicinity of Columbia.[27] Wilson had already been battling the divisions of Buford's cavalry, recently joined in to cover the Confederate rear. There was no reason not to believe that Forrest had also arrived. This kind of information would make for a number of sleepless nights. The idea of contending with the likes of Nathan Bedford Forrest was enough to chill the bones of any officer in George Thomas's army.

Forrest Links Up with the Remnants of Hood's Army

Wilson's intelligence was right. Earlier in the day at Lillard's Mills, located between Shelbyville and Columbia on the Duck River, Forrest had crossed over a portion of his command, including prisoners and cattle, putting him within easy reach of Hood's army. Due to the rising waters, which quickly became impassable, Forrest's personal crossing was prevented, forcing him "to push his way down the north bank of the river to Columbia, where he arrived on the evening of the 18th" with his ordnance trains and artillery.[28] "It was then, during the night, the redoubtable battle flag of Major General Forrest reappeared among his men."[29]

With the arrival of the renowned Confederate cavalry commander on the field, Wilson's fading prospects to capture Hood before he could reach the Tennessee was rapidly slipping through his fingers. From this point forward, all dealings with the Army of Tennessee would undergo drastic changes. Although Wilson had paid dearly in lives given in battle under his command, with the addition of Forrest in the game the stakes had suddenly been raised. And with *this* hand, there would be no bluffing.

4

Monday, December 19, 1864
Columbia, Tennessee

December 19: [Confederate] Army headquarters still at Mr.
Vaught's. The army, and such trains and artillery as were
not crossed over yesterday, occupied the day in crossing
Duck River—Lee first, Cheatham next, and then Stewart.
The enemy's cavalry appeared on [the] opposite side of
Rutherford's Creek. —Journal of the Army of Tennessee

Hood's Army Continues Crossing the Duck River; HQ Remains in Columbia

Monday, December 19–1864 Fought the enemy nearly all day on the
[Rutherford] creek, withdrawing in the afternoon and crossing Duck River,
leaving Stewart on the north bank, who, however, also withdrew that night
and crossed"[1] (Itinerary of Cheatham's Army Corps).

"[The Federal Cavalry] resumed the march at 7:00 a.m., and continued
to Rutherford's Creek, where we dismounted, marched by the right flank one
mile, and succeeded in crossing the Sixth Illinois on the wreck of the burnt
railroad bridge, when the fragments floated away and the balance of my command were compelled to ford the stream some distance above. Moved two
miles below on the enemy's flank, the Sixth Illinois skirmishing until dark;
then the command encamped for the night"[2] (Report of Col. Datus Coon,
2nd Iowa Cavalry, Commanding Second Brigade, of operations from September 30, 1864, to January 15, 1865).

Headquarters Department of the Cumberland.
In the Field, December 19, 1864
8:30 a.m. Brig. Gen. T.J. Wood, Commanding Fourth Army Corps, near Spring Hill;

General: On account of the bad state of the weather this morning, the major general directs that your corps remain in camp today, and attend to getting up your trains, if there are any behind, issuing provisions and making preparations for continuing the pursuit tomorrow....

WM. D. Whipple
Brigadier General and Chief of Staff

Unknown to Maj. Gen. Thomas, his order for Wood to "remain in camp today" would soon be overruled by circumstances beyond the control. Regardless of "the bad state of the weather this morning" (8:30), certain segments of the army would be unable to stand down and resupply as directed. Due to the fact that Thomas's message was not received by Wood until later in the day—at 12:30 p.m.—Wood was unaware of its existence until after he had arrived at Rutherford Creek at 9:30 a.m. By then the Federal cavalry advance under Hatch was already in the field and into a hard fight at the banks of Rutherford's Creek that lasted nearly the entire day, a fight that drew Wood's infantry forward within rifle range and under the muzzles of a four-gun Confederate battery manned by Cheatham's rear guard.

Wood's Fourth Army Corps Held at Rutherford Creek and a Sharp Engagement Ensues

December 19th; the whole [Federal] command had a hotly contested fight at Rutherford's Creek. The Ninth was in line with the whole brigade, and was engaged nearly all day. The rebels had destroyed the bridge, and a new one had to be built over this creek, which was much swollen by the recent heavy rains, before we could cross or advance. This enabled the enemy to hold their position and keep us in check as long as they did, and they did fight stubbornly and bravely at this time for the purpose of holding us in check as long as they possibly could, to enable their straggling forces to gain a safe distance on their retreat, as it was apparent to them that this was their last bold and desperate stand before crossing the Tennessee River, infantry and cavalry on both sides being engaged and considerable artillery firing being indulged in. From this time on we had skirmishing until we reached Columbia; here there was considerable firing across the river, mostly by artillery.[3]

The intensity of the battle at Rutherford Creek was greatly increased with the weather turning much colder as the day wore on. No one, it seemed, was spared from the penetrating cold that engulfed them. Due to the lack of blankets, overcoats, and footwear, the sufferings borne by the Confederates was particularly severe. "Rains all day, very cold" (G.L. Griscom Diary, 9th Texas Cavalry). "When as children we shed tears when reading of Washington at Valley Forge; of his men leaving bloody tracks in the snow. Little then did we dream that we would witness similar scenes. The sufferings and hardships endured by Hood's Army on the retreat were greater than any endured by our revolutionary forefathers. We cannot even now think of them without emotion."[4] "The enemy is much demoralized. About one-third of what remains of Hood's Army is without arms and as many are without shoes. Thus far, we have taken from them over 60 pieces of artillery and a large number of prisoners, perhaps 9,000 up to date, including the captured in hospital"[5] (Journal of the Fourth Army Corps).

What was sorely missing in supplies from Hood's army was, with a great deal of effort and continuing patience, made relatively available to Thomas. Much to the relief of Wilson's cavalry, a measure of the needed goods and provisions had finally arrived in the Union camp on the night of the 18th. The men being somewhat rested and reequipped, "the pursuit was resumed [the following morning], not withstanding a heavy storm of rain and snow then prevailing." Due to the harsh weather on the 19th, by order of General Thomas the balance of the Cavalry Corps remained in bivouac while Hatch pushed on ahead, seeking out the best way for the Federals to cross Rutherford Creek when it became time for them to move out. "The country had been entirely denuded of supplies for both men and horses; the haversacks and forage-bags were empty, and there was no alternative but to wait for the supply trains which had been ordered forward, and which joined [the Federal army] late in the night [the 18th]. But during the night the rain turned into a snow storm and by order of General Thomas the larger part of the cavalry corps remained in bivouac the next day, while Hatch was trying to repair the railroad bridge"[6] (James Harrison Wilson, Major-General, USV, Brevet Major-General, USA, "The Union Cavalry in the Hood Campaign").

The Federal army had their work cut out for them that day, with both infantry and cavalry becoming engaged with the Confederates of Cheatham's rear guard on the opposite side of the river. Facing further hindrance, James Wilson put it to the point. Logistical problems seemed insurmountable. At 6:00 that morning, he had sent a desperate note to Gen. Thomas describing the gravity of the circumstances he had been thrust into. On his shoulders the lion's share of responsibility had fallen. No doubt frustrated and pressed with a high degree of anxiety, Wilson faced yet another antagonist at least as serious as the failing supply trains: the constant threat of infectious demoralization was hampering every step the army took. Although his cavalry divisions could take a certain degree of pride in their conduct and success thus far, the army as a whole was confronted by more painful obstacles than they had bargained for. As a consequence, it was the responsibility of the cavalry commander to keep his men from stumbling into the morass of sinking morale. At that moment, his command was "entirely without rations" and nearly out of ammunition. He could hardly take another step forward without them. All he could do was exercise an exasperated patience. "With the exception of Hatch's Division, my [Wilson] command is entirely without rations and nearly without ammunition. I confidently expected the trains here last night, but I learn that the troops and trains ... [of the infantry Corps] so encumbered the road that it was impossible for our supplies to reach us."

Hatch Pushes on Ahead

Two hours later that morning, Wilson's orders reached him. Thomas's stated intention for the army was that it should draw back from the chase temporarily and refit for the days just ahead. According to his plan there would be little battle action for Wilson or anyone else in Thomas's army that day. Although Wilson was acutely aware that the continuous lack of supplies and ammunition was crippling every effort of the cavalry to reach Hood before he could cross the far-off Tennessee, after a day of rest and resupplying they would (according to Thomas) gain the upper hand, overtake Hood, and capture his weary army. How things actually worked out was quite different from what Wilson or Thomas had anticipated.

Nevertheless, while the majority of Wilson's cavalry rested, the unstoppable U.S. cavalry division under Brig. Gen. Edward Hatch would not be dictated to by harsh weather or the lack of supplies. In spite of it all, Hatch reconstructed a bridge from the remains of the original (and another one which had been torched by the Confederates), crossed over Rutherford Creek "with his whole command" the next morning, and closed the distance to the flooded Duck River, just missing the trailing elements of Hood's army, which had passed over prior to his arrival.

Communication from Thomas to Wilson early in the day called for a time of semi-rest and resupplying: "On account of the bad weather ... remain where you [Wilson] are and reconnoiter the country ... get up your ordnance and other trains, issue ammunition and other provisions for continuing the pursuit tomorrow"[7] (addressed to "Headquarters Department of the Cumberland, In the Field December 19, 1864[,] 8 a.m. Major General J.H. WILSON: Commanding Cav. Corps, Mil. Div. of the Miss., 3 Miles beyond Spring Hill"). Wilson should have known there was one officer under his command who paid little heed to the elements. Persistent, resolute Edward Hatch could not stay out of the action. By the following morning his entire command was over the creek and Hatch was on his way to Columbia, the flooded waters of the Duck River the only obstacle stopping him. "Meanwhile the pioneers of the [Federal] cavalry were not idle. Those of Hatch's division, by dint of hard work, soon made the railroad bridge passable for skirmishers, and by the morning of the 20th had built a floating bridge out of the debris of another railroad bridge. This enabled him to cross the [Rutherford] creek with his whole command, but a few miles beyond he was again stopped by the Duck

River, which was also at flood. The delay of the pursuit at Rutherford Creek was short, but it gave the enemy a breathing spell, which was of great value to him"[8] (James Harrison Wilson, Major-General, USV, Brevet Major-General, USA, "The Union Cavalry in the Hood Campaign").

Seven Miles North of Columbia

Close on the heels of the Confederates, Wood's Fourth Infantry Corps was on the road early on the morning of the 19th, reaching the northern bank of the flooded waters of Rutherford Creek only moments behind Hatch, who was then engaged in skirmishing with enemy combatants on the opposite bank. Stating that the rain, having begun days previously, was still pouring down and thereby creating impossible marching conditions for both wagon and infantry, Wood had little encouragement to report as Hatch's cavalry divisions sped by, Columbia-bound. Although assured by Thomas that the cavalry would soon be off the pike and out of his way, maneuvering through the thick mud took much longer than anyone had anticipated. "General Hatch's cavalry is still passing, and interferes much with the movements of our troops," grumbled an angry General Wood.

Around 9:00 a.m. Hatch's cavalry reached the banks of Rutherford Creek, engaging the Confederates of Cheatham's corps acting as rear guard entrenched on the opposite side. Half an hour later, Wood arrived, noting with more disappointment that "the bridge has been destroyed and the enemy holds a high and commanding line of hills ... parallel with the creek," situated under protection of earthworks. Aggravated even further, Wood observed that because of the presence of a Confederate four-gun battery and a hill packed with sharpshooters he was unable to build the much-needed bridge. In addition, "the rains have so swollen this creek that it is impossible to ford it, being fifteen feet in most places." And then came the gloomiest news of all: "the pontoon train has not yet come up and we can hear nothing of it"[9] (Journal of the Fourth Army Corps). Owing to the creek's "steep and abrupt banks" and its overflowing stream, as well as the fact that the pontoons were a day's journey behind them, the Union infantry found Rutherford Creek impassable:

> The weather was very inclement. During the night of the 18th the rain poured down in torrents, and the morning brought no improvement to the weather of the night. During the night I [Wood] received instructions from the commanding general of the forces informing me, first, that the cavalry, then encamped in my rear, would move at 6 a.m., pass to the front, and that I should move out at 8 a.m. ... at the appointed hour the corps was in motion.
>
> The rain still fell in torrents, flooding the earth with water and rendering all movements off the pike impossible. The head of the column advanced three miles and a half and arrived at Rutherford's Creek. This is a bold and rapid stream, usually fordable, but

subject to rapid freshest, and the heavy rains of the preceding twenty-four hours had swollen it beyond a possibility of it being crossed without bridges. To construct these it was necessary we should first occupy the opposite bank of the stream. As the head of column approached the creek the hostile fire from the southern bank opened with musketry and artillery. To clear the enemy from the opposite bank at the turnpike crossing, where the bridge for the passage of the artillery and trains had to be constructed, it was necessary to pass troops over, either above or below, and as the pontoon train was not yet up, every expedient that ingenuity could devise was resorted to effect the desired object. Rafts were constructed and launched, but the current was so rapid that they were unmanageable. Huge forest trees growing near the margin of the stream were felled athwart the stream, with the hope of spanning it in this way and getting some riflemen over; but the creek was so rapid and the flood so deep that these huge torsos of the forest were swept away by the resistless torrent. In these efforts was passed one of the most dreary, uncomfortable, and inclement days I remember to have passed in the course of nineteen and a half years of active field service[10] [Report of Brig. Gen. T.J. Wood, USA, commanding Fourth Army Corps].

Under the harassing presence of Confederate sharpshooters situated in close proximity, elements of the Union Fourth Army Corps spent the day hard at work, felling trees and constructing rafts, entirely hopeful, "almost certainly" in expectation of crossing over by the next morning.[11] Unfortunately, things did not go as well as expected.

By mid-afternoon there had been no progress. Wood remained stranded on the northern bank of Rutherford Creek and within enemy rifle range. "Headquarters: Second Division, Fourth Army Corps, Rutherford's Creek, December 19th, 1864–2:30 PM.... The officer in charge of the bridge builders reports that he has failed in putting a bridge across the creek.... The creek is rapidly rising. Enemy's sharpshooters still in our front."[12]

At about the same time, Wood, having been informed that General Hatch had accomplished a crossing of Rutherford Creek, sent orders for the Second Division to scout the area. If it was clean of Confederate presence, nothing at hand was to be spared in the obtaining construction materials, not even civilian homes. The order included a command to "commence building a bridge at once ... [and] tear down houses, use everything to facilitate the building of the bridge," and to stay in advance of Hatch's dismounted cavalry.[13] "Rutherford's Creek, swollen by the rain and having steep and abrupt banks, could not be forded. The pontoon train was behind, and did not arrive till the next day. The enemy occupied a strong position commanding the site of an old bridge. General Hatch succeeded in crossing a few skirmishers on the ruins of the upper railroad bridge, about a mile from the pike, but, after some skirmishing, withdrew them to the north bank after dark"[14] (Report of Bvt. Major General James H. Wilson, USA, commanding Cavalry Corps, Military Division of the Mississippi, of operations October 24, 1864–February 1, 1865). "The weather had now become icy cold, and Rutherford Creek could not be crossed without pontoons. The colored regiment, which had been detailed and trained as pontooniers, became demoralized by the cold, and it was almost impossible to make any headway. The ropes froze and the planks were covered with ice the moment they touched the water."[15]

Reports later in the afternoon were less than encouraging, noting that, although no enemy pickets were found on the opposite creek bank, "about one regiment of the enemy [still] occupied the hill ... commanding the pike and the crossing of the stream." Further woes included the report of a rapidly moving current, a further rising of the stream, and a final observation: "The current is very swift and creek still rising. It is not practicable to bridge the stream ... even should the enemy not oppose the working party."[16]

Regardless of his strenuous efforts, Hatch's crossing produced slight effect or change in the general state of affairs, other than the putting forth of "a few skirmishers on the ruins of the old railroad bridge" where the Confederate troops (Cheatham's) were holding a strong position. Following a short round of skirmishing, after dark Hatch fell back across the river, having accomplished little. "Major General Wilson: I [Hatch] have succeeded in crossing Rutherford's Creek with dismounted men; not being in force, the enemy drive slowly. I have gone into camp here ... near Duck River bridge."[17]

As for Maj. General John Schofield's 23rd Union Infantry Corps (having recently arrived from the environs of Nashville to the flooded Harpeth and lagging terribly far behind) one short, desperate message from "Franklin, December 19, 1864," to "Brigadier General Whipple, chief of staff, Department of the Cumberland," said it all: "Harpeth is rising very fast, and I am apprehensive the trestle may be washed away. Where are the pontoons?"[18] Later that evening Schofield's superior replied, making sure that Wilson's long-awaited trains (much more imperative than Schofield's far-off infantrymen) would have total freedom of movement down the pike: "Get your troops across Harpeth and attempt to come no farther today, but leave the road clear for General Wilson's trains.... Be in readiness to march early tomorrow."[19]

In the meantime, around 4:00 p.m., Hood's main body, including his sorely depleted supply trains, had safely made the passage over the Duck River. As would be expected, Forrest had been in the thick of things at Rutherford Creek, positioning his cavalry to oppose Hatch's advance, which he succeeded in doing. Later in the afternoon, after Hood had successfully crossed the Duck, Forrest and his command passed over, setting up camp in Columbia. "On the morning of the 19th the enemy was reported at Rutherford's Creek in strong force. I [Forrest] immediately commenced disposing of my troops for the purpose of preventing his crossing. Everything being across Duck River I was ordered by General Hood to withdraw my command at 3:00 o'clock, which I did, and went into camp at Columbia" (Report of Maj. Gen. Nathan B. Forrest, CSA, Commanding Cavalry, of operations on North

Alabama and Middle Tennessee Relating to the Battle of Nashville). "On the 19th, Major General Forrest having come up, I resumed command of my division, which was posted on the left of Cheatham's Corps to guard the crossings on Rutherford's Creek. During the day we had some skirmishing with the enemy, but held our position until 4 p.m., when, they having succeeded in crossing a force in our front of our infantry pickets, our whole force was withdrawn to the south side of the Duck River" (Report of Brigadier General James R. Chalmers, CSA, Commanding Cavalry Division, for operations November 17 to December 12, 1864).

> Hdqrs. Cavalry Corps, Mil. Div. of the Miss. In Camp, Eight miles North of Columbia, December 19, 1864
> 4:30 p.m., Brigadier General Whipple, Chief of Staff:
> General:
> Hatch succeeded in crossing two regiments dismounted over Rutherford's Creek, and drove the rebel cavalry back upon their main line. Prisoners and one man belonging to our navy just escaped say Lee's corps marched by the Pulaski pike from Columbia this morning, but that Cheatham's and Stewart's were in camp when he left. Forrest, with about 7,000 cavalry, is lying between Rutherford's Creek and Duck River. He could be dislodged quite easily by crossing a division of infantry on the pike and Hatch by the ruins of the railroad bridge.
> Very respectfully, your obedient servant,
> J.H. Wilson, Brevet Major General[20]

Later that evening, Thomas replied. Operations in pursuit of Hood's army would continue as planned. Wilson would move out as advised. There would be no change or hesitation. As for Wood's infantry, having failed to make the crossing, there was nothing to do but wait for tomorrow.

> Headquarters Department of the Cumberland, Near Spring Hill, December 19, 1864
> 9 p.m.
> Maj. Gen. J.H. Wilson, Comdg. Cavalry Corps, Military Division of the Mississippi:
> Your dispatch of 4:30 p.m. today is received. As I wish the troops to advance in the morning, if possible, I will instruct General Wood to advance by the main road, if he can cross the creek, whilst you move Hatch's division by the ruins of the railroad bridge, as you suggest.
> Geo. H. Thomas, Major General, U.S. Volunteers[21]

Citing further the impact of Chalmers' division during the previous day's action, Forrest later recounted that Chalmers "was constantly and severely engaged every day while protecting the rear of General Hood's army until he crossed Rutherford Creek." Cheatham's stubborn rear guard (augmented by the arrival of Forrest and after checking the Federal advance over Rutherford Creek) crossed the Duck River later that evening following a heated disagreement with Forrest as to whose right it was to cross first. Cheatham then encamped that night with the rest of Hood's army at Columbia. "When we arrived at Columbia, Gen. Cheatham was crossing his men on the pontoon bridge, and Gen. Forrest started to cross some wagons also, but Cheatham objected, and the two fiery generals had hot words mixed with oaths, before Forrest gave way, and let Cheatham finish crossing."[22]

During General Hood's disastrous retreat from Nashville, in December, 1864, the following incident, which I have never seen in print, occurred at the pontoon bridge crossing Duck River into Columbia. The writer was standing barefoot, wet and shivering by the side of the only piece saved by his battery—waiting for a gap in the surging mass that was constantly pouring across—into which he might fall, and do his share of the struggle to reach the opposite bank. [Stewart's] Corps had about finished crossing when a commotion was observed among Cheatham's troops—and just before the head of his column moved onto the bridge, General Forrest, who had been sitting quietly on his horse, evidently much disgusted at the state of affairs, trotting quickly up to Cheatham, said: "General Cheatham, it is my turn to cross ahead of you, sir." Cheatham replied: "I think not, sir. You are mistaken. I intend to cross now, and will thank you to move out of the way of my troops." Forrest grew furious, and pulling his pistol—the same long barreled weapon that we saw him use so effectively on the heads of Bates' division, at the disgraceful retreat from Murfreesboro the week before—spurred his horse close up to Cheatham, and said, "If you are a better man than I am, General Cheatham, your troops can cross ahead of mine." Forrest, with his pistol, had the best of Cheatham, and a tragedy was only prevented by the timely interference of General Stephen D. Lee, who, alighting from an ambulance (he had been painfully wounded in the leg a few days before), pushed in between the two disputants, and advising General Forrest to cross over, pacified the chafing Cheatham. My companion and messmate, J.W. Noyes, and I, moved across the bridge and on to camp about a mile south of Columbia, picking out the wet and muddy spots along the road, so as to prevent unnecessary wear and tear of our pedal extremities. We took Headquarters Kitchen in the rear, and gaining the good graces of the negro cook, sampled the savory dishes ahead of the generals, and through her kindness slept under the stove that night. The incident at the bridge and barefooted march to Pulaski next day, over the frozen pike road, both left lasting impressions on our minds that only death will obliterate.[23]

Other participants, with apparent equal certainty, recalled the event quite differently. Although witnesses of a particular incident may never fully agree in detail, the scene, engulfed in a cloak of mystery, beckons across the fading years, and the intrigue grows steadily on. "When he [Carrick W. Heiskell, 19th Tennessee Infantry, CSA] rejoined the army, after twelve months on crutches, Hood was retreating from Nashville. He witnessed what came very near being a bloody conflict between Forrest and Cheatham, when they quarreled over which of them should cross the river at Columbia first, each contending that he had precedence; guns were cocked all along the line of infantry, but Forrest at length gave Cheatham the right of way, and the incident closed."[24] "I shall never forget the passage of Duck River—Washington crossing the Delaware was insignificant."[25] "We continued our retreat across the Duck River to Columbia, the Corps alternating as rear guards to the Army."[26] (Report of General J.B. Hood

Forrest and Walthall Placed in Command of the Rear Guard

Having put most of his army across the Duck River, General Hood decided the time had come to strengthen the rear guard with a chosen array of troops fit for the task. If he was to continue south and lead his army out of Tennessee, he must have a rear guard that could keep the enemy at bay and give him plenty of room to maneuver. As it turned out, the combination of a select infantry and Forrest's cavalry would constitute a new and formidable rear guard, which would conduct the army from Columbia to the Tennessee. One somber condition was laid in plain view for all who would fight alongside Forrest as rear guard. Those who would volunteer for this duty might well be sacrificing their lives for the saving of the army:

When Hood's army reached Columbia, Tenn., it was in a most disastrous plight. Hood sent for General Walthall, who, on the way to his headquarters, accompanied by Major Sanders, met General Hood in company with Lieutenant Hampton and Dr. Darby, his medical director, at which time Hood said to Walthall that he must take command of the rear and enable him [Hood] and his army to escape across the Tennessee River; and, if necessary for the safety of his army, the rear guard must perish in the attempt to save it. Major Sanders is now the only survivor of that interview; but this statement was published by him in 1881 and again in 1885, when General Walthall and Dr. Darby were both living. It is absolutely true and correct.

When General Walthall was ordered to take charge of the rear guard, General Hood gave him the authority to select such commands as he chose, to consist of eight brigades of infantry, and to select his staff officers. He selected Major Sanders for his adjutant general, Maj. George S. Storrs for his chief of artillery, and Lieutenant E.T. Freeman as inspector general and for the remainder continued his old division staff.

Hood's army was protected by the infantry rear guard under the command of general Walthall, and the cavalry under the command of General Forrest, General Forrest, by virtue of his superior rank, being in command of the entire column. The rear guard was in daily contact with the Federal troops, which pursued relentlessly, and [we] crossed the Tennessee River near Tuscumbia, Ala., December 28, 1864.[27]

"Across the [Duck] river General Hood rode up to the officer in charge of the Fourth, who at that time was commanding the Brigade, and asked, 'What Brigade is this?' Upon being informed, 'Strahl's,' he said: 'I desire to organize a strong infantry reserve under General Walthall to cooperate with the Cavalry, and under General Forrest cover the retreat of the Army until I get across the Tennessee; and I know no troops I can call upon with greater confidence in its being well done than you Tennesseeans. Will this Brigade volunteer for that duty?' Upon being answered in the affirmative, he said: 'Then report to Col. Feild.'"[28]

The Fourth Tennessee, Strahl's Brigade, Cheatham's Corps was typical of that of Hood's entire army, "ill-clad" and shoeless. By 4:00 the following morning the Fourth Tennessee, a meager 200 of whom were fit for duty, were at the front guarding the crossing of the Duck River before Columbia. "The soldiers were without rations—the day bitterly cold."[29] After days of ceaseless exertions the Confederates had finally crossed the Duck into relative security. At least for the present, all imminent danger was past, minus one ceaseless, ever-present peril: the weather. It was "one of the coldest nights of the war."[30] "[T]here was a slow rain falling, and the weather was very much colder. We took up the line of march very dispirited. Rations were hard to get and not much when we got them. Shoes were scarce, and the clothing of many threadbare. We were certainly a rather unpresentable lot. The morale of the army was not good by any means. We felt that we were beaten and unable to rally or make a stand. The march from Columbia to Pulaski was made in constantly slow falling rain in connection with a falling temperature and did not seem to be in a hurry, for my recollection is we went but a few miles that day [December 20]."[31] To some in Hood's army, as well as for the many pitiful Union prisoners on hand, it was the worst cold they had ever experienced. The comfort of food, clothing, and shelter was simply unavailable for blue and grey alike. "Hundreds made the march with clothing hardly sufficient to hide nakedness, barefooted, or with their feet wrapped in an old rag or piece of blanket. The winter was intensely cold, the ground frozen, hard and stiff. Almost every step tore and bruised their feet, whilst many did in reality, leave a bloody track every time they put their feet down from Columbia to the Tennessee River."[32]

Years later, at the turn of the century, Confederate veteran William Gibson of the 6th and 7th Arkansas Infantry recounted the ordeal in a letter of correspondence to Carrie McGavock of Franklin, Tennessee. Looking back over the years that had passed since those terrible days, Gibson recalled the relentless cruelty of the time, in which so many comrades were brought to the point of a shocking, pitiful, embarrassment as to their haggard and worn appearance:

You reminded me of the severe weather that followed Franklin. Indeed the remembrance of that winter is burned into my memory as with a hot iron. Whilst around Nashville with a four inch sleet on the ground, which seemed would never melt, and from Nashville back to Corinth I was barefooted with sleet, rain & snow the whole way without winter clothing, my pants frozen and shredded to the knees and so worn that I was ashamed to go to a house to ask for clothes or to be seen by a lady. I think I can truthfully say that I bled for our country every step of the way from Nashville to Corinth, and this was but the experience of hundreds of my comrades."

During his stay at Mr. Vaught's in Columbia, Hood, reflecting on recent events and in the hearing of his physician, Dr. Charles T. Quintard, related his uncertainty as to the conclusion of the army's endeavors during the recent campaign. How could such a splendid army with so promising a future come to such ruin? No doubt his perplexity was shared by many:

> One officer remarked to the General in my [Dr. Quintard] presence, that while God was on our side so manifestly that no man could question it, it was still very apparent that our people had not yet passed through all their sufferings.
>   The General replied that the remark was a just one. He had been impressed with the fact at Spring Hill, where the enemy was completely within our grasp, and not withstanding all his efforts to strike a decisive blow, he had failed. And now again at Nashville, after the day's fighting was well nigh over, when all had gone successfully until the evening, our troops had [suddenly] broken in confusion and fled.[33]

There seemed to be no satisfactory answer on hand for the failure at Spring Hill that eventful November night nor for the disastrous outcome of the entire campaign. How could it have happened? Who was to blame? Could the fault lie hidden within the huge, all-encompassing realm of war with all its complexities? Was it the fault of a few or even of one? These considerations and many others would reverberate from those dark days of 1864 well into the 20th century, with many of the answers to its most intriguing questions still lying just out of reach. Who could give an adequate answer that would satisfy all concerned? For highly respected Confederate general Alexander Stewart, the decision to invade Tennessee in the autumn of 1864 was regarded as acceptable, at least in theory: "I deem it proper to say that after the fall of Atlanta the condition of the army and other considerations rendered it necessary, in my judgment, that an offensive campaign should be made in the enemy's [Sherman's] rear and on his line of communications. It is not my purpose, nor does it pertain to me, to explain the reasons which prompted the campaign, but simply to express my concurrence in the views which determined the operations of the army."[34] "[I]f we had captured Schofield [at Spring Hill], as could easily have been done at a trifling loss, we would have taken Nashville without a battle and pushed on into Kentucky, and, while I [Stewart] do not claim that it would have changed the result, yet it would certainly have prolonged the war and thrown an uncertain factor into the great problem. It seemed then, as it looks now as we glance back over the scene, that a hand stronger than armies had decreed our overthrow."[35] "We all could see that our army was reduced to less than half the men and officers in the last thirty days, had lost nearly all of its artillery, and ordnance, and the morale of the remainder of our army, as to its success in any move, was at a low ebb, and the final end seemed to be only a question of a few months time. Yet every man expressed his determination to do his duty, until that time should come. After a good night's rest we moved slowly and steadily in the rear of everything except the rear guard."[36]

During the early stages of Hood's proposed Tennessee Campaign in the fall of 1864, the thought of a Confederate army pushing northward through Tennessee had sent shivers up the spine of Federal authorities, including the resolute U.S. Grant, who had become so irritated with the idea as to make arrangements for a visit to Thomas's Nashville headquarters to personally oversee the operations there. At the time, General John Bell Hood and his Army of Tennessee moving into Northern territory was one serious threat to be reckoned with. Union cavalry commander James Wilson recalls his feelings at the time, which undoubtedly were not unlike most of his contemporaries: "Had Hood advanced at once [and not been held up at Gadsden, AL] with his three corps of infantry and his cavalry in better condition, he must have overthrown Thomas and overrun both Tennessee and Kentucky…. Fortunately for us, Hood lost a whole month at Gadsden, waiting for ammunition, supplies and recruits, while Forrest was making a senseless raid toward the Cumberland River. It was this delay and this raid … that gave Thomas time to assemble all his forces for a sturdy defense." As to his estimation of Hood's capabilities as an army commander, and particularly in his planning and attempted execution of the campaign, Wilson's statements contain an unexpected theme of respect; a certain tone of esteem for the enemy's talents and personal character as a soldier:

> Although a soldier of great personal courage and prowess, there is no doubt that he was looked upon by his contemporaries as possessing but limited ability and lacking the necessary experience for the great responsibilities thus imposed upon him. It was customary in both the Confederate and Federal armies after his advancement to decry his abilities, and this may account in some degree for the failure of his bold undertakings, but it has always seemed to me that they were ably planned and needed nothing but heavier battalions, greater resources, and better subordinates to make them successful.
>
> Alas for Hood! He passed out [of Tennessee] broken-hearted at last by the weight of his misfortunes. His courage and undoubted ability as a leader and a general deserved better luck.[37]

By the end of the day, late in the evening on the 19th, things had neither progressed nor improved for T.J. Wood's struggling engineers, he reporting that it was "impossible … to get a man across the [Rutherford] river on a raft," having already lost two rafts and two men in the attempt "owing to the swiftness of the current."[38] Having been ordered by Thomas the night before (in coordination with Wilson's cavalry) to "push forward your command across Rutherford's Creek tomorrow morning and move directly against Forrest, who is said to be in camp between Rutherford's Creek and Duck River," Wood's infantry was soon to learn that Forrest was already gone.

And as if that was not enough, the hours ticked away with no real change taking place. By midday the badly needed supplies were nowhere to be seen. "[T]he pontoon train that General Thomas thought would be up last night has not yet come as far as Rutherford's Creek." Noting also that the Confederates had left Columbia heading southward, another ominous bit of news was relayed. Forrest's cavalry was in dangerous proximity and could easily be seen on the Duck's opposite bank. Moreover, the river had risen so high and fast that the likelihood of making a crossing was unthinkable. And, as usual, the pontoons had still not arrived. "The enemy took up his pontoon bridges over Duck River at daylight this morning. The river is very much swollen; it is too deep and swift to bridge with timber ... [and as] we will have to wait for the pontoon train to come up ... it will be impossible to cross the Duck River today.... It now commences to rain hard, with a prospect of raining all night." Should it rain without a letup the river would certainly rise even higher.

By 4:00 in the afternoon the Union army had settled in for the long wait. A message from Thomas stating that the pontoons would arrive that night brought little comfort. "Have just heard form General Thomas. He reports that the pontoon train will be up tonight. This [Wood's] corps has already been delayed thirty-four hours waiting for the pontoon train to cross the Harpeth River, Rutherford's Creek, and now Duck River. The enemy has, therefore, gained so many hours in his retreat. It was most difficult for us to bridge the Harpeth and Rutherford's Creek for the passage of infantry." By midnight the weather had improved but little. A ceaseless downpour made all progress impossible. "The roads off of the pike are impassable for wagons; they cannot be moved at all"[39] (Journal of the Fourth Army Corps).

For two days the fleeing "rebels" had withstood everything the bitter weather and the Federals could throw at them. And to exacerbate matters for Thomas, Forrest was now on the field. From this point forward, the working out of this remarkable scenario would undergo a striking transformation. What had been previously perceived as a walkover by the Union army was suddenly vanishing from their grasp. One thing was certain; Thomas was running out of time, quickly. After a full day of unsuccessful attempts to construct bridges over the swollen waters of Rutherford Creek—most of them being swept away in the swift current—the rain continuing to fall, the river rising, and the weather turning much colder, Wood received an expected message from a General Elliot, who was directed to build a footbridge over Rutherford's. According to Elliot it would be "impossible to build a bridge over the creek; the water is too deep and swift and still continues to rise"[40] (Journal of the Fourth Army Corps).

A little past midnight an order was delivered from the Union commander to an exasperated Gen. T.J. Wood. George Thomas had called off the movement forward. Wood's infantry, soaked to the bone and no closer to their objective than they had been that morning, went into a damp, frigid camp. All the infantry's endeavors of the past few days to bag Hood seemed fraught with impossibilities. Hood was neatly walking away.

5

Tuesday, December 20, 1864
Hood Quits Tennessee, Heading South

The Confederates Compete the Crossing of the Duck River; Hood Evacuates Columbia for Pulaski; HQ at Pulaski

December 20: Everything over the [Duck] river this morning. The march was resumed on the Pulaski pike—Lee in front (Stevenson commanding), Cheatham next, and General Stewart in rear. General Forrest, with his cavalry and a division of infantry under command of Major General Walthall (composed of Ector's, Strahl's, Maney's, Granbury's, and Palmer's brigades), directed to oppose the advance of the enemy's cavalry. General Stevenson's corps camped within two miles of Pulaski, and the other two corps in his rear, and in order of march. Army headquarters at Mr. Jones, Pulaski [Journal of the Army of Tennessee November 14, 1864-January 23, 1865, Campaign in North Alabama and Middle Tennessee, p. 673].

Headquarters ... Mrs. Brown's House, Duck River Crossing
December 20, 1864–12 a.m.
Brig. Gen. W.D. Whipple, Chief of Staff:

General: My advance has been here [Duck River] some time, the last of the enemy—Forrest, Cheatham, and Loring—having left during the night. A few mounted men can be seen on the other side of the river. Mrs. Brown, a very intelligent woman, who conversed with many of their generals, says they will make no stand this side of the Tennessee River. Duck River is very high, and therefore cannot be passed at any point without the aid of a bridge train; one should be sent forward at once. We shall have no difficulty laying it near the turnpike crossing. Most of the rebels have probably gone by the Pulaski road.

Very Respectfully, your obedient servant, J.H. Wilson, Brevet Major General[1]

The Majority of Wilson's Cavalry Briefly Held at Rutherford Creek

[A]t daylight [we—Federal cavalry] were again in motion down Rutherford's Creek. Marched two miles, when I was ordered to dismount my command and construct a crossing from the fragment of a railroad bridge which the rebels had destroyed the day previous. This work was completed and my command across at 12 p.m. and the pursuit again resumed. The Seventh and Ninth Illinois were dismounted and deployed on foot, while the remainder of the brigade followed mounted to Duck River, opposite Columbia. On arriving here [we] found the enemy had crossed his rear guard in comparative safety at 4 a.m., leaving a small party, with a piece of artillery, as rear guard in the town upon the opposite side. A light skirmish between the above named regiments and the enemy, accompanied by light cannonading from both sides, closed the operations of the day, when the command encamped to await the arrival of the pontoons. During the skirmish the Seventh Illinois discovered where the enemy had abandoned four pieces of artillery by tumbling it into Duck River over the abutment of the old bridge. It was afterward taken out by the infantry[2] [Report of Col. Datus Coon, 2nd Iowa Cavalry Commanding Second Brigade, of operations from September 30, 1864, to January 15, 1865].

Others also commented: "It was sleeting, and freezing to everything, and bitter cold."[3] "On the 20th we [Confederates] marched twenty-three miles in a cold rain."[4] "A day of darkness and gloominess to me. I feel in bidding farewell to Columbia that I am parting with my dearest and most cherished hopes"[5] (Dr. Charles Todd Quintard).

The Effect of Forrest's Arrival

General Forrest, who had been operating around Murfreesboro, came in on the 18th of December. The inspiring effect of his presence was felt by all, and was thus described by my Adjutant, Captain W.A. Goodman, a man of brilliant intellect, cool in battle and untiring in his devotion to the cause and the discharge of his duty: "At no time in his whole career was the fortitude of General Forrest in adversity and his power of infusing his own cheerfulness into those under his command, more strikingly exhibited than at this crisis. Broken and defeated, as we were, there were not wanting many others as determined as he to do their duty to the last, and who stood out faithfully to the end; but their conversation was that of men who, though determined, were without hope, and who felt that they must gather strength from despair; but he alone, whatever he may have felt (and he was not blind to the danger of our position), spoke in his usual cheerful and defiant tone, and talked of meeting the enemy with as much assurance of success as he did when driving them before him a month before. Such a spirit is sympathetic; and not a man was brought in contact with him who did not feel strengthened and invigorated, as if he had heard of a reinforcement coming to our relief.[6]

Prior to withdrawing from Columbia on the 20th, General Hood relieved General Stevenson, guardian of the army from Spring Hill to Columbia, of the responsibility of directing the rear guard. Placing Forrest in command of the guard, Hood evacuated Columbia with orders for him to "hold the town as long as possible," and to cover the army's retreat by moving "in the direction of Florence Alabama, via Pulaski, protecting and guarding his rear"[7] (Report of Maj. Gen. Nathan B. Forrest, CSA, Commanding Cavalry, of Operations In North Alabama and Middle Tennessee Relating to the Battle of Nashville). Not expected to bear the entire weight of protecting the army's withdrawal, Forrest was to be assisted by a division of infantry consisting of eight brigades under the command of Major General E.C. Walthall. "To aid me in this object he [General Hood] ordered Major General Walthall to report to me with about 1,900 infantry, 400 of whom were unserviceable for want of shoes"[8] (Report of Maj. Gen. Nathan B. Forrest, CSA).

On the morning of the 20th of December, 1864, General Hood sent a member of his staff to General Walthall, who had established his headquarters at the residence of Nimrod Porter, near Columbia, with the urgent request that he call at army headquarters immediately. General Walthall at once rode to headquarters and the writer accompanied him. On the pike, as Walthall approached army headquarters, he met General Hood on his horse in company with Dr. Darby, who was the medical director of the army. Hood said to Walthall substantially as follows[:] "Things are in bad condition. I have resolved to organize a rear guard. Forrest says he can't keep the enemy off of us any longer without a strong infantry support, but says he can do it with the help of three thousand infantry with you to command them. You can select any troops in the army. It is a post of great honor, but one of such great peril that I will not impose it on you unless you are willing to take it; and you had better take troops that can be relied upon, for you may have to cut your way out to get to me after the main army gets out. The army must be saved, come what may, and if necessary your command must be sacrificed to accomplish it."

Walthall, in reply, said: "General, I have never asked for a hard place for glory nor a soft place for comfort, but take my chances as they come. Give me the order from the troops, and I will do my best. Being the youngest Major General in the army, I believe, my seniors may complain that the place was not offered to them, but that is a matter between you and them."

General Hood said in reply: "Forrest wants you and I want you."

General Forrest rode up during the conversation in time to understand what had been said, and he remarked: "Now we will keep them back."[9]

Hood gave verbal orders for Walthall to take any troops he desired, and he selected eight brigades, estimated at 3,000 effective, as follows: W.S. Featherston's, J.B. Palmer's, D.H. Reynold's, of Strahl's (commanded by Col. C.W. Heiskell), Smith's (commanded by Col. C. Olmstead), Maney's (commanded by Col. H.R. Feild), Ector's (commanded by Col. George D. Coleman), and Quarles' (commanded by Brig. Gen. George D. Johnston). These brigades reported to Walthall, who had them inspected and a report of effectives made. The eight brigades numbered 1,601 effectives. General Walthall issued the following General Order No. 1 from "Headquarters

Infantry Forces in Rear of Army of Tennessee, Columbia, Tenn., December 20, 1864" (p. 715):

> The brigades of this command will be temporarily united as follows: Featherston and Quarles, under command of Brigadier General Featherston; Ector and Reynolds, under command of Brigadier General Reynolds; Strahl and Maney, under the command of Colonel Feild; Smith and Palmer, under command of General Palmer.
>
> This command will stand in line in the following order: Featherston on the right, then Feild, Palmer and Reynolds in the order they are named.
>
> By command of Major General Walthall, D.W. Sanders, Assistant Adjutant General.

The field return of this command's effectives was as follows: Featherston, 498; Reynolds, 528; Palmer, 297; Feild, 298; total, 1,601 [1,621]. The organization of this rear guard is given in detail for two reasons. General Hood, in his report and also in his book, incorrectly reports the names of the brigades that composed this command and a correct statement has never heretofore been given.[10] The situation the rear guard was placed in could be adequately described only as a probable suicide mission. With his worn-out "effectively mounted men"—a force of less than 1,900 infantry and eight pieces of artillery—Forrest was expected to check the advance of an army composed of a 10,000-man cavalry corps and three infantry corps. Walthall's ears must have burned upon hearing these words of Gen. Hood: "It is a post of great honor, but one of such great peril that I will not impose it on you unless you are willing to take it; and you had better take troops that can be relied upon, for you may have to cut your way out to get to me after the main army gets out. The army must be saved, come what may, and if necessary your command must be sacrificed to accomplish it." A more sober and grave situation has hardly been imposed upon a soldier. The fate of an army was placed in his hands.[11]

Hood's decision to place General Forrest in command of the rear guard (coming as an outcome of consultation on the night of the 19th) was a product of the commanding general's apprehension over the destiny of his exhausted army. The vicious weather, the impossible traveling conditions, the dire state of the army in general, and the unceasing attempts of George Thomas to capture them all added up to a possibility of fearsome consequences. Responding to Hood, Forrest's advice was simple, direct, and forceful. If Hood could not of a certainty hold his army intact within Tennessee, he should pull out immediately. Remaining there under such ominous conditions was certain to bring disaster.[12]

In conference with General Hood, Forrest had laid out a plan, clear and unambiguous. His command, accompanied by the reinforcement of a sizable portion of Hood's infantry, would see to the safe withdrawal of the army, providing it protection, time, and opportunity for a relatively unhindered escape to its crossing over the Tennessee River.[13] Hood, of necessity, agreed. Far too many difficulties faced the army for it to remain in Tennessee another day. The campaign was over. The army was broken. Hood had gambled it all and lost. Nothing could be done to reverse it. "After the fight at Nashville, I at first hoped to have been able to remain in Tennessee on the line of the Duck River; but after arriving at Columbia I became convinced that the condition of the Army made it necessary to cross the Tennessee River without delay; and on the 21st [20th] the Army resumed the march for Pulaski, leaving Major General Forrest, with the Cavalry, and Major General Walthall ... at Columbia as a rear guard"[14] (Report of General J.B. Hood). "On the morning of the 20th of December ... [Hood] directed me with these troops to report to Major General Forrest for service under his orders in covering the retreat of the Army.... These Brigades were all greatly reduced in numbers"[15] (Report of Major General Edward C. Walthall, CSA).

The infantry Brigades chosen by Walthall to cover the rear of Hood's army for the duration of the retreat were haggard indeed: one third of them were without shoes or blankets, with little or nothing to eat, and many were so footsore they were prevented from participating in combat. Mercifully, they were relieved to ride with the wagons. Despite their gaunt and pitiful condition, Walthall's selected brigades were destined for the following days, in concert with Forrest's spirited cavalry, to so chastise the Federal army that to his credit the Union commander would be compelled to commend them for their unyielding tenacity in consistently repelling the numerous attacks brought against them throughout the long retreat from Nashville to the Alabama border. "The [Confederate] rear guard ... was undaunted and firm, and did its work bravely to the last,"[16] General Thomas said.

As for Hood's selection of the most capable officer to lead the rear guard infantry, he had chosen well. Regardless of the army's dismal condition, his decision to place Walthall in command over the brigades protecting the army's withdrawal was certainly the correct one. "General Walthall, [was] one of the most able division commanders in the South,"[17] according to Hood. "[I]t was a splendid command, led with consummate skill and courage. 'Walthall was the youngest division general in the Army of Tennessee, and when he drew his sword in command over the rear guard to cover its retreat, there was not a soldier in it, from the commanding general down, who did not believe he would do it or perish in the effort."[18] "For several days the ground was covered with snow, and numbers of the men made the march without shoes, some had no blankets, and all were poorly clad for the season; but despite these difficulties and privations there was no complaint. Every day there was a skirmish or a combat, in which the cavalry and artillery of Forrest participated with the infantry of Walthall. The danger was a common one, and the two arms of the service were alike conspicuous for courage and endurance. The Federal advance was beaten and punished day by day...."[19]

Following the arduous but ineffective efforts of Hatch's Fifth Division the previous day to cross Rutherford Creek and attack the Confederate rear guard located in a strong position "commanding the site of an old bridge," the next morning the indefatigable Hatch was again in the saddle and on the move. But, regardless of his efforts, after crossing Rutherford Creek and pushing on he was held up once more. Having raised its water level in the constant rain, the Duck River would also be impossible to get over, and without pontoons there was no hope of crossing. For Wilson's cavalry, these setbacks must have been the most depressing series of events. "The morning of the 20th General Hatch constructed a floating bridge out of the debris of the lower railroad bridge and crossed his entire command, but the enemy had succeeded in getting everything across Duck River the night before. This stream, being also much swollen, could not be crossed until the pontoon bridge was laid"[20] (Report of Major General James H. Wilson, USA, commanding Cavalry Corps).

But again, as predicable as the rising sun, Hatch would not be stopped: "On the morning of the 20th, before daylight, [I] threw dismounted men on the road to Columbia and built a bridge to cross the creek, taking over my Parrott guns. The enemy, under the impression that we were close upon him, the night before took up his pontoons and left his rear guard of about 300 men and a battery, threw two of the guns into the river, and attempted to escape with the other two to the east, when the Second Iowa were sent in pursuit, capturing the guns, six ambulances, a few wagons and cattle, and scattering the rear guard of Texas cavalry"[21] (Major General Edward Hatch, U.S. Army). Late on the afternoon of the 20th, well after all Confederate presence had departed Columbia, Federal cavalry forces under General Hatch suddenly appeared opposite the river, firing a terrible, indiscriminate artillery barrage upon the town. Forrest, now in command of the rear guard, drew near to the river's edge, raised a flag of truce, and rode calmly out in open view of the Federals, personally informing Hatch that his cannonade was aimed only at "noncombatants and the wounded of both armies" still held up in the town. The Confederate army had long since vacated the area. Any further shelling was useless and a danger to innocent victims.

With a striking sense of compassion in light of such dreadful conditions, Forrest presented an offer: a prisoner exchange of the nearly 2,000 Federals he had on hand. Most, if not all, of them were "without blankets or proper clothing for the inclement season," and without doubt they were close to dying from overexposure. As the Confederate army was taxed to its limits, wholly undersupplied, and with no relief in sight, it could not guarantee the lives of its prisoners. If Thomas wanted them saved, now was the time. For many, it was their final and only hope of survival. After waiting a full two hours for a response, the answer from Thomas arrived: offer refused. There would be no prisoner exchange, not even of those Forrest held on parole that he had previously offered for a trade.

As ascertained later from Forrest, as many as one-fourth of his prisoners may have "perished from exposure" resulting from that decision. Those remaining alive were left to suffer the current privations and the merciless weather conditions. As a consequence, many of his prisoners were permanently disabled. All was not a total loss, however; at the conclusion of the dialogue with Hatch at the river's edge, the shelling of Columbia ceased. There was at least some consolation to be found in that.[22]

> Headquarters Cavalry Corps, Mil. Div. of the Mississippi, Near Columbia, Tenn., December 20, 1864–3:45 p.m.
> Brigadier General Whipple, Chief of Staff, Department of the Cumberland:
>
> General: General Forrest came to the river-bank, under a flag of truce, and requested an exchange of prisoners. I have just sent an officer to inform him that I have no prisoners to exchange.
>
> Very respectfully, your obedient servant,
> J.H. Wilson, Brevet Major General, Commanding[23]

In *Ninth Regiment Illinois Cavalry Volunteers* there is the following account:

> The Federal troops were not long … coming to Duck River, on the opposite side of which was Columbia, and we could see the long lines of Hood's supply trains slowly moving away. A sharp fire was taking place over the river. General Hatch, with a few staff officers and orderlies, were well in front on the skirmish line, and as we came in sight of the town a large number of Confederate troops were seen on the opposite bank. While we halted a moment to view the scene the crowd parted and we saw artillery just in the act of being fired at our little squad. General Hatch said quickly, "Scatter, boys, they are going to shell us." As he spoke, the blue wreaths of smoke from their guns were seen, and the shot whistled over our heads. We were so close that they shot too high, so we galloped back unscathed. It was not long ere we saw a white flag approaching our line, and a party was sent out to meet them. They brought a message from General Forrest saying he wanted to meet General Hatch. (The bridge over Duck River had been burned by the rebels in November.) General Hatch soon went forward to the river side, and Forrest appeared on the abutment on the other side, and calling across, said, "You are shelling your own wounded men and prisoners and the women and children in the town"; also that "he wanted to exchange some prisoners." This simply showed how wily was the Confederate chieftain, for while General Hatch was communicating with General Thomas, the Confederate trains were moving away in safety. When after this delay the Federal soldiers finally crossed the river there was no one in Columbia but the wounded of both armies and the women and children.[24]

According to the official report of Major General Forrest, "The enemy appeared in front of Columbia on the evening of the 20th and commenced a furious shelling upon the town. Under a flag of truce I proceeded to the river and asked an interview with General Hatch, who I informed by verbal communication across the river that there were no Confederate troops in town, and that his shelling would only result in injury to women and children and his own wounded, after which interview the shelling was discontinued."[25]

Around 5:00 p.m. at the Warfield House, where Forrest had set up his headquarters, Major General Walthall, covering the rear at Forrest's command, was ordered to send 200 men to picket along the Duck River in front of Columbia, near the mill and the place where the Confederate pontoon bridge had been laid. Federal troops, evidently of Hatch's division, had appeared over the river, making no significant trouble other than loosing the above-mentioned artillery barrage upon the town. With the flooded river between them, there was little more the Federal army could do. And with the added knowledge that Columbia was empty of the enemy, options for success on the 20th of December had dwindled to nothing. Walthall's pickets could rest easy. Their services would not be needed nor would they be faced with the prospect of sacrificing their lives that the army might live. "No effort was made to effect a crossing in my front, "[26] said Major General Edward C. Walthall in his report.

Wood's Infantry Crosses Rutherford Creek and Camps Before the Duck River

Beginning the night of the 19th and continuing throughout the 20th, as Wilson's cavalry under Hatch was engrossed in a strenuous effort to cross the rushing waters of Rutherford Creek and engage the enemy, Union general Thomas J. Wood's Fourth Infantry Corps was occupied in the laborious task of bridge building. By the "early forenoon of the following day, the 20th, two bridges for infantry were constructed across the stream [Rutherford Creek], one at the turnpike crossing, by Colonel Opdycke's brigade, of the Second Division, and the other by General Grose's brigade, of the First Division. As soon as these were completed the infantry of the corps was passed over, marched three miles, and encamped for the night on the northern bank of Duck River," waiting, as usual, for the arrival of the pontoons[27] (Report of Brigadier General Thomas J. Wood, USA, commanding Fourth Army Corps, of operations October 26, 1864–January 5, 1865).

Headquarters Fourth Army Corps, Near Columbia, Tenn., December 20, 1864–2 p.m.
Brigadier General Whipple,
Assistant Adjutant-General and Chief of Staff:

General: This corps is now forming on the north bank of Duck River opposite Columbia, and is only prevented by the want of a pontoon train from crossing the river and continuing the pursuit of the enemy. It is much to be regretted that we have no pontoon train here. The river is quite high and appears to be rising, and it appears to me the only way to cross it will be by a pontoon bridge, as it will take a long time and much trouble to construct any other kind. There is no indication that there is any enemy on the south bank of the river, and every indication and report goes to show that he has retreated. It is reported that his pontoon bridges over Duck River were taken up at daylight this morning. I constructed two passage-ways for infantry, about half a mile apart, over Rutherford's Creek. If the creek does not fall today, so as to be fordable, the rear corps should build a bridge for the passage of wagons and artillery, which we had not time to do.[28]

Respectfully, yours,
THE. J. WOOD,
Brigadier General, Commanding

With the rising waters of the Duck River between them and the enemy, for once it seemed that the Army of Tennessee could retire beyond the immediate reach of the Federals in relative safety. And with the added bonus of Nathan Bedford Forrest on the field and in command of the rear guard, the fortunes of the day had turned highly in favor of the Confederates. Although greatly dispirited, the army's successful and unopposed crossing of the Duck River had become all that they had hoped. Without pontoons on hand, Thomas, Wilson, and the entire Federal Infantry Corps could only stare across the flooded river, fuming.

Headquarters Department of the Cumberland, Rutherford's Creek, December 20, 1864 8:30 p.m. Maj. Gen. J.H. Wilson, Comdg. Cavalry Corps, Military Division of the Mississippi:

The major general commanding directs me to say that you did perfectly right in telling Forrest you had no prisoners to exchange with him. Major General Schofield has been directed to build a trestle bridge across Rutherford's Creek, and the pontoon train will be up with you tomorrow morning early, if the mules are able to haul it. If at all possible the major general commanding desires the army to be across Duck River before tomorrow night. Hood cannot possibly get all his troops and trains across the Tennessee River before we can overtake him, if we get across Duck River tomorrow.

Very respectfully, your obedient servant,
Robt. H. Ramsey, Assistant Adjutant General[29] [Journal of the Fourth Army Corps].

In a side incident to the fighting taking place, at an unknown point during the day a particularly irritating message began buzzing its way along the Federal lines of communication. It seemed that things back in Nashville had taken a turn for the worse. "Numerous" roving bands of Federal cavalry units were preying on the civilian population. A suggestion was put forth to the authorities that "these men get into camp and under control."

Headquarters Post of Nashville, Nashville, Tenn., December 20, 1864 Major Beaumont, Assistant Adjutant General, Cavalry Corps:

I am informed that between our picket line and Brentwood Hills there are numerous bands of dismounted cavalry wandering about and committing all manner of depredations. I would respectfully suggest that some step be taken to get these men into camp and under control, that an end may be put to this evil.

I am, Major, very respectfully, your obedient servant,
Jno. F. Miller, Brigadier General.[30]

There is no known written correspondence on hand to indicate the matter was ever taken seriously enough to effect a change.

6

Wednesday, December 21, 1864

Alignment of Three Federal Infantry Corps Attempted—Washington vs. Thomas

Confederate HQ in Pulaski

"December 21: [Confederate] Army headquarters still at Mr. Jones,' Pulaski. Stevenson's corps marched across Richland Creek and went into camp; Cheatham's and Stewart's corps camped on this side" (Journal of the Army of Tennessee, November 14, 1864–January 23, 1865, Campaign in North Alabama and Middle Tennessee). "We saw numbers of privates and some officers trudging along with feet as bruised and bloody almost, as of beef steak and swollen to twice their natural size. That they could even stand without walking was a mystery to us. Others had wounds bleeding and sore, with nothing to eat. At Pulaski the last rations of unbolted flour and fat meat were issued."[1]

"Cold, icy rain"

"It rained on us almost daily from Columbia to the Tennessee River, cold icy rain and the men were wet to the skin day and night. The army moved slowly during the day, and camped at night. We heard some little fighting occasionally with the rear guard."[2]

The Seventh and Ninth Illinois were dismounted and deployed on foot, while the remainder of the brigade followed mounted to Duck River, opposite Columbia. On arriving here found the enemy had crossed his rear guard in comparative safety at 4:00 a.m., leaving a small party, with a piece of artillery, as rear guard at the town upon the opposite side. A light skirmish between the above named regiments and the enemy, accompanied by light cannonading from both sides, closed the operations of the day, when the command encamped and awaited the arrival of the pontoons. During the skirmish the Seventh Illinois discovered where the enemy had abandoned four pieces of artillery by tumbling it into Duck River over the abutment of the old bridge. It was afterward taken out by the infantry[3] [Report of Col. Datus Coon, 2nd Iowa Cavalry, Commanding Second Brigade, of operations from September 30, 1864, to January 15, 1865].

Columbia, Tenn., December 21, 1864
[Confederate] Maj. D.W. Sanders, Assistant Adjutant General, Walthall's Division:

Major: Citizens report that the enemy are trying to effect a crossing at Johnson's Knob, about two miles above this place. Johnson's Knob is on the opposite bank on the river and commands a large extent of the country on this side. Reports say that the enemy are digging down the bank at that point.

Very respectfully, H.R. Feild, Colonel,
Commanding, Maney's and Feild's Brigades.[4]

"I had so set my heart upon success ... [and] my heart has been very rebellious"[5] (Jones's residence, Pulaski, TN, General John Bell Hood).

"This has been a terrible day"

"This has been a terrible day ... exceedingly cold rain in the morning and snow in the evening. So many of our poor boys are bare footed that there is great suffering and my heart bleeds for them. The citizens of Pulaski have done all they could to provide shoes"[6] (Dr. Charles Todd Quintard).

Federal Infantry Operations at the Duck River Suspended Because of Harsh Weather

Late in the evening of the 20th another factor weighed heavily in the escalating level of difficulties experienced by the Federal army; the atrocious weather, their constant, merciless enemy, had turned severely cold. Added to the already wretched conditions plaguing both armies, by early morning on the 21st snow was on the ground. What had been a knee-deep sea of mud and sludge in and around the Franklin-Columbia pike was soon to be covered with a layer of snow and ice. As a result, the agonizing movements of Wood's infantry became even more cumbersome. With the weather again turning against them, making it impossible for the army to safely maneuver, Wood called for a temporary halt. For the Federal army stretched out along the major roads of Middle Tennessee, the 21st of December 1864 would be a day of much-needed rest. Unable to continue the chase, for the time being Wood's infantry corps halted. "During the night of the 20th the weather became bitterly cold. Wednesday, the 21st, [Federal Infantry] operations were suspended, and the corps remained quietly in camp, as the pontoon train, detained by the swollen streams, the inclement weather, and the miserable condition of the roads, had not been able to get to the front. The day was bitterly cold, and the rest which the command gained by laying in camp was much needed after their arduous and laborious service of the many preceding days"[7] (Report of Brig. Gen. T.J. Wood, USA, commanding Fourth Army Corps).

Although Wood's corps had pulled aside for a well-deserved time of rest, infantry corps commanders Schofield and Smith at the same hour were approaching Rutherford Creek with orders to build a bridge over the creek in order to be over the Duck River by the morning of the 21st. Regardless of the mounting complications, the Union army had no choice: whenever possible the forward movement must continue at all costs. In a dispatch dated the previous morning, General Thomas had directed operations for the immediate crossing of Rutherford Creek "as rapidly as possible," in anticipation of commencing the fording of the Duck by the morning of the 21st.

Alignment of Three Federal Infantry Corps Attempted

In the interim General Schofield's 23rd Infantry Corps, in company with General A.J. Smith, both having plodded in the wake of the two previous armies, had recently arrived at Rutherford Creek. In response to the added presence of more men and material, Thomas instructed them both to "build a trestle bridge over Rutherford's Creek so that artillery and train can cross," the goal being the crossing of the Duck River by the next night. If the three infantry corps were successful in carrying out their orders, by the night of the 21st his entire army would be over the Duck River and prepared to engage Hood. "It is the desire that the entire Army be over the Duck River by tomorrow night [the 21st], in which case it is to be hoped that the greater part of Hood's Army may be captured, as he cannot possibly get his teams and troops across the Tennessee River before we can overtake him"[8] (Maj. Gen. George Thomas, Journal of the Fourth Army Corps).

Pontoons Arrive at Rutherford Creek

Regardless of the feasibility of his plans, things were moving, predictably, far too slowly. Thomas lamenting over the lack of pontoons, his army had languished on the north side of Rutherford Creek for what had seemed an endless wait, watching helplessly as opportunities to confront Hood's rear guard and Forrest's arrival escape them time and again. According to the latest information, the pontoons would arrive sometime that afternoon. Fortunately for the Federal army, the trains arrived as expected, and by 1:00 p.m. the work for the crossing of Rutherford Creek was set in motion.

Although it would be hours before the crossing could be completed, with the pontoon's arrival the interminable waiting was over. Once the entire train was laid across the stream the Federal army would be passing over the swiftly flowing waters of Rutherford Creek and moving on to the Duck River. With a new surge of effort on all fronts the pursuit would be renewed. Regardless of the myriad complications facing the Federals, the capture and subjugation of Hood's army was still a definite possibility. Nevertheless, the ever-present delays seemed never-ending. "The last of Forrest's command and Bate's rebel division of infantry arrived opposite Columbia, on the north bank of the Duck River, from Murfreesborough, yesterday. If we could have had a pontoon train to enable [us] to cross Rutherford's Creek when we arrived there, we could have captured the most of this force.... It will be dark before it is [completely] laid over the creek.... [O]nly part of the [pontoon] train has arrived on this side of the river ... [and] it will be impracticable to commence laying the bridge [over Duck River] before morning ... [so I] will commence work on it at 5 a.m."[9] (Journal of the Fourth Army Corps).

Although the pace was quickening, dissatisfaction and frustration still hung over the troops. The sluggishness in bringing the pontoons forward had a specific cause, and it wasn't due to fierce weather alone. During the insufferable waiting period it had come to the attention of Thomas's staff that a major blunder on the part of the Federal commander had severely crippled the army's movements for days. "We have been delayed another day in the pursuit of the enemy on account of the pontoon train not being up with us," commented a disgruntled Federal officer. The slowness demonstrated the past few days in bringing up the trains had become a source of major anxiety of the highest priority.

As reported, Federal commander George Thomas, apparently awakening from a drowsy slumber on the 17th, had mistakenly ordered his trains to press forward from Nashville and connect with the army via the Murfreesboro pike instead of down the Franklin pike, where the army was actually situated. After the trains had covered fifteen arduous miles in the direction of Murfreesboro, going entirely in the wrong direction, the mistake was discovered. Turning about, the column took to crossing the rain-soaked fields and "a country road, which was almost impassable," in a strenuous effort to intersect the Franklin pike and connect with the army. The hours lost retracing their progress, combined with the horrific traveling conditions, had held up Federal pursuit for days. Although it is doubtful that the prevention of this one embarrassing incident would have guaranteed an overall victory during the initial stages in the pursuit of Hood's army, it nevertheless impeded Union progress to the point, at times, of overshadowing it with an intolerable despondency. "By this mistake we have been delayed about three days in pursuit of the enemy, and have missed many splendid opportunities to inflict severe blows upon the enemy, perhaps to annihilate him"[10] (Journal of the Fourth Army Corps).

Wilson's cavalry fared no better. The Duck River was a formidable obstacle and could not be crossed without pontoons. The accidental delay had cost Thomas dearly. "The Duck River proved impassable for the National cavalry till the single pontoon-train of the army could be brought forward. And this, owing to the condition of the roads and a mistake which had started it in the wrong direction, involved a further delay"[11] (James Harrison Wilson, Major-General, USV, Brevet Major-General, USA, "The Union Cavalry in the Hood Campaign").

Thomas Ordered by Washington Superiors to Hasten the Pace

Sentiments in far off Washington only confirmed Thomas's anxiety. The current perception of Federal leadership from the capital was unanimous: Thomas was simply unaware of the critical nature of his operations against Hood. The Union's success in this phase of the war was worth any cost to achieve it. He must be brought up to date with the facts and move his troops much more speedily to accomplish the desired results more quickly. "Old Slow Trot" would have to pick up the pace.

Washington, December 21st, 1864, 12 p.m. via Nashville
Major General Thomas:

Permit me, General, to urge the vast importance of a hot pursuit of Hood's army. Every possible sacrifice should be made, and your men for a few days will submit to any hardship and privation to accomplish the great task. If you can capture or destroy Hood's army, Sherman can entirely crush out the rebel military force in all the Southern States. He begins a new campaign about the 1st of January, which will have the most important results, if Hood's army can now be used up. A most vigorous pursuit on your part is therefore of vital importance to Sherman's plans. No sacrifice must be spared to attain so important an object.[12]

H.W. Halleck
Major General and Chief of Staff

Thomas, on the other hand, was not to be spoken down to, by the Chief of Staff or anybody else. Comfortable in their cozy offices far from the pain of an extremely rigorous march, away from the ceaseless suffering and the stench of death that had pervaded the air for weeks, they could counsel or advise, coerce or flatter, it made little difference to him. General Thomas responded without delay.

Headquarters Department of the Cumberland
In the Field, December 21, 1864

Maj. Gen. H.W. Halleck,
Washington, D.C.:

Your dispatch of 12 p.m. this day is received. General Hood's army is being pursued as rapidly and as vigorously as it is possible for one army to pursue another. We cannot control the elements, and, you must remember, that to resist Hood's advance into Tennessee, I had to reorganize and almost thoroughly equip the force now under my command.

On the verge of chiding his superiors, Thomas reminded them that since the victory at Nashville, with troops but "partially equipped," he had been able to drive the retreating Confederates past the Duck River and over streams in the most difficult weather conditions, all without the aid of pontoons or a suitable transportation of supplies and ammunition. "I am doing all in my power to crush Hood's army, and, if possible, will destroy it; but pursuing an enemy through an exhausted country, over mud roads, completely sogged with heavy rains is no child's play, and cannot be accomplished as quickly as thought of."

In another bold statement, Thomas pointed out that had he not been relieved of the bulk of the army's men and supplies (having been sent to Sherman) his overall situation would be more conducive to a successful accomplishment. In fact, he asserted, he was facing a far greater danger than in any previous engagement. The lack of men, reliable transportation, and supplies only aggravated the matter. "Although my progress may appear slow, I feel assured that Hood's army can be driven from Tennessee, and eventually be driven to the wall, by the force under my command." Thomas concluded his remarks, again bringing to the minds of his superiors that they shouldn't expect too much from overly exhausted, outnumbered troops conducting a winter campaign with limited supplies: "In conclusion, I can safely state that this army is willing to submit to any sacrifice to oust Hood's army, or to strike any other blow which would contribute to the destruction of the rebellion"[13] (Geo. H. Thomas, Major General).

The authorities in Washington would just have to understand the severity of the situation. No doubt the thought may well have crossed his mind that if they became too dissatisfied they could look elsewhere for a more determined and capable commander. As for Thomas, he was sure of one thing: no one could be doing more under the present circumstances than the Army of the Cumberland. Fortunately for him, the Federal establishment responded to his messages with full appreciation of his tireless efforts under the most trying conditions. The heat, however, must be turned up.

Washington, December 22, 1864–9 p.m.
Major General Thomas,
In the Field:

I have seen today General Halleck's dispatch of yesterday and your reply. It is proper for me to assure you that this Department has the most unbounded confidence in your skill, vigor, and determination to employ to the best advantage all the means in your power to pursue and destroy the enemy. No Department could be inspired with more profound admiration and thankfulness for the great deeds you have already performed, or more confiding faith that human effort could accomplish no more than will be done by you and the gallant officers and soldiers of your command.[14]

Edwin M. Stanton
Secretary of War

General Ulysses S. Grant, poised to take on General Robert E. Lee the following spring, minced no words in relating his objectives, including the defeat and capture of the Army of Tennessee. Hood was within reach, his army ripe for the picking. If there was ever a time to strike with everything Thomas had, it was now. "You have the congratulations of the public for the energy with which you are pursuing Hood. I hope you will succeed in reaching his pontoon bridge in Tuscumbia before he gets there.... You now have a big opportunity, which I know you are availing yourself of. Let us push on and do all we can."[15] Upon receiving General Grant's dispatch on the 24th, Thomas, perhaps relieved at the understanding that had been reached, reaffirmed his unwavering commitment to continue the struggle, ever hopeful to the eventual outcome: "I am now, and shall continue to push Hood as rapidly as the state of the weather and roads will permit, [being] "very hopeful that either General Steedman or Admiral Lee will reach the Tennessee in time to destroy Hood's pontoon bridge, in which event I shall certainly be able to capture or destroy almost the entire army now with Hood."[16]

The dialogue was familiar. During the weeks before the battle of Nashville Thomas had endured similar experiences. In a private moment with Wilson he had stated, in essence, that if they would stop treating him like a child and simply let him do his job and use his own judgment he would soon take the necessary steps to engage the enemy. If they wanted a replacement, fine. But in any case he would not act against his own judgment. George Henry Thomas must have been a man of remarkable patience to have endured such continual prodding.[17]

Hood's Contrition

Later on, in the bitter cold of the evening of the 21st just a few miles down the pike, an unusual drama was beginning to unfold. General Hood and his immediate staff, including Dr. Charles Quintard, physician and chaplain of the army, had gathered at the home of one "Honorable Thomas Jones," where Hood had become headquartered. At the conclusion of a baptismal service in which Dr. Quintard had baptized four of Jones's children, Dr. Quintard recorded in his journal, "Mr. Jones joined us for prayers in General Hood's room." It is not difficult to envision what might possibly take place in such a case. The command structure of a defeated army, bearing the shame and confusion of being in full retreat after a total failure to bring off an all-important campaign, are assembled together in a secluded place, a deep sense of the certainty of their critical condition wrapped around them like a shroud. All the ingredients for an explosive, acrimonious setting would be present. One careless, well-aimed word could enflame the entire scenario.

But this was to be a prayer meeting, not a court session, a time of self humbling, an hour set apart to the Lord, when anything so trifling as petty personal glory would be ground to dust before the awesome presence of a holy God who holds all life in his hands and renders to every man according to his works. There is no record that strife or debate accompanied this gathering. Even if there had been smoldering fires, slowly burning just below the surface, ready to explode at the slightest provocation, General Hood extinguished them all in a moment by a single act of contrition. Taking full responsibility for the failed campaign, the general humbled himself before his subordinates: "I am afraid that I have been more wicked since I began this retreat than for a long time past. I had so set my heart upon success, and had prayed so earnestly for it, had such a firm trust that I should succeed, that my heart has been very rebellious. But, let us go out of Tennessee, singing hymns of praise." This was a truly remarkable acknowledgment.

Finished describing this unusual scene, Quintard brought his journal entries to a close. The weather, to which the army was ceaselessly exposed, had become increasingly colder. Many of those "poor boys" were nearly naked and barefoot. The citizens of Pulaski had done everything in their power to provide shoes, but even all they were able to do could not alleviate the intensity of the misery. The suffering was too deep, too widespread, and too profound to be alleviated by a pair of shoes. Thus ended Wednesday, the 21st of December 1864, on the Columbia-Pulaski road where two opposing armies lay shivering on the frozen ground, encamped within mere miles of one another (preceding information according to *Doctor Quintard, Chaplain, C.S.A., and Second Bishop of Tennessee*, edited and extended by The Rev. Arthur Howard Noll, University Press of Sewanee, 1905).

7

Thursday, December 22, 1864

Racing through Columbia

During the night of the 21st, between midnight and daylight, the pontoon train came up.[1]—Report of Brig. Gen. T.J. Wood, USA, commanding Fourth Army Corps

After a Series of Delays the Federal Fourth Corps Crosses Duck River, "The Rest of the Infantry" Poised to Cross

Major General George Thomas wrote, "The [Union] Fourth Corps crossed Duck River today, and has advanced about two miles beyond town, in the direction of Pulaski. Cavalry will cross by daylight tomorrow, [the 23rd] and the rest of the infantry during the day. Prisoners, on being questioned, stated substantially that Hood's army is greatly demoralized, nearly half of which is unarmed.... I shall push forward rapidly in the morning, and endeavor to overtake him before he reaches the Tennessee River."[2]

"The enemy succeeded in crossing Duck River on the morning of the 22nd" (Report of Maj. Gen. Nathan B. Forrest, CSA, Commanding Cavalry, of operations In North Alabama and Middle Tennessee Relating to the Battle of Nashville). As for the Confederate army under Hood, the 22nd of December 1864 was, for the most part, a day of trudging over miles of frozen ground while determining which routes would best service the army's retrograde movement due south. Keeping a tight rein on its progress, Hood encouraged his men to "push forward as far as you can" and cross Sugar Creek. Alabama and safety would soon appear.

Confederate HQ Remains at Pulaski

December 22. Army headquarters at Pulaski. Stevenson' s [Lee's] corps was directed to move forward on the Lamb's Ferry road, in rear of the pontoon train, and camped about eight miles from Pulaski. General Stewart's corps camped in rear of Stevenson's about six miles from Pulaski, and General Cheatham's on Richland Creek, in the immediate vicinity of town. The wagon train [was] ordered to move at daylight toward Bainbridge, by the Powell road[3] [Journal of the Army of Tennessee].

Various quotes follow in regard to subsequent movements:

On the 22nd, the enemy having effected a crossing of Duck River, and the rear guard, under Major General Forrest, having commenced its retreat, this division (which had been consolidated into a brigade) moved down the Campbellsville pike, on the left flank of the infantry, and on the following day moved still farther down that pike without molestation from the enemy"[4] (Report of Brigadier General James R. Chalmers, CSA, Commanding Cavalry Division, for Operations November 17 to December 12, 1864).

Headquarters, December 22, 1864–8 a.m.
Lieutenant General Stewart, Commanding:

General: General Hood directs that you move your command at once while the ground is frozen, marching some eight or ten miles out on Lamb's Ferry road. Get all your wagons out to that point, and artillery; gather forage there, and collect your rations at that point. General Hood desires to see you at once.

A.P. Mason, Colonel and Assistant Adjutant General[5]

Six miles and a half from Pulaski, Lamb's Ferry Road,
December 22, 1864–1 p.m.
General J.B. Hood, Commanding Army of Tennessee:

General: At this point I take the right-hand or Powell Road; it intersects the Florence Road four miles this side of Lexington and is five miles shorter; has not been traveled, and is the best route, with a good ford over Sugar Creek. I have sent an officer to examine the lower ford, and, if not fordable, will send boats sufficient to bridge it, and to remain till ordered to be taken up by you. Will camp tonight sixteen miles from Pulaski. Have already passed the worst portion of the road, and will make better speed tomorrow.

I have the honor to be, general, very respectfully, your obedient servant,
S.W. Presstman, Lieutenant Colonel and Actg. Chief Engineer, Army of Tenn.[6]

Headquarters, Pulaski, December 22, 1864
Lieutenant General Stewart, Commanding: Sunset

General: ... General Hood says you must judge for yourself when you arrive at this point, six miles and a half, as to which will be the best road for you to move by. Push forward as far as you can tomorrow, and after crossing Sugar Creek send your best teams back to get the ordnance trains over that creek.

Yours Respectfully,
A.P. Mason, Colonel and Assistant Adjutant General[7]

[We] continued our march on the 22nd and 23rd, through snow and very cold weather.[8]

During the late night of the 21st and into the following morning the long-awaited Federal pontoon trains finally arrived and were quickly laid across the river. The Federal infantry corps, commencing its movement across the Duck River by early morning, began the day skirmishing with Confederate pickets and capturing "quite a number of prisoners."

So soon as it was light enough to work the morning of the 22nd a sufficient number of pontoons (they were canvass) were put together to throw across the river a detachment of the Fifty-first Indiana to clear the opposite bank of the enemy. This service was handsomely performed by the detachment, and quite a number of prisoners was the result of the operation. So soon as the opposite bank was cleared of the enemy Colonel Streight commenced to lay down the bridge, and completed the work with commendable celerity, though, owing to the inexperience of the troops in such service and the extreme coldness of the weather, more time was consumed in doing it than could have been desired[9] [Report of Brig. Gen. T.J. Wood, USA, commanding Fourth Army Corps].

December 22.—7 a.m., [The Federals] open fire upon the enemy's pickets across Duck River. After considerable firing we succeeded in crossing the Fifty-first Indiana Infantry across the river in pontoon-boats. They soon drove back the enemy's skirmishers and captured a few prisoners. These skirmishers were left by the enemy as a party of observation. The Fifty-first Indiana behaved very well, and lost 1 man killed and 7 or 8 wounded[10] [Journal of the Fourth Army Corps].

During a period of prisoner interrogation, the Confederates who fell captive to the Federal army informed them of Hood's plans to cross the Tennessee, at least in part, at Decatur, Alabama, a port city on the Tennessee River (located appoximately 35 miles southeast of Florence) as well as a center for the shipment of cotton by railway. Armed with this bit of uncertain information, the Federals continued their bridge work throughout the day. Nevertheless, apart from the number of available boats on hand, the bulk of the army, of practical necessity, would again have to wait for the completion of the pontoon bridge, however long it took. "8 a.m … the troops that are to lay the bridge know nothing about the work. It will, therefore, be necessarily slow"[11] (Journal of the Fourth Army Corps). As Wood's Corps, bogged down at the Duck River, worked feverishly in the construction of a bridge, miles behind them in Franklin the same situation was faced by the Union army's supply trains opposite the rising waters of the Harpeth.

Franklin, December 22, 1864,—9 a.m.
General W.D. Whipple:

The bridge [over the Harpeth] will be finished in half an hour. It has been an awful job to complete it.[12]

W.W. WRIGHT,
Chief of Engineers

By 6:30 p.m. the bridge over the Duck River was finally completed and the infantry began the crossing of its first corps. Although progress had finally been initiated, the ever-present slow, laborious effort to get fully across remained a seemingly insurmountable obstacle. As a consequence, the precarious situation on the north bank of the river improved precious little during the late night hours. Delays had again impeded Wood's progress to a crawl. "6.30 p.m., the pontoon bridge just completed. This corps will move over it at once; the cavalry will follow, and commence to cross at 5 a.m., tomorrow [the 23rd]. General Thomas verbally directs that as soon as the cavalry gets over tomorrow we 'press on' after the enemy to move out the Pulaski pike…. [T]he cavalry will move on our flanks…. The pontoon bridge is a very poor one, and may break down before all of our artillery and trains pass over it…. All [the trains] must be over by 5:00 a.m. tomorrow to allow the Cavalry to cross"[13] (Journal of the Fourth Army Corps).

As soon as the bridge was completed Wood's Fourth Corps began crossing. Its first priority included getting over most of the artillery and a sufficient amount of ammunition, along with the baggage trains to enable a quick resumption of the pursuit—all before the Federal cavalry had begun its crossing on the following morning. On the 22nd Wilson sent the following directive to his Brigadier Generals, outlining the order of cavalry movement to be taken the next day:

Special Field Orders, Headquarters Cavalry Corps, Military Division Of The Mississippi
Near Columbia, Tenn.
December 22, 1864

I. Brigadier-General Hatch's division will begin crossing Duck River as soon as the bridge is completed.
II. Brigadier-General Hammond's brigade will follow the Fifth (Hatch's) Division.
III. Brigadier-General Croxton's brigade will follow General Hammond's.
IV. Colonel Harrison's brigade will follow General Croxton's.
V. The Cavalry Corps will go into camp two miles beyond Columbia, upon ground to be designated by the inspector of the Cavalry Corps.

By order of Brevet Major General Wilson[14]

Wilson's cavalry moved out early the next morning at 5:00 a.m. as scheduled, followed later in the day by Thomas's discontented foot soldiers tramping the Pulaski pike, keeping with his order to "press on after the enemy" once the bulk of the army (especially the cavalry) had forded the river. But by midnight of the 23rd Wilson's cavalry had still not fully crossed. Moreover, the remaining artillery and supply trains were yet to pass over, a task ideally to be accomplished before the rest of the cavalry took possession of the pontoons. After marching southward Thomas's Fourth Corps settled into a freezing bivouac along the Pulaski pike a few miles south of Columbia.

December 23—5 a.m., the bridge is in such a bad condition and the descent and ascent of the banks so slippery that it is most difficult to get on and off of the bridge. Since midnight, when the last of General Elliott's division crossed, we have been able to cross but three batteries and a few wagons. The rest of our artillery and the greater part of our train is [yet] to cross, but the bridge must now be given up to the Cavalry Corps, which is just ready to cross.

   7 a.m. [Wood] directed division commanders to march as soon as the cavalry passes. It will be at least 9 o'clock [p.m.] before all of the cavalry gets over the river, even if the bridge does not break or have to be repaired. It was very cold last night; this morning it is a little warmer. The roads off the turnpike are yet impassable.

Wilson's Cavalry Begins Its Crossing, Which Is Uncompleted by Nightfall

"2 p.m., the cavalry is very slow crossing the bridge. It is very probable that it will not all be over before dark, therefore orders are given to division commanders to march down the Pulaski pike about five or six miles [in the rear of the cavalry] and camp for the night"[15] (Journal of the Fourth Army Corps). After a brief skirmish in a gorge some five miles south of Columbia the Fourth Corps bedded down for the night. At dusk on the 23rd orders arrived for the Fourth Corps' latest movements. The following day Wood's infantry was to work in close conjunction with the Federal cavalry. Wilson felt confident that his cavalry would be over the river by dark and would move out at 5:00 the next morning, renewing the chase. "Immediately after the passing of the cavalry, Wood's Corps would move down the Pulaski pike in full pursuit, with elements of Wilson's cavalry on either flank. That was the plan"[16] (Journal of the Fourth Army Corps).

Forrest Checks the Advance of the Enemy Outside Columbia

On the evening of the 22nd and, aware of the sudden presence of Union forces possessing the possibility of a superior numerical advantage on the southern side of the Duck River, Forrest and the rear guard immediately pulled back, skirmishing with the enemy, Forrest's infantry under Walthall moving on the Pulaski road, Jackson's and Buford's cavalry divisions protecting the army's rear with Chalmers on the right flank moving toward Bigbyville and "a few scouts thrown out on the left flank" (Report of Maj. Gen. Nathan B. Forrest, CSA, Commanding Cavalry, of Operations in North Alabama and Middle Tennessee Relating to the Battle of Nashville).

Soon enough Union troops had closed the distance. Some three miles south of Columbia "near Warfield's" the Federals approached, "opening warmly" with artillery fire upon Forrest's pickets and causing him to fall back to a well-defended point a few miles in the rear. Finding cover in a gorge between two hills situated on either side of the road, Forrest took a position. With Federal forces in a continuing struggle to get their army across the river in full, the Confederate rear guard was all that stood between them and Hood. Much to the relief of the Confederates, Forrest's cavalry for the duration of the day held the upper hand south of Columbia, protecting Hood's withdrawing army and widening the ever-closing gap between them. Too shrewd to allow himself to be drawn into combat hastily, Forrest pulled back. There would be plenty of opportunity in the following days for a full confrontation.

At about the same time, some distance up the pike where Hood's army trudged along, a Confederate surgeon stopped by the roadside to warm himself: "December 22, 1864, was exceedingly cold weather, and spitting snow. I saw where a fire had been near the road and rode out to the old stump, found a few embers and kindled them up. Gen. Hood and escort rode up and asked permission to warm, which was granted, he at the same time making the remark that he had only one foot to get cold."[17]

"I will take care of that"

For Thomas, the 22nd brought an unexpected bit of encouragement in the form of a message from Gen. Grant. Both Grant and the general public were pleased with his performance. Even more, if things were to continue as they were Hood would soon be cut off, and a major portion of the Confederate army would fade away into history.

City Point, Va., December 22, 1864
Major General Thomas
Nashville, Tenn.:

You have the congratulations of the public for the energy with which you are pushing Hood. I hope you will succeed in reaching his pontoon bridge at Tuscumbia before he gets there. Should you do it, it looks to me that Hood is cut off. If you succeed in destroying Hood's army, there will be but one army left to the so-called Confederacy capable of doing us harm. I will take care of that and try to draw the sting from it, so that in the spring we shall have easy sailing. You now have a big opportunity, which I know you are availing yourself of. Let us push and do all we can before the enemy can derive benefit either from the raising of negro troops or the concentration of white troops now in the field.[18]

U.S. Grant, Lieutenant-General

8

Friday, December 23, 1864
Alabama within Sight

Confederate Army HQ Six Miles from Lexington, Alabama

"December 23: [Confederate] Army headquarters on Powell's Ferry road, six miles from Lexington, Alabama. The army, after the day's march, camped as follows: Stevenson's corps at the intersection of the Lamb's Ferry road with the Powell road, four miles from Lexington; General Stewart in rear, on the Lamb's Ferry road; General Cheatham moved on the Lawrenceburg road" (Journal of the Army of Tennessee, November 14, 1864–January 23, 1865, Campaign in North Alabama and Middle Tennessee, p. 673). "Friday, December 23. Marched about twenty miles on the Lewisburg road"[1] (Itinerary of Cheatham's Army Corps).

Columbia, Tenn., December 23, 1864—8 P.M.
Major General H.W. Halleck,
Washington, D. C.:
The Troops Are Still Crossing Duck River, And Are Close Up To The Enemy's Rear Guard, On The Pulaski Road. I Hope To Get The Whole Force Across Tomorrow And Continue The Pursuit. The Railroad Bridges Between Spring Hill And This Place (Five In Number) Have Been Destroyed, But The Construction Corps Is Hard At Work, And I Am In Hopes They Will Have The Road Repaired Up To Columbia In The Course Of Four Or Five Days…. General Mccook … With General Long Will Soon Join General Wilson, Thus Increasing My Cavalry Force Sufficiently To Enable Me To Completely Destroy Forrest, If I Can Overtake Him, Which I Shall Make Every Exertion To Do.[2]
Geo. H. Thomas,
Major General, U.S. Volunteers, Commanding

Headquarters Fourth Army Corps, Columbia, Tenn., December 23, 1864–1.30 P.M.
Brigadier General Whipple, Chief Of Staff:

General: I have the honor to report that I am just starting on the march. I wish to move six or eight miles out on the Pulaski pike, to get out of the way of the cavalry and such other troops as may cross tonight. I do not think the cavalry will all get over the river much before dark. Please allow the remnant of my artillery and trains to cross the pontoons tonight.[3]

Very respectfully, your obedient servant,
TH. J. WOOD,
Brigadier General, Commanding

December 23—Brigade commenced crossing at 12.30 a.m.; crossing very bad. The Sixth Ohio Battery G, First Ohio, and First Kentucky Battery, and Battery E, First Michigan, and one piece of Battery B, Pennsylvania, crossed, when the bridge broke; at daylight the cavalry was ordered to cross before the other batteries.[4]

Wood's Artillery and Wagons Held at the Duck River

As mentioned previously, early the next morning Federal infantry advancement on the north bank of the Duck River had changed little. Wilson's cavalry, having been given first priority to cross, had created yet another holdup for Wood. The remaining artillery and wagons would have to stand aside until the entire cavalry corps had passed to the front. Afterward, the wagons were to regroup and file out behind them. This further setback cost the Federal army added time, holding back the infantry's march down the Pulaski pike for several more hours. With Wilson taking the entire day and into the next for the cavalry to finish crossing, Wood finally went into an icy camp on the night of the 23rd. It was hoped that by the next morning the way would be clear for the wagons and remaining infantry. "Friday, the 23rd, I rested near Columbia, awaiting for the cavalry to complete its passage of Duck River, till midday, when, the cavalry not being yet over, I informed the commanding general I would move the corps a few miles to the front that afternoon, encamp for the night, and wait the following morning for the [remaining] cavalry to move out..."[5] (Report of Brig. Gen. T.J. Wood, USA, commanding Fourth Army Corps).

A glance at a moment of relaxation in Union camp life on the 23rd of December 1864, on the Columbia-Pulaski pike, reveals what many would recall years later. The long delays at the river crossing had provided time for some journaling, an official report, and a letter home. "About noon the bugle sounded the march but afterward sounded the dinner call. In partaking of my frugal repast today, prepared by 'Mat' my intelligent contraband & found several worms in one hard tack. This issue of crackers is worse than usual."[6] "[C]rossed the Duck River, and encamped five miles south of Columbia on the Pulaski Pike"[7] (Report of Col. Datus Coon, 2nd Iowa Cavalry, Commanding Second Brigade, of operations from September 30, 1864, to January 15, 1865).

> Camp near Columbia, Tenn. December 23rd, 1864
>
> Respected Father, We have been in the saddle almost constantly day and night since the first of the month in pursuit of the rebel General Hood. We are in good spirits but much fatigued, and need rest badly, but I suppose there will be no rest for us until we capture the rebel army or drive it back to its starting point. Almost every day since we started on this raid we have been fighting the enemy more or less, and have lost several good men. I have not time to give you full details of our proceedings up to this date, but will endeavor to do so when I write you again. You will find here a list of losses of Company E during this month:
>
> Killed: Capt. Volney Hobson (Shot Through The Heart) [On North Side Of Franklin, 17 December Across The Harpeth River], Sergeant Frank Ricks (Shot In The Head) [Killed While Carrying The Regimental Colors 17 December, At West Harpeth].
>
> Wounded: Sergeant Madison Grose, In Shoulder, Slight, Sergeant George P. Helvis, In Breast, Mortally, John A. Sheckles, In Leg, Slight, Amos H. Allee, In Thigh, Mortal [Captured 1 December; survived incarceration At Cahaba Prison; Died 14 May, 1865, At Vicksburg, Mississippi, Where He Is Buried], Harrison Jackson, In Hand, Severe, Samuel Sweigart, In Shoulder And Neck, Severe.
>
> Missing: Wyatt Crandall, Charles O. Nixon, Nathan O. Hill, Wm. Leisure, K. Mendenhall [Captured 1 December; Died At Cahaba Prison; Buried At Marietta, Georgia], Harvey Jackson, Thos. Laboyteaux [Captured 1 December; Cahaba; Lost In *Sultana* Explosion, 27 April, 1865; Body Not Recovered], Rob't. Gilbreath.
>
> W.S. Julian [*New Castle (IN) Courier*, Thursday, January 5, 1865].

With additional delays expected, around 2:30 p.m. the Federal infantry began marching down the Pulaski pike, intending after a few miles to camp for the night alongside the road, evidently preparing for a more organized and energetic pursuit in the morning. Early in the evening however, the advance troops of Federal infantry suddenly found themselves confronted by the rear guard of Hood's army, who were ready and waiting for them. Forrest's cavalry would hold the Federals off until the vanguard of Confederate infantry had safely vacated Pulaski. "December 23, received orders to march toward Pulaski as soon as the cavalry was out of the way, my division marching in rear of the corps. The rear guard of the enemy stubbornly resisted our advance, and we succeeded in advancing but five miles during the day"[8] (Report of Brigadier General Samuel Beatty, USA, Commanding Third Division).

Federal Advance Troops Confront Confederate Rear Guard Near Lynnville

In a directive written on the morning of the 23rd, "three miles north of Lynnville," General Chalmers was instructed to take his cavalry division in the direction of Columbia, where Federal troops were forming, and "hold the enemy in check as long as possible." A remnant of the Confederate forces, including their trains, were still in the vicinity of Pulaski, much too close to the advancing Federal army. Under these orders and with the aid of Buford, Jackson, and the rear guard infantry of Walthall's division located near Lynnville, Chalmers was to fall back toward Columbia and engage the enemy in a strong, defiant stand, leaving the impression that he had purposed to occupy the town.[9] "On the night of the 23rd I [Forrest] halted my command at and near Lynnville, in order to hold the enemy in check and to prevent any pressure upon my wagon train and the stock then being driven out."[10] Soon, with both armies on the same side of the river and equally determined, the coming collision would become unavoidable.

"General Wilson says that all of his Cavalry will be over the river by dark, and that he will move out at 5 o'clock in the morning [the 24th]. The Cavalry will move in advance of this [Infantry] Corps, and as soon as it passes by the [Infantry] Corps will move. It has been very cold today"[11] (Journal of the Fourth Army Corps). Regardless of the cold or anything else that had the capability of hampering their progress, Hood's army was on the move. The Alabama line lay just ahead and, with its crossing, recovery and rest. But that hour had not yet arrived. By the time they had come within reach of safety, the army was tottering on the brink of exhaustion.

"Two [Union] scouts from these headquarters who crossed the river yesterday and have been some seven miles south of this place have just come in.... [T]he entire rebel Army has gone on the turnpike ... to Pulaski ... [and] it is reported that they were to divide the infantry going to Lamb's Ferry, eighteen miles below Florence, while their transportation and artillery go to Decatur.... [T]he artillery horses have all given out, and the guns are being hauled by oxen.... The bulk of the [men] are very much out of spirits; they are without shoes, and would give themselves up, if pushed."[12] As for the Confederate troops, they were on their own. No reinforcements or supplies were to be expected. On December 23, in response to an earlier message from General Hood, General Beauregard related the disagreeable news to his besieged subordinate: "General J.B. Hood: I regret to inform you that no reinforcements can possibly be sent to you from any quarter. General Taylor has no troops to spare, and every available man in Georgia and South Carolina is required to oppose Sherman ... [so] you must retire at once behind the Tennessee River."[13] How those last words must have stung, from that day onward.

The weight of responsibility for the failed campaign was sufficient to crush many a man, regardless of his strength or wisdom. The burden pressing down on General Hood during those awful days must have been massive. Even so, he handled it well, the tramping multitude at his side, departing

Tennessee and all that was lost, "singing hymns of praise" upward and beyond the ice-covered heavens. Those hymns scattered over the frozen countryside must have been the oil and the wine for many a distressed and hopeless soul living within hearing distance and huddled around their smoldering firesides in that terrible winter of 1864. What they heard, if they heard anything at all, was known only to them but no doubt was indelibly seared into their conscience, lasting a lifetime. To them it was given. As for us, we can only imagine, piecing together the broken fragments of the puzzle as best as we can. The strained, dry voices of a mighty host, rising up ten thousand strong, carried heavenward on the frozen air are gone forever. But their memory remains, and their hymns of praise are eternal. And on snowy, windswept nights their coarse, hollow voices can still be heard, carried aloft on the Columbia-Pulaski pike. It took a special breed of men to sing their way out of a shocked and distraught Middle Tennessee that winter. Has the like ever been seen or heard?

9

Saturday, December 24, 1864
Richland Creek

Confederate Army HQ Near Bainbridge, Alabama

"December 24: [Confederate] Army headquarters at Mr. Joiner's, eleven miles from Bainbridge, on the main Bainbridge road. Stevenson's corps reached and camped on Shoal Creek and Stewart's in his rear. General Cheatham has not yet come into the main road from the Powell road" (Journal of the Army of Tennessee, November 14, 1864–January 23, 1865, Campaign in North Alabama and Middle Tennessee). "Saturday, December 24.— Marched fourteen miles today, leaving ten miles to make to the river"[1] (Itinerary of Cheatham's Army Corps).

> Everyday's march brought us nearer the Tennessee River, and now the news reached us that the river was very high and that Yankee gunboats were up the river ready to destroy any bridge that we might throw across. This was very plausible, for we knew there were boats in the lower Tennessee and that there had been an abundance of rain, and that all the rumors were possible.
>
> Distress and worry of that sort are contagious and most of the men were filled with gloom.
>
> The prospect for reaching the south bank of the Tennessee was not good. We could now hear rumors of fighting in the rear, more or less, and some wounded were brought forward. It was said that we could not re-cross at Florence. We finally reached Shoal Creek, a large stream flowing out of the Tennessee and emptying into the river about ten miles above Florence. Here we heard for the first time the name Bainbridge, a name that in a few hours was on the lips of the entire Army.[2]

"We [Confederates] marched twenty miles on the 24th."[3] "Our gallant rear guard, after they left Columbia, had a battle at Richland Creek."[4] "On the following morning, the 24th, I [Wood] was detained till 12 p.m., waiting for the cavalry to come up and move out. Shortly after the cavalry had passed out through my camp Brevet Major General Wilson sent me a message to the

144

effect that he had found the ground so soft that he could not operate off of the turnpike, and begging that I would not become impatient at the delay he was causing in the movement of my command. At 12 p.m. the road was free of the cavalry, when the corps was put in motion and marched sixteen miles that afternoon, and encamped two miles south of Lynnville"[5] (Report of Brig. Gen. T.J. Wood, USA, commanding Fourth Army Corps).

Fourth Army Corps "We Will Now Be Able to Move Rapidly"

"7 a.m., the [Union] Cavalry still passing by. Division commanders directed to march and follow it as soon as it has passed.... 11:50 a.m., the head of our [Infantry] column [is] just starting on the march.... We will now be able to move rapidly"[6] (Journal of the Fourth Army Corps). It had been a long haul for the Union troopers. From Nashville to Columbia, in a pursuit plagued by horrific weather and equally bad transportation and logistical troubles, the Federal infantry as a whole had seen little action, regardless of the weight of pressure put on Hood's retreating riflemen. Now, with the lesser rivers behind them and miles of open country in their front, the way was finally cleared for free, unhindered movement. No one could have known what lay just ahead. But in the event that the Federal infantry, beset with more unforeseen difficulties, should fall still farther behind, Thomas was yet not without aid. At the first possible opportunity, regardless of the obstacles, the powerful forces of Wilson's staunch cavalry regiments racing to the front would surely swoop down upon the struggling remnants of Hood's tattered ranks, overcome them, and force their surrender.

Following the construction of the bridge spanning the Duck River, the Federal army was again on the move. But with Hood nearing the Tennessee the prospects for bringing him to bay had become slim indeed. For Thomas and the Union army under his command, time was quickly running out. The Confederate rear guard under Nathan Bedford Forrest, although weakened numerically with each encounter, had proved itself more than a match for the onrushing Federal cavalry. Regardless of the conditions surrounding it, the rear guard simply would not yield. Somehow, at every phase of the pursuit it seemed to snatch victory out of the mouth of certain defeat—and there appeared to be little the Union army could do to change the situation. "[T]he bridge was completed by the evening of the 23rd, and that night ... [the Cavalry] crossed to the south side of the river, and early next morning resumed the pursuit. Hood's reorganized rear guard, under the redoubtable Forrest, was soon encountered by the cavalry advanced guard, and he was a leader not to be attacked by a handful of men, however bold"[7] (James Harrison

Wilson, Major-General, USV, Brevet Major-General, USA, "The Union Cavalry in the Hood Campaign"). In spite of his optimism, Wilson's setbacks were not over. Beset by the forces of nature and the restraining power of the Confederate rear guard, the Union cavalry movements under his command were again brought to a near standstill. "1 p.m., received note from General Wilson, who states that he cannot move on the side of the turnpike, owing to the nature of the ground; that his progress has been slow, as he has been constantly skirmishing with the enemy"[8] (Journal of the Fourth Army Corps). "The [Federal] cavalry has been skirmishing with the enemy's rear guard as the dead horses lying in the roadside indicate."[9]

"On we [Confederates] marched, through ice and rain and snow, sleeping on the wet ground at night. Many thousands were barefooted, actually leaving the prints of blood upon the ground, as the enemy pressed us in the rear. When we left the pike at Pulaski we had an awful road, strewn with dead horses and mules, broken wagons, and worse than all, broken pontoons. We counted as we passed them, one, two, three, to fifteen."[10] "[Federal infantry] marched with the division, in rear of General Croxton's command, as far as Lynnville, when my brigade was ordered to march by the left flank, to gain the rear of the enemy's lines, and drive him from a strong position on Richland Creek, but was prevented by the unfordable condition of Richland Creek, when I dismounted my command and engaged the enemy at long range for half an hour. During this skirmish the rebel General Buford was wounded by the Seventh Illinois. Camped for the night"[11] (Report of Col. Datus Coon, 2nd Iowa Cavalry, Commanding Second Brigade, of operations from September 30, 1864, to January 15, 1865).

> Three Miles from Lynnville, December 24th, 1864 11:40 a.m.
> Brig. Gen. T.J. Wood, Commanding Fourth Corps:
>
> General: From the nature of the ground I find it impossible to move off the turnpike, and as the head of my column is constantly skirmishing with the enemy's rear guard my progress is necessarily slow. I beg, therefore, that you will not become impatient, as I am pushing forward as rapidly as possible.[12]
>
> Very respectfully, your obedient servant,
> J.H. Wilson, Brevet Major General, Commanding

The Confrontation at Lynnville

At approximately the same time that Wilson's cavalry was coming into more difficulty with the roads, the rear guard of Hood's army moved steadily on, well aware of the vulnerability of the precious wagons and stock that they were protecting. Soon Forrest's rear guard would take yet another stand just south of Lynnville, Tennessee:

December 24, while bringing up the rear of our army, the enemy charged my rear guard at Lynnville with a heavy force and threatened to break over all opposition, when the Sixth Texas, hastily forming, met and hurled them back, administering a most wholesome check to their ardor. At the moment this occurred our columns were all in motion, and it was of the utmost importance to break the charge of the enemy on our rear. Too much credit, therefore, cannot be given the Sixth Texas for gallant bearing on this occasion. Had it failed to check the enemy, my brigade and probably the entire division, taken at a disadvantage, might have suffered severely. At Richland Creek, where the cavalry took position later in the day, I was assigned a position on the right of the railroad and in front of the creek. Soon afterward, however, the enemy moving as if to cross above the bridge, I was withdrawn to the south side of the creek, and taking position on the hill near the railroad, skirmished with the enemy in my front, holding him in check until our forces had all crossed the creek. We were then ordered to withdraw, and, passing through Pulaski, again crossed Richland Creek, and camped near Mr. Carter's for the night [Report of Brig. Gen. Lawrence S. Ross, commanding Ross's Brigade, CSA, Operations of October 24– December 27, 1864].

Walthall's infantry again played a key role in this new round of fighting, engaging the advance forces of Wilson's cavalry divisions and his forward infantry units, holding them in check for several hours, "skirmishing with the enemy's rear guard," as Wilson put it. At the close of the contest Walthall retired, eventually withdrawing to a more advantageous position on the banks of Richland Creek in preparation for a full encounter. "On the 24th, Wilson's cavalry corps, <u>ten thousand strong</u>, and Wood's division of infantry, crossed, and the pursuit began in earnest. There was heavy fighting during the day, in which both infantry and cavalry were engaged" ("Forrest and His Campaigns," *SHSP* 7, no.10 (January–December 1879), 482).

The Engagement at Richland Creek

On either side of the turnpike stretching from Columbia to Pulaski the countryside lay rutted, chopped, and heavily obstructed by dense woods, creating yet another hindrance to Federal pursuit. To the Confederates' advantage the pike ran through valleys and gorges, providing many a useful location for defensive purposes. Even so, Wilson pushed on. Another confrontation was in the making. The battle at Richland Creek was about to commence. "The rear guard had thus a clear road and when pressed could fall back rapidly. The country on the right and left of the pike, very broken and densely timbered, was almost impassable; the pike itself, passing through the gorges of the hills, was advantageous for the enemy; with a few men he could compel the pursuing force to develop a front almost anywhere"[13] (Report of Bvt. Major General James Wilson, USA, Commanding Cavalry Corps). "The enemy was closely pressed and every opportunity was seized upon to bring him to bay. In the vicinity of Lynnville, the country being somewhat more open, he was driven back rapidly, and at Buford's station while General Hatch was engaging him upon the turnpike, Croxton struck him in the flank, captured one flag [by the hands of Medal of Honor recipient, Cpl. Harrison Collins, Co. A, 1st Tennessee Cavalry] and a number of prisoners; wounded General Abram Buford, and drove his cavalry rapidly beyond Richland Creek"[14] (James Harrison Wilson, Major-General, USV, Brevet Major-General, USA, "The Union Cavalry in the Hood Campaign").

Perceiving that the Federals were drawing near, Forrest got moving quickly. Using Capt. John Morton's Tennessee artillery battery to the greatest advantage, he placed six guns (with Armstrong's Brigade supporting) on the pike covering his entire front, positioning them across the creek and up by the roadside leading to the bridge. As Walthall's infantry covered the passage over the creek, the remaining cavalry brigades of Chalmers, Buford, and Ross's Texans were positioned along the flanks of the artillery, Chalmers and Buford being placed "in line with and to the left of the artillery, while Ross's brigade was on the right." Having placed his guard in such complete concealment, Forrest inspected his lines. Morton's Battery turned and faced the enemy, waiting for the Federal advance. The wait was not a long one. Upon the arrival of Federal cavalry, an intense artillery duel soon developed, followed by the dismounting of two Federal guns and an attempted flanking of the Confederate right by a crossing of the creek, causing an eruption of fire and lead in an aggressive confrontation with Jackson's division that lasted several hours. In the end, as darkness began to fall, prohibiting any further pursuit, the Federals, repulsed with heavy losses, temporarily fell back. As for the Confederates, except for the wounding of General Buford (by the Seventh Illinois) their losses were relatively light[15] (Report of Colonel Datus E. Coon, Second Iowa Cavalry).

Soon after the engagement had opened, Union reinforcements poured in, all intent upon showing the Southerners their superior ability to withstand Forrest's ferocity and cunning. Having blunted the Union offensive and seeing no justification to continue, Forrest eventually chose to withdraw, removing his forces south to Pulaski without further conflict. Throughout the previous 36 hours the fighting had raged on without a letup. The Confederate rear guard suffered significantly, being heavily pressed by Union cavalry flanking attempts and the onrush of infantry. But, remarkably, the rear guard had held its ground in each encounter, yet not without the inevitable and irreplaceable losses.

Around 5:00 that afternoon Major General Wilson, although having declared from headquarters in mid-afternoon that he was "driving the enemy [Forrest] rapidly," his efforts had nonetheless produced little effect on the day's outcome. In reporting to General Whipple, Wilson remarked with some irritability, "We have driven Forrest all day without bringing him to an engagement." Nevertheless, Wilson had "driven him back" on two accounts at Richland Creek where "Croxton got in on their left and compelled them to retire…. Our progress has not been as rapid today as I expected, but it was rather from the difficult nature of the country than the resistance of the enemy." Indeed, Wilson concluded his remarks with a message that he would be out on the pike at an early hour, resuming the pursuit with further attempts at outflanking the fleeing army of Confederates.[16]

With the day spent and having made little or no advancement, Wilson positioned his cavalry into camp a half-mile south of Lynnville, fronted on the pike by Hood's rear guard, whose numbers, according to the Union accounts, consisted of "seven brigades of infantry" and Forrest's cavalry brigades. Wilson's stalled movements along the pike "owing to the nature of the ground" and of his "skirmishing with the enemy" differ greatly from the view of the day's activities from Forrest's standpoint. By moving his units back toward Columbia and confronting the enemy directly, Forrest had taken the initiative, going on the offensive with both infantry and cavalry in the face of a powerful artillery exchange, outmaneuvering the attempted flanking charges of Wilson's cavalry divisions and driving them back across the river.

On the morning of the 24th I ordered the infantry [Walthall's] back toward Columbia on the main pike and my cavalry on the right and left flanks. After advancing about three miles [to Lynnville] the enemy was met, where a severe engagement occurred and the enemy was held in check for two hours. [Afterward] I retreated two miles, where I took position at Richland Creek. Brigadier General Armstrong was thrown forward in front and General Ross on the right flank. Chalmers and Buford formed a junction, and were ordered on the left flank. Brigadier General Armstrong was ordered to the support of six pieces of my artillery, which were placed in position immediately on the main pike and on a line with Buford's and Chalmers' divisions and Ross' brigade, of Jackson's division.

After severe artillery firing on both sides, two pieces of the enemy's artillery were dismounted. The enemy then flanked to the right and left and crossed Richland Creek on my right, with the view of gaining my rear. I immediately ordered Armstrong and Ross, of Jackson's division, to cross the bridge on the main pike and move around and engage the enemy, who were crossing the creek. Both Buford and Chalmers were heavily pressed on the left, and after an engagement of two hours I ordered them to fall back across Richland Creek. I lost 1 killed and 6 wounded in this engagement. The enemy lost heavily. Brigadier General Buford was wounded in this engagement, and I ordered Brigadier General Chalmers to assume command of Brigadier General Buford's division together with his own. I reached Pulaski without further molestation[17] [Report of Maj. Gen. Nathan B. Forrest].

Later that evening, Wilson's superiors put to rest any concerns regarding his apparent inability to get the job done as quickly as expected, approving his plan to get an early start in the morning yet advising him as well to "continue a pretty strong force covering your right." His efforts were "not considered slow" but actually "quite satisfactory to the commanding General."[18] Wilson's final orders that night were summed up in one, brief line: "The Cavalry Corps will move tomorrow in pursuit of the enemy … [and] every effort should be made to push the enemy as rapidly as possible."[19]

As Forrest held his position on the evening of the 24th, adeptly fending off the incessant cavalry attacks at the army's rear, Hood's leading elements—some having spent the morning collecting and repairing broken pontoons found along the roadside—had marched to within a mere eleven miles of Bainbridge, Alabama, on the main Bainbridge road. The Tennessee, and safety, although now within sight, yet remained just out of reach. As to the Confederate infantry rear guard, after the standoff at Richland Creek it withdrew to the outskirts of Pulaski for the rest of the night. On the following morning it resumed its duties, watching the army's back.

> I [General Walthall] was directed when I arrived at Richland Creek to prepare to hold the crossing should the Cavalry, which was retiring slowly, be so pressed as to make it necessary for them to pass over before night. I posted my command in strong position on the creek, about seven miles from Pulaski, and remained there till 8 o'clock at night, when I was ordered to retire to the outer line of earth works, near the town. I remained there till daylight next morning, when I withdrew, and passing through Pulaski left the Pike and took the road heading to Bainbridge on the Tennessee River. The roads now were almost impassable[20] [Report of Maj. General Edward C. Walthall, CSA].

Impassable roads were not the only obstacles in Hood's path on the 24th. The dilapidated condition of his pontoon trains had become so serious a threat that special attention was directed to the securing of an adequate number of reliable pontoons. Earlier, during the first week of December, Hood had wisely made a precautionary decision, selecting a portion of his army under the command of Brigadier General P.D. Roddey to remain in the rear "for the purpose of … building a bridge over the [Tennessee] river at Decatur" in the event a retreat southward from Tennessee might become necessary should the campaign fail.[21] On the 24th of December 1864 on the Columbia-Pulaski pike it was definitely necessary.

Roddey's subsequent efforts at holding the enemy in check near the proposed crossing point while simultaneously destroying Federal rail lines, "driving back three gunboats that appeared at Decatur" with "only a section of smooth-bore six-pounder guns and a few sharpshooters" (in addition to preparing a traversable roadway for Hood's footsore army), had proved invaluable. The hope was that all essential precautions and preparations for the crossing would be completed on time, for there was no time to lose.[22]

Federal Navy Wreaks Destruction and Threatens Hood's Crossing

Out ahead of Hood's army another serious threat was mounting. The ominous sounds of reverberating artillery booming off in the distance chilled the men to the bone. Rapidly approaching Yankee gunboats working their way downriver would soon be upon them. Admiral S.P. Lee was in the process of wreaking havoc among the Confederate defensive works on the Tennessee around Florence, Alabama, which, according to Federal belief, was the most likely point of Hood's crossing. Admiral Lee would spare no effort at destroying everything in his path in order to prevent Hood from reaching his crossing point as well as the securing of Lee's much-needed Union supplies and Federal troop transports that were due in shortly. In a message dated from the 27th Admiral Lee reported to Thomas on his recent activities:

Major General THOMAS:

I arrived here on the 24th, and destroyed a new fort and magazine; no guns. Have been several miles above Florence, and have destroyed all the enemy's visible means of crossing below Florence. I found the enemy have field pieces, probably protecting a crossing at foot of Mussel Shoals, six miles above Florence, which want of water prevented my reaching. The rebels crossed their prisoners at Garner's Ferry, twelve miles below Florence, on the 19th instant. I destroyed over a dozen flats and pontoons there; nothing but one flat at Florence. I learned that Hood took some pontoons with him, and others go adrift. Hood has earthworks at Florence, made last spring; saw two on each side. No guns ... [L]ooked finished. Hood's troops arriving near Florence are said to declare that they don't know where his main army is; that they had orders to scatter and care for themselves; that no Tennessee troops have come to this river since Hood's defeat; that 100 wagons and a great many troops were grievously disappointed at my destruction of the ferry boats at Garner's Ferry, which obliged them to move thence up river. Today I destroyed two guns and caissons at Florence Landing, and found a battery of several field pieces on heights over left bank at Boone's Ferry. Neither of these places was occupied yesterday. Enemy is doubtless coming in, seeking crossing. Your two telegrams of the 21st were received tonight. Your transports with provisions arrived here today, and will remove to Eastport tomorrow, where they will be well protected. I will immediately dispatch an iron-clad and gun-boats to convoy your troops up from Paducah. If any are there, or expected, shall keep up active patrol of river above and below.

S.P. LEE
Flagship Fairy, Tennessee River, off Chickasaw, Ala. December 27, 1864
Acting Rear Admiral, Commanding.[23]

As for Hood's gaunt rear guard, there had been little if any relief. Forrest had been fighting without a break for nearly ten days (from December 15 to the 24th), extricating his command from the disaster at Nashville while shielding the army from the unremitting flanking assaults of Wilson's cavalry, as well as keeping the rear guard out of reach of the onrush of Wood's Infantry Corps, struggling down the pike, never more than just beyond the margin of danger. Rarely has a rear guard action been placed in such threatening conditions. "But each Confederate officer and man appeared to act and fight as if the fate of the army depended on his individual conduct.... [N]ever were there manifested higher soldierly virtues than by Forrest's heroic band [on the retreat of the army from Columbia to the Tennessee River]."[24] The daring accomplishments and fortitude of the rear guard under Forrest's command under such prolonged adversity during those fateful days seem to be without parallel in the historical record. Through the determined efforts of this band of half starved, bludgeoned, virtually frozen remnants of the Army of Tennessee, what was left of its ebbing life was saved to fight another day.

Upon arrival near Pulaski, the pitiless, frigid rain had turned to snow, then ice, the surface mud of the pike becoming a frozen layer of mire, severely hampering all forms of transportation or movement. Wagons, horses, and bleeding, barefoot men worked their way along, each step sinking deeper through the crusty sheet of frozen mud down into a thick river of sludge. Progress crept along with agonizing effort and was achieved only with the utmost exertions. As night fell and the temperature with it, Hood's army and Forrest's rear guard drew into the seclusion of a nearby wood, its ground frozen solid. Even the trees were partially covered with a coat of ice. Building a fire of any size was now impossible. Without rations, warmth, or dry clothing, the Army of Tennessee sprawled out over the frozen ground and sought an unattainable time of rest. "The road from Pulaski to Bainbridge was as bad as it could be, the country through which it runs almost entirely denuded of forage and Army supplies. Both men and horses suffered greatly"[25] (Major General James H. Wilson, USA, Commanding Cavalry Corps).

A few miles behind Hood's army the relentless bluecoats surged forward, struggling down the Columbia-Pulaski Pike. The forces under the command of George Henry Thomas were not about to lose the one opportunity they possessed, however elusive. In spite of the setbacks, Thomas was moving ahead. In a message dated the 24th at 4:00 p.m. Thomas's priorities of men over supplies became evident. The trains would wait for the troops to pass.

Headquarters Fourth Army Corps, Duck River Bridge, December 24, 1864—4 P.M.
General Wood:

Our trains are just getting in with six days' rations. I [William H. Sinclair, assistant adjutant general] saw General Thomas, but he would not give an order for supply train to pass to the exclusion of other trains. The bridge broke many times last night and this a.m., but is working well this p.m. The troops of A.J. Smith are all over, but not his batteries. The cavalry train is passing now, and will get over by dark, if the bridge continues to work well; then Smith's batteries pass over; then comes our turn. If nothing happens to the bridge tonight the rations will get up tomorrow. I would suggest, however, that the men be a little saving of their rations, for fear of some accident. We will do everything we can to get the rations forward, though. They are just going to work putting down another bridge. Fished out three pieces of artillery from the river this morning.[26]

I am, your obedient servant,
Wm. H. Sinclair
Assistant Adjutant General

About an hour later, some two-and-a-half miles south of Lynnville, General Wood relayed to his superior the situation his Fourth Army Corps was faced with. The slow-moving cavalry was still impeding his movements and he was in desperate need of provisions. Those rations may not have been top priority to George Thomas, but from Wood's standpoint they were all-important. He had just enough "subsistence" for one more day. If he could not become adequately supplied he would not be held responsible for the results. The army would begin to come apart and the pursuit would unravel into a crawl:

General [Whipple]: My Leading Division Is Just Going Into Camp. We Were Not Able To Leave Camp Before 12 O'clock, On Account Of Being Delayed By The Cavalry. We Have Marched Sixteen Miles And A Half Today. General Wilson Is Going Into Camp One Mile And A Half In Advance. The March Will Be Resumed In The Morning As Soon As The Cavalry Get Out Of The Road For Us. All Information Goes To Show That The Enemy Is Covering His Retreat With Seven Brigades Of Infantry, Commanded By Walthall, And Forrest's Cavalry. The Enemy's Pontoon Train Camped Twelve Miles From Columbia Wednesday Night, And Left There Thursday Morning. I Hope We Will Yet Be Able To Strike The Enemy Before He Reaches The Tennessee River, Provided We Can Be Supplied With Subsistence. I Therefore Respectfully Urge That My Wagons Be Allowed To Move Up, As We Will Be Out Of Subsistence Tomorrow Night.

Very Respectfully,
Th. J. Wood
Brigadier General, Commanding

The army however, remained on its original course. Time was all-important, with none to waste. Whipple's reply was brief, showing little sign of any change in plans.

Brigadier General T.J. Wood, Commanding Fourth Army Corps:

General: Your dispatch of 5 p.m. this day received. The major general commanding directs that you continue to push on and that he will do everything in his power to get up your train and that of the cavalry.

Very respectfully, your obedient servant
WM. D. Whipple
Brigadier General and Assistant Adjutant General

The army would forge ahead, with or without the necessary supplies.

At about the same time, the forward elements of Union cavalry were out and on the move. With scouts patrolling the far front, the following report was brought in: "The force in our front, or in front of the cavalry, is the enemy's rear guard, and consists of seven brigades of infantry and Forrest's cavalry. The enemy's pontoon train camped on Wednesday night at Mr. Foster's, twelve miles south of Columbia, and left there early Thursday morning for Pulaski. All information obtained in the road goes to show that the enemy intends to cross the Tennessee River at Lamb's Ferry, that he will lay his pontoon at that point, and that he will not make a stand north of the river"[27] (Journal of the Fourth Army Corps). Encamped that night at his headquarters near Richland Creek, Wilson's order for the following day was typical. After designating the order of pursuit, he summed up the basic force that had driven them since the beginning of it: "Every effort should be made to push the enemy as rapidly as possible."[28]

Unknown to Union intelligence and contrary to their expectation, Hood's rear guard was preparing to do the unanticipated. Just where Federal scouts had obtained the information that Hood's army would not make a stand north of the river is not certain, but wherever it had come from it surely misled them. Knowing something of Forrest's character they might well have doubted the notion that he would shun unavoidable confrontation. He was well known for taking a stand, regardless of the odds.

Christmas Eve

At the close of the day, Christmas Eve 1864, the general staff of the Army of Tennessee again found itself before God in prayer. It is doubtful that we will ever know the specifics of that meeting. But there is one thing we can be quite certain of: it must have been truly heartrending. The past month had been brutal and they were all living in its ever-present shadow. So much lost at so high a price. Who could forget the sign posted by the roadside that had greeted them only a month before: "Tennessee, a free home or a grave." It's no wonder that they met together for prayer. Where else could they have found comfort? "Just at the close of day I [Dr. Quintard] found my friend, Major General Clayton, camped by the road side and not knowing General Hood's location, I decided to accept his most cordial invitation to spend the night with him. It was Christmas eve. After supper the General called up all his staff and couriers and we had prayers."[29]

Composed in agony and anguish of the soul, the following verses from the book of Psalms would have been a fitting depiction of the depth of suffering experienced during those stirring days wherein children, lost in an ocean of blood, stood in empty doorways gazing through hollow eyes in silent astonishment as whole cities gone up in flames emptied out their inhabitants into the blackened streets, and the sun, turning its back on them, descended into dark night.

Psalm 69, Selected Verses:

A Psalm of David

Save me, O God; for the waters are come in unto my soul.

I sink in deep mire, where there is no standing: I am come into deep waters, where the floods overflow me.

I am weary with my crying; my throat is dried: mine eyes fail while I wait for my God.

They that hate me without a cause are more than the hairs of my head: they that would cut me off, being mine enemies wrongfully, are mighty: that which I took not away I have to restore.

O God, thou knowest my foolishness, and my sins are not hid from thee.
Let not them that wait for thee be put to shame through me, O Lord Jehovah of hosts: let not those that seek thee be brought to dishonor through me, O God of Israel.

Because for thy sake I have borne reproach; shame hath covered my face.

I am become a stranger unto my brethren, and an alien unto my mother's children.

For the zeal of thy house hath eaten me up; and the reproaches of them that reproach thee are fallen upon me.

When I wept, and chastened my soul with fasting, that was to my reproach.

When I made sackcloth my clothing, I became a byword unto them.

They that sit in the gate talk of me; and I am the song of the drunkards.

But as for me, my prayer is unto thee, O Jehovah, in an acceptable time: O God, in the abundance of thy lovingkindness, answer me in the truth of thy salvation.

Deliver me out of the mire, and let me not sink: let me be delivered from them that hate me, and out of the deep waters.

Let not the waterflood overwhelm me, neither let the deep swallow me up; and let not the pit shut its mouth upon me.

"Deliver me out of the mire, and let me not sink…."

10

Sunday, December 25, 1864
Anthony's Hill
(King's Hill, or Devil's Gap, Tennessee)

Confederate Army HQ at Bainbridge, Alabama, on the Tennessee River

"December 25: [Confederate] Army headquarters at Bainbridge, on the Tennessee River. The pontoon was being laid across the river as rapidly as the arrival of the boats would allow. General Cheatham came into the main road this morning, and in rear of Stevenson's corps moved to the river, where a line covering the bridge was formed, Cheatham occupying the right and Stevenson the left. General Stewart's corps, upon arriving at the point where Cheatham's corps came into the main road, was put into position so as to protect both roads"[1] (Journal of the Army of Tennessee, November 14, 1864–January 23, 1865, Campaign in North Alabama and Middle Tennessee).

Hood's Vanguard Crosses Shoal Creek, Alabama

"Sunday, December 25th—Moving at daylight we [Confederates] soon reached Shoal Creek, two miles from the river. After great difficulty, on account of the high water and rough ford, we succeeded in crossing, and bivouacked between the creek and river. This corps was at once put in position, and built works that night to protect the bridge in case the enemy should move on us from below, which was thought not improbable. Heard the gunboats all day in the direction of Florence"[2] (Itinerary of Cheatham's Army Corps). "The [Confederate] army spent Christmas on the march, the most cheerless one of their lives."[3] "A sad and gloomy day; a day of clouds and

156

rain."[4] "Two Miles and a half, South of Lynnville, TN. December 25; 7 a.m. "[D]irected [Federal infantry] division commanders to march as soon as the cavalry moves and we can get the road.... We have but one day's rations now in the haversacks of the men. Our supply train [is] breaking.... General Wilson is informed that we can go no farther until we can get rations"[5] (Journal of the Fourth Army Corps).

By the 25th the roads had become horrific. With the constant rain and tramping men they were nearly impossible to maneuver through, the thick mud no less than knee deep. Several valuable stores of Confederate supplies, including ammunition, had of necessity been destroyed. Anything not of the utmost priority was summarily cast aside, the pike littered for miles with various pieces of unnecessary accessories sinking in the deep mud or strewn carelessly along the roaside. Hood's advance guard soon reached Shoal Creek, a short distance across the Alabama state line. "The country from Sugar Creek [TN] to the Tennessee River was as desolate and destitute as the unbroken wilderness. What few inhabitants were left seemed to be totally without any means of subsistence. On the evening of the 25th of December, the fragments of our Army began to arrive at Bainbridge."[6]

Leaving Forrest's cavalry brigades to protect the army's rear, the soldiers in the van of Hood's army approached Shoal Creek, Alabama, "two miles from the river," the wagons and critically important pontoon trains along with them. One thought occupied the minds of those men. Wilson—with his terrifying 10,000-man cavalry force, along with the pervasive threat of a stalking, determined, well-equipped (from the Confederate perspective) Federal infantry—was still uncomfortably close. Moreover, the distinct sound of gunboats firing in the distance was plainly heard throughout the day. It must have had a chilling effect on Hood's army and what remained of its fragile morale.

If the Southern army was to be saved from the Federal vise closing in on them, Forrest with his comparatively small force would have to step forward again and secure a decisive victory, assuming that they possessed sufficient time and means to stay well in advance of the enemy. The situation surrounding them remained dangerous in the extreme. Nonetheless, in spite of the impending hazards, certain units were compelled to wade through the bitterly cold creek that confronted them. Others had built bridges, but for these there was no other choice.

Federal Gunboats Drew Near

"On Christmas Day I waded Shoal Creek, which seemed to me to be one hundred yards wide and the water very swift. To prevent being washed downstream, I had to secure a pole to brace myself. I removed my clothes except my shoes ... to protect my feet from the rough cutting rocks.... I fastened my clothes on the end of my gun and held them above the water. I suffered from the extreme cold of both wind and water.... [T]he main Army did not cross where our regiment crossed Shoal Creek. Bridges were built at other places.... Two gunboats came in sight but a few shots from our batteries turned them back."[7]

As "fragments" of the Confederate army approached the vicinity of Shoal Creek, W.G. Davenport of the 6th Texas Cavalry, Ross's Brigade, Jackson's Division, witnessed an unusual scene. According to Davenport's testimony, General Hood, probably accompanied by his staff, rode into the company of several soldiers who had gathered together. As they beheld their commanding officer, waiting for a word from him, General Hood, "looking worn and tired but with kindly words for all,"—in a manner reminiscent of Robert E. Lee— said to them, "Boys, this is all my fault."[8] By acknowledging his responsibility for the failed campaign Hood had relieved his men from forever carrying that heavy load. They would never have an occasion to blame themselves. It was all his fault. In the near future he would turn again to this admission, declaring that he alone was responsible for the failed campaign's conception as well as its execution. That being said, on they marched, over the icy creek to Bainbridge, Alabama:

> When our troops arrived at Bainbridge, my Brigade, on the 24th [25th] of December was ordered to the Tennessee River to protect our pontoon bridge gang, who were preparing for us to cross as soon as possible. The Federal Cavalry was trying to drive the bridge gang away from their position. Our Brigade, en route to the river had to cross Shoal Creek without delay; so we proceeded to ford this creek, about one hundred and fifty or two hundred yards wide, very swift and rocky bottom, with some ledges of rock on the bottom. The depth was from knee-deep to armpits perhaps. It was bitter cold, and when we had gotten across, our clothes were frozen stiff.... It was a touching scene to witness a thousand and more of our boys without shoes and leaving their bloody footprints on that cold and frozen ground as they trudged their weary way. Cut off from supplies, they could not get clothing. Many of the poor fellows got shoes after the battle of Franklin. At Tupelo, MS., shoes were issued to the barefoot men. But many could not wear them because of their sore feet.[9]

On the morning of the 25th Forrest stole away from the presence of Wilson's cavalry long before the Federals had finished breakfast and broken camp. Outwitted and obviously embarrassed, Wilson summed up his explanation by stating that the Confederates had gotten away before dawn because of having nothing to cook, comparing their pitiful flight to Napoleon's miserable retreat from Moscow. Commensurate with his never-failing eagerness, Wilson's implacable cavalry was saddled and in pursuit "as soon as it was light enough to see their hands before them."[10]

Pushing Through Pulaski; The Federal Cavalry Launches Out

I [Harrison] have the honor to report that on the 25th instant, this [Federal] brigade had the advance in pursuit of the enemy, moving out of camp ten miles north of Pulaski at 5 a.m. The enemy's rear guard was struck about two miles from camp, when active skirmishing commenced. The Fifth Iowa Cavalry was in [the] advance, drove the enemy from every position, and when near Pulaski charged gallantly through the town, saving the bridge across Richland Creek, which the enemy had fired, and which he was attempting to hold with a heavy force until destroyed. I immediately ordered two guns in position and deployed along the creek, obliging the enemy to withdraw[11] [Report of Col. Thomas J. Harrison, Eighth Indiana Cavalry, commanding First Brigade, of operations December 25, 1864].

"We haven't got trees"

At about the same time as the "active skirmishing" had been taking place at Richland Creek between the Fifth Iowa and the Confederate rear guard, a rare display of humor coming from General Forrest played out. Amid charges of injustice leveled their way, a brief dialogue ensued between the rank and file and General Forrest, all in the middle of an artillery barrage, no less. The accusation directed at the general was critical. According to the rank and file, there were just not enough trees to go around. Why should the officers get all the trees? "[A]t Richland Creek, Tenn., when the enemy's artillery was hurling shells like handfuls of marbles about us ... General [Forrest] coolly dismounted and stepped behind the only tree in the vicinity, a movement which all of us longed to make, but dared not in his presence. One of the men said to him: 'Come out from behind that tree, General. That isn't fair; we haven't got trees.' 'No, but you only wish you had,' laughingly replied Forrest. 'You only want me out to get my place.'"[12] Who could blame them?

The Confederate Rear Guard Standoff at Anthony's Hill

Harrison's Brigades Ambushed at Anthony's Hill

Crossing the bridge [over Richland Creek] I [Colonel Harrison] followed up the pursuit rapidly, dislodging the enemy from strong positions, until reaching the head of a narrow gorge, some seven miles [south] from Pulaski, where the enemy had taken up position on a high hill behind strong barricades. His position was admirably selected, being hidden from view by heavy timber until within a few feet of it.

Supposing that the enemy would retire from this position, as he had from others on a flank movement from us, I deployed the Seventh Ohio Cavalry on the right and the Sixteenth Illinois Cavalry, all dismounted. These regiments moved upon the enemy most gallantly, when suddenly he opened from a masked battery of three guns and charged over his works, in two lines of infantry with a column of cavalry, down the main road. Before this overpowering force my men were obliged to fall back about half a mile, when we checked the enemy, and receiving support, drove him back.

I regret to state that Company I, Fourth U.S. Artillery, were obliged to abandon one gun and limber at this time. The battery had been placed in position by General Wilson's order. The stand made by the enemy at this point was to save his train, as we had driven his rear guard sharp upon it. From prisoners I learn that this rear guard consisted of seven brigades of infantry and one division, Jackson's of cavalry, all under General Forrest. In the hasty evacuation of Pulaski, [the] train of five cars loaded with arms and ammunition [was left behind or destroyed], and it is reported he left near town, two locomotives in good order.

For six miles below Pulaski the road was strewn with abandoned artillery ammunition, and burning and abandoned wagons. I think he saved some twenty wagons entire. We captured during the day 1 captain, 2 lieutenants, and some 50 or 60 men, also some 150 wounded at Pulaski.

Our casualties, mostly from the Fifth Iowa Cavalry, consisted of 3 killed, 18 wounded, and 5 missing. In charging the bridge at Pulaski the Fifth Iowa cavalry lost 3 killed and 3 wounded.

Brevet Major General Wilson expressed himself much pleased with the operations of the brigade during the day. The officers and men of the brigade behaved admirably; they are men who can be relied upon[13] [Report of Col. Thomas J. Harrison, Eighth Indiana Cavalry, commanding First Brigade, of operations December 25, 1864].

Two-and-a-Half Miles North of Lynnville, Tennessee, on the Columbia-Pulaski Turnpike

As for Wood's Fourth Corps, things had improved little. By midmorning of the 25th, and after many frustrating delays, Wood's famished infantry was finally on the move again, heading straight for Pulaski. "We [the Federal infantry] have but one day's rations now in the haversacks of the men. Our supply train is on the other side of Duck River and the pontoon bridge is constantly breaking.… 9:10 a.m. The Cavalry is now out of the way, and the head of our column starts for Pulaski"[14] (Journal of the Fourth Army Corps).

In spite of the ongoing difficulties, the Union infantry corps plodded on in the wake of Hood's withdrawing army. The sluggish movement of supplies would just have to pick up and reach them whenever possible. With an early morning promise from General Thomas for an increased effort at bringing up the wagons, the infantry moved out for Pulaski, arriving in the surrounding area by mid-afternoon.

Sunday morning, the 25th, the [Federal Infantry] corps followed closely on the heels of the cavalry, passed through Pulaski, from which the cavalry had rapidly driven the enemy's rear guard, and encamped for the night six miles from the town, on the Lamb's Ferry road. The corps marched sixteen miles on the 25th, the last six miles on a road next to impracticable from the depth of the mud. As we could not have the use of the turnpike farther south than Pulaski, I ordered all the artillery of the corps but four batteries, to be left at Pulaski, using the horses of the batteries left to increase the horses of the pieces taken with the command to eight, and of the caissons to ten horses each. I also ordered that only a limited number of ammunition wagons, carrying but ten boxes each, should accompany the command. These arrangements were necessary on account of the condition of the road on which the enemy had retreated.

Without extra teams to the artillery carriages and lightening of the usual load of an ammunition wagon, it would have been impracticable to get the vehicles along; a vigorous pursuit would have been impossible[15] [Report of Brig. Gen. T.J. Wood, USA, commanding Fourth Army Corps].

"1:15 p.m., General Wilson has crossed Richland Creek and is pushing on after the enemy. He meets with considerable resistance.... Our head of column is just beginning to cross the creek, and we will follow closely in support of the Cavalry. We leave the turnpike at Richland Creek. The road from here is almost impassable for wagons and artillery"[16] (Journal of the Fourth Army Corps).

Impassable or not, Wood's Fourth Army Corps was as determined as Wilson's cavalry. Later in the day, Wood related to Wilson his situation, outlining his plan for the next day. In time it had become increasingly clear for both cavalry and foot-soldier: Without rations they weren't going anywhere. "I [Wood] will move my corps south of Richmond [Richland] Creek three or four miles, as I may find the ground suitable for campaign, and halt for the night. I will be out of rations tonight, and it will be necessary for me to halt here until our supply train comes up. General Thomas has promised to push it forward as rapidly as possible, but it is uncertain when it will arrive here, though I trust it will arrive some time tonight or tomorrow morning. I will be glad to know your condition in reference to rations, and your intentions in reference to future movements, as I wish to keep the corps up in supporting distance of the cavalry."[17] However, unknown to Wood, Wilson, or anybody else in the Federal ranks, there was a stunning surprise being planned for them that afternoon. Major General Forrest was setting up for a fight: "Just before sundown on Christmas day, Forrest, in a fit of desperation, made a stand on a heavily wooded ridge at the head of a ravine"[18] (James Harrison Wilson, Major-General, USV, Brevet Major-General, USA, "The Union Cavalry in the Hood Campaign").

By the 25th of December the situation had become increasingly perilous for the Army of Tennessee. Although the van of the army was approaching the Tennessee River, the main body of infantry, with the wagons, still limped far behind. It was hoped the quality and number of pontoons on hand would be sufficient to bridge the river and carry them to safety. The alternative was unthinkable. Far in the army's rear an encounter between Forrest's rear guard and a segment of Wilson's massive cavalry corps was brewing. Before long it would boil over into a major confrontation.

Anthony's Hill

On the morning of the 25th, after destroying all the ammunition which could not be removed from Pulaski by General Hood and two trains of cars, I ordered General Jackson to remain in town as long as possible and to destroy the bridge at Richland Creek after everything had passed over. The enemy soon pressed General Jackson, but he held him in check for some time, killing and wounding several before retiring. Seven miles from Pulaski I took position on King's [Anthony's] Hill, and awaiting the advance of the enemy, repulsed him with a loss of 150 killed and wounded besides capturing many prisoners and one piece of artillery. The enemy made no further demonstrations during the day. I halted my command at Sugar Creek, where it encamped during the night[19] [Report of Maj. Gen. Nathan B. Forrest, CSA].

Pressing hard with his cavalry, James Wilson had pushed through Pulaski earlier that morning ("on the keen jump") without serious incident. Reaching the outskirts of the town in the wake of the Confederate withdrawal, Wilson's troopers lunged ahead barely in time to save the bridge spanning Richland Creek the Confederate rear guard had torched behind them, in effect achieving a significant advantage by saving his army a great deal of time and energy.

My advance, Colonel Harrison commanding, drove the rebels through this place half past 8 on the keen jump. Forrest, with Jackson's and Buford's division, is scarcely out of sight. Everything has gone on the road to Lamb's Ferry, the original intention of going to Decatur having been abandoned for fear they would be intercepted. They are trying to reach Florence. I will crowd them ahead as fast as possible. They are literally running away, making no defense whatever.

I will open communication with the column in the direction of Huntsville. The rebels have destroyed a large quantity of ammunition, but the bridge across Richland Creek has been saved, thanks to the gallantry of Colonel Baird, commanding Fifth Iowa[20] [J.H. Wilson, Brevet Major-General].

"1 p.m., head of [the infantry] column arrives at Pulaski, having marched eleven miles since 9:10 a.m. General Wilson drove the enemy's rear guard through Pulaski very rapidly, and his advance arrived at Richland Creek (in the outskirts of the town) just in time to save the bridge over the same on the Lamb's Ferry and Florence road. The enemy had set it on fire and it was burning"[21] (Journal of the Fourth Army Corps)

Anthony's Hill, Harrison's Report, Reprise

The enemy's rear guard was struck about two miles from the [Union] camp, when active skirmishing commenced. The Fifth Iowa Cavalry was in advance, drove the enemy from every position, and when near Pulaski charged gallantly through the town, saving the covered bridge across Richland Creek, which the enemy had fired, and which he was attempting to hold with a heavy force until destroyed.

Crossing the bridge I followed up the pursuit rapidly, dislodging the enemy from strong positions, until reaching the head of a narrow gorge, [Anthony's Hill] some seven miles from Pulaski, where the enemy had taken position on a high hill behind strong barricades. His position was admirably selected, being hidden from view by heavy timber until within a few feet of it[22] [Report of Colonel Thomas J. Harrison, Eighth Indiana Cavalry, commanding First Brigade, of operations December 25, 1864].

The Powerful Federal Army Amasses Its Forces

By 1:15 p.m. Wilson's riders had crossed over the creek. Moving his corps rapidly down the pike, Wood's infantry closed in behind, as Generals A.J. Smith and John Schofield brought up the remaining mass of Union infantry from Columbia. The mighty Federal army was gathering strength, pouring down the weather-beaten pike like a torrent, preparing for a final, combined assault on the rear of Hood's columns. If Thomas could gain the necessary ground with only a portion of his forces engaged, the outcome would be almost certain. All that stood before them was Nathan Bedford Forrest, a battle-fatigued, exhausted Confederate cavalry, and the starving remnants of a footsore, bleeding infantry. Earlier in the day Forrest's rear guard had fallen back to "a strong position on Anthony's hill, seven miles beyond Pulaski," coolly waiting for the approaching Federal advance that was sure to come. It was only a matter of time.[23]

After passing through Pulaski and saving the bridge over Richland Creek, Harrison took the lead, renewing the pursuit of Hood's harried army. Very much aware of the need for infantry support when confronting the likes of Forrest, Wilson fired off an order to the Fourth Army Corps: "3:30 p.m. (two miles from Pulaski) received a dispatch from General Wilson stating that the enemy has given him a check; that he is strongly posted, with his front covered with rail barricades; that Forrest's Cavalry and eight brigades of infantry are in his front, and he wishes the assistance of our infantry. We [Wood's infantry corps] push forward as rapidly as possible to General Wilson's assistance"[24] (Journal of the Fourth Army Corps).

Anthony's Hill: Accounts Merged

By mid-afternoon Harrison had come upon "the enemy strongly entrenched at the head of a heavily wooded and deep ravine, through which ran the road." "Strongly entrenched" was an apt description. All across the hill's heights and down along its ridges Forrest had posted Walthall's brigades of Featherston and Palmer, with Jackson's cavalry covering the flanks. Two infantry brigades were placed in reserve under protection of timber breastworks. A line of skirmishers lay hidden along the slopes. Well concealed, Forrest waited calmly. Around 1:00 p.m. Harrison's dismounted regiments of the Seventh Ohio, the Sixteenth Illinois, and the Fifth Iowa made their way over the ground, advancing in broken ranks and driving back the skirmishers posted on the hillsides as Wilson's cavalry closed in from behind the forward ranks of infantry.

Leaving the impression that they were isolated and that the main body of the guard was absent, the Confederate skirmish line withdrew into a gap between the hills, allowing the dismounted Federal cavalry to approach to within fifty deadly paces. Drawing closer, Harrison was forced to an uneasy standstill. Something was amiss. Things were all too quiet. Pausing briefly, he peered through the thick mist, waiting for Wilson's support of Hatch, Croxton, and Hammond to arrive before attempting a general advance. Suddenly it seemed as if the whole hillside exploded in their faces. A terrible blast of artillery hidden in the dense woods was loosed, raking the Federals' exposed ranks with canister. At the same instant, Walthall's skirmishers released a ferocious volley upon the scattered Union lines, extending from their front to their exposed flank, immediately succeeded by an even deadlier blast from the main line of Confederate infantry.

Shocked by Forrest's fierce barrage, Harrison's dismounted cavalry began a feeble resistance, quickly falling back to the rear in confusion. Simultaneously, several hundred of Walthall's rear guard infantry leaped over the barricades and emerged from the woods, rushing forward and compelling Harrison's immediate withdrawal, killing and capturing many while taking an artillery piece of the Fourth U.S. Artillery. In a headlong charge Walthall's brigades drove the bluecoats back through the way they had come, disordered and bewildered at such an avalanche of fire and lead. Soon after the initial onrush of Walthall's infantry, the Eighth Indiana regrouped, and returned fire, halting the Confederates. "These [Union] regiments moved upon the enemy most gallantly, when suddenly he opened from a masked battery of three guns, and charged over his works, in two lines of infantry with a column of Cavalry, down the main road. Before this overpowering force my men were obliged to fall back about half a mile, when we checked the enemy, and, receiving support, drove him back"[25] (Report of Colonel Thomas J. Harrison, Eighth Indiana Cavalry, commanding First Brigade, of operations December 25, 1864).

By 4:00 p.m. the fighting had subsided. Recognizing the rapidly approaching columns of enemy cavalry regiments of Hatch's division pressing his flanks, Forrest quickly called off the chase and ordered a timely retreat.

Moving swiftly, the rear guard slipped away, carrying off a number of prisoners, the captured artillery piece from Company I, Fourth U.S. Artillery, with its eight horses, and three hundred cavalry horses.[26]

Anthony's Hill, Ninth Regiment
Illinois Cavalry, A Memoir

Christmas Day; we had our last fight, and Forrest made his last stand. This was on the hill near Ross' farm. The Second Brigade was passing through a narrow valley, just about wide enough for our Regiment to form a line across it. Here we found corn and fodder in abundance, and as we had not had opportunity to feed for some time, General Hatch halted his division, with each regiment in line closed up behind each other, thus showing a regimental front which completely filled this narrow valley. We had taken the bridles off our horses, and they were eating. Our brigade, with the Ninth Illinois Cavalry in the front, was the advance of our division with another division still in the advance of us. General Forrest had laid a trap for this advance division, and they ran right into it. Forrest closed in on them and completely routed them, and sent them back whirling and disorganized upon us, but our blockade of the valley stopped them. The rebels sprang their trap too soon, or they would have surrounded and taken in the whole advanced division. General Wilson came riding back, hunting for General Hatch, who was with the Ninth, then the head of the column. General Wilson seemed much surprised to see General Hatch feeding his horses, and told him that Forrest had routed the advanced division and would soon be back on him (Hatch). General Hatch told General Wilson not to be alarmed, that Forrest knew too much to attempt to come back, and he could not get to us anyway, for we had the valley blockaded. General Wilson then ordered General Hatch to move his division to the front and advance. As we moved forward, the Ninth in the front, and coming in sight of the hill (Ross' farm), we saw the rebels pulling up the hill, by hand, some artillery they had just captured. General Wilson kept hurrying General Hatch, and when he saw the rebels pulling up this artillery he said to General Hatch, "There they are; hurry up!" Hatch then said to Wilson, "General, if you will let me take my own course, I will carry that hill in twenty minutes." Wilson said, "All right; go ahead." General Hatch then ordered Captain Mock to dismount the Ninth, and to move up the hill on the right of the road, as far as he could safely, in front of the enemy, and to make it as hot for the rebels as he could. At the same time, the Seventh Illinois Cavalry was also dismounted and directed to advance up the hill on the left of the road and in a line with the Ninth. The Second Iowa Cavalry was sent mounted to our right, and to strike the left and rear of the enemy. The Twelfth Tennessee Cavalry was sent mounted around the enemy's right flank, and the Sixth Illinois Cavalry was left in our rear as a support. The rebels had made a strong breastwork in our front, on the hill, by tearing down log houses and using rails, and with the two had made very formidable works. The Ninth advanced up the hill to within seventy-five yards of the rebels, keeping up a heavy fire all the time as they advanced. The enemy being in too heavy force for the Ninth to go any farther, they remained there under cover of logs and trees, and kept up a heavy fire on the rebels to hold them there, and prevent them from reinforcing their flanks, and in about twenty minutes we heard the firing and welcome shouts of the gallant Second Iowa coming in on the flank and rear of the rebels, then the Ninth rose up, and with a shout moved forward and carried the rebel works, and the enemy fell back. By this time it was dark, and the fighting ended. We went out some five miles and got forage and returning, went into camp on Ross' farm. There was captured here a number of prisoners, several pieces of artillery and a quantity of small arms, the latter having been abandoned by the enemy[27] [Report of Datus Coon 2nd Iowa Cavalry].

"[M]arched with the division, in rear of Colonel Harrison's and General Hammond's commands, reaching Pulaski at 11 a.m., and passing beyond some six miles, when the enemy was found in force. A light skirmish ensued when the advance was repulsed. My brigade immediately dismounted, and after a heavy skirmish of an hour drove the enemy from a strong position protected by a barricade of rails, and encamped for the night"[28] (Report of Col. Datus Coon, 2nd Iowa Cavalry, Commanding Second Brigade, of operations from September 30, 1864, to January 15, 1865). "Christmas again. The last one for me in the [Union] army. This is the Sabbath too, but notwithstanding we continue the march. Passed through Pulaski and took the Lawrenceburg road, which is about knee deep in mud. In fact, the road is almost impassable. The Rebs destroyed wagons, guns and everything pertaining to an army, indicating they were closely pushed."[29] "On Christmas day we [Confederates] left Pulaski, setting fire to the bridge there when we left. The rascals came up, and put the fire out, and crossed over and attacked us on the first hill. We gave them a good drubbing, however, capturing some of their artillery. We made a forced march then to Sugar Creek, only a few miles from the Tennessee River, wading the creek in a late hour of the night and bivouacked at the edge of a valley, half a mile or so from the creek."[30]

Anthony's Hill, Wilson's Report

"Just before sundown on Christmas day Forrest, in a fit of desperation, made a stand on a heavily wooded ridge at the head of a ravine, and by a rapid and savage counter-thrust drove back the skirmishers of Thomas Harrison's brigade, capturing one gun, which he succeeded in carrying away, as the sole trophy of that desperate campaign. This was the last flicker of aggressive temper shown by any part of Hood's beaten and demoralized army."[31] "Thus we toiled on, till Christmas Day, cold, drizzly and muddy we [Confederates] camped on the bank of Shoal Creek, and our corps [Stewart's] formed line of battle to protect the rear and let all cross, if the bridge could be made."[32] "Christmas day and Sunday, was very sad and gloomy. I had prayers at General Clayton's headquarters, after which I rode down to the river and watched the work of putting down the pontoons. Some one brought me a Christmas gift of two five dollar gold pieces from Mrs. Thomas Jones of Pulaski."[33]

The treacherous roads leading south to Sugar Creek were appalling, impeding Forrest's every move, the horses being literally pushed through a river of mud. At times the sludge ran so deep it reached their undersides and it appeared as if the animals were actually swimming through the thick mire. Walthall's soldiers fared no better, sloshing down the waist-deep pike, heading toward the icy stream as sleet poured down upon their defenseless bodies and night closed in. By 1:00 the next morning they had reached the chilly banks of Sugar Creek. Surely frostbitten and dressed in nothing more than rags, at least in these icy waters they could wash the thick, heavy mud of the pike from their freezing clothes and bodies. With another brief victory to their credit, Forrest's rear guard was finally allowed a much needed breather. "The brilliancy and vim of the Confederate charge astonished the Federals so much that they attacked no more that day. Forrest then retired to Sugar Creek and halted for another fight."[34]

Sharing the same sufferings, Wilson remembered the "untold hardship of advance, battle, and retreat. Men and horses had suffered all the rigors of winter; snow, rain, frost, mud, and exposure." As night fell, a layer of ice formed a half-inch thick upon the ground. With the constant movements along the pike amid the relentless rain, the roads had become a sea of ice-covered mud, freezing the legs of the horses and disabling them for any further use, with hundreds of them having lost their hoofs. To further the misery, there remained little if any food to be had from the surrounding countryside, the war having ravaged and decimated the heartland of Middle Tennessee. It seemed that no one was spared the hardships of those days. As one of Hood's Tennesseans put it, "When this work [at Anthony's Hill] was done, commenced that long, cheerless march, through that half ice and half water, down the winding road to Sugar Creek. The icy pathway; the bloodstained track; the crashing tramp; the sad moan of that unhappy household, one of whose sons lay sleeping at Franklin, another of whom, true to his colors was about to turn his back on the home of his youth; that tedious march after various movements of the day—all these testify the soldierly qualities of those resolute men."[35]

Later in the day (the 25th) after a regrouping of his command, Wilson was advised to "go no further" until the supply wagons had come up, which at best, due to the deplorable roads, would be by mid-morning the next day at the earliest. With the setback at Richland Creek and Forrest's furious resistance at Anthony's Hill, the constant lack of supplies combined with the atrocious weather and impossible traveling conditions, things again looked depressingly bleak for Thomas's army. Despite its admirable yet futile attempts to entrap Hood, the Confederates yet remained just beyond reach. Still, confidence remained unshaken. As referenced above, "Major General Wilson expressed himself much pleased with the operations of the Brigade during the day. The officers and men of the Brigade behaved admirably; they are men who can be relied upon"[36] (T.J. Harrison, Colonel Commanding Brigade).

But tomorrow was another matter. Despite Thomas's determined efforts to remain "close upon the heels of the enemy" and "to press him as long as there is a chance of doing anything," things were not to improve any time soon. Nevertheless, as always, he stood firm. "I have my troops well in hand, and well provided with provisions and ammunition."[37] Thomas's troops may have been "well in hand" as he put it, with plenty of provisions and ammunition to go around. But nothing could change the desperate state of their immediate surroundings. The miserable weather persisted, affecting everything and everybody. "It has been raining since 1 p.m. today, and this will make the roads even worse," noted a weary Union officer[38] (Journal of the Fourth Army Corps).

Far in the rear, John Schofield's Army of the Ohio struggled along. Crossing his troops over the Duck River at Columbia and repairing the broken-down bridges, Schofield reported that the way was now clear for Wood's supply trains to pass. But it was anybody's guess as to when they would actually reach the front.[39] (Evidently, the earlier attempt at merging the three Union armies with Wilson's mighty host of seasoned cavalry was simply not possible. Far too many obstacles defied them and their extraordinary efforts.) As much as everyone would have it be, the ordeal was not yet over. Somewhere south of Pulaski, at 10:00 a.m., Wilson fired off a message to the chief of staff, General Whipple: "There seems to be little doubt that the rebels have gone to Bainbridge, eight miles above Florence, fearing a flank movement.... Two corps (Stewart's and Lee's) went by this road, the Florence road to Lexington; Cheatham's went toward Lawrenceburg, striking the old military road, eight miles below Lawrenceburg. The people say the rebels are suffering immensely.... The rebels have lost eighteen generals killed, wounded, and captured, since they started north. They acknowledge sixty-eight pieces of artillery lost."[40]

The people were right. Johnny Reb was wounded to the core of his being.

11

Monday, December 26, 1864

Sugar Creek

The Confederate Pontoon Bridge Completed and Laid Across the Tennessee River

"December 26 ... The pontoon was completed by daylight on the 26th instant, and the [Confederate] army was occupied two days in crossing—Lee's and Cheatham's corps on the 26th, and Stewart's and the cavalry on the 27th. On the 28th the pontoon was withdrawn. The march was resumed, upon striking the Memphis and Charleston railroad, immediately down the road, in the order of crossing the river to Burnsville, Mississippi"[1] (Journal of the Army of Tennessee, November 14, 1864–January 23, 1865, Campaign in North Alabama and Middle Tennessee).

"Monday, December 26.–The pontoon across the river was completed this morning after working on it all night, General Cheatham supervising in person, and about sunrise the trains began to cross. By night most of our wagons and artillery had crossed. Leaving orders for his troops to move across at 3 o'clock the next morning, General Cheatham came over about 7 o'clock at night and slept some two miles from Bainbridge. Two gun-boats came up the river in the afternoon to within two or three miles of the bridge, but were driven back by our batteries"[2] (Itinerary of Cheatham's Army Corps).

The Confederate Army Begins Two-Day Crossing of the Tennessee River

"Upon Hood's advance into Tennessee, the Federals in evacuating their positions so hurriedly left much valuable material and stores behind them ... and also a pontoon bridge, which [later] proved to be of great value to us.

169

The boats had been floated down to Bainbridge, and by the time our pontoon train had arrived, we had a bridge completed. Had we have had to wait for our pontoons … Bainbridge would have been noted in history as the place of the surrender of Hood's Army. Before light on the morning of the 26th the trains began to cross."[3] "Wretched weather, roads muddy, hunger, and marching most trying on the troops," was not limited to the winter months alone during the Southern army's evacuation from Tennessee. The same had been true earlier in October as Hood made his bold advance into Tennessee:

> Passing over Sand Mountain we arrived before Decatur, Ala., on the afternoon of the 26th [Oct.] and formed line of battle. The weather was wretched, the roads muddy, and the marching most trying on the troops. The 27th and 28th were equally as bad, and the regiment being kept in position and moved frequently as the line was moved to the right, and the enemy throwing some shell meanwhile, made our stay in front of Decatur most uncomfortable, especially as we expected to attack or to be attacked at any moment. The men had no chance to cook and suffered from hunger. We left this position at 3 o'clock on the afternoon of the 29th and marched nine miles on the Tuscumbia road, camping in Florence County[4] [Report of Col. Ellison Capers, 24th South Carolina Infantry].

By the end of December the hardships common to both armies had taken their toll. Following the horrific carnage at Franklin and exposure to ruthless weather conditions combined with a relentless running battle covering nearly a hundred miles of desolate terrain, both armies were on the edge of collapse. The survivors, men and animals alike shivering in the cold, found little comfort. Many must have been reduced to mere skeletons.

> From that time till the Tennessee River was reached … [t]he weather had become worse and worse; it was cold and freezing during the nights, and followed by days of rain, snow, and thaw.
> The country which was poor and thinly settled at best had been absolutely stripped of forage and provisions by the march of contending armies. The men of both forces suffered dreadfully, but the poor cavalry horses fared still worse than their riders.
> Scarcely a withered corn-blade could be found for them, and thousands, exhausted by overwork, famished with hunger, or crippled so that death was a mercy, with hoofs dropping off from frost and mud, fell by the roadside never to rise again. By the time the corps found rest on the Tennessee River it could muster scarcely 7,000 horses fit for [Union] service[5] [James Harrison Wilson, Major-General, USV, Brevet Major-General, USA, "The Union Cavalry in the Hood Campaign"].

Wood's Infantry Situated on the Lamb's Ferry (Florence) Road, Six Miles from Pulaski

At the conclusion of a period of almost two weeks of near starvation, the scarcity of supplies had become serious in the extreme. The men and horses of Thomas's army were famished. And as Hood's army was reported to have begun its crossing over the Tennessee, the situation confronting the Federals was bleak indeed. Not a moment too soon, circumstances for the Northern army suddenly improved as the long overdue supplies finally reached the Union camp late in the afternoon. It must have been a most welcome sight to their weary, bloodshot eyes. "Owing to our rapid pursuit of the enemy, the difficulty of getting our train across Duck River, and the almost impassable condition of the roads, our supplies did not overtake us until late in the afternoon of the 26th, when they were at once distributed to the command, and every preparation made for an early advance on the morrow"[6] (Report of Brigadier General Samuel Beatty U.S. Army Commanding third Division).

But before the "early advance on the morrow" would be undertaken, the Federals had an unexpected appointment with destiny. Coming as a result of the shellacking the Yankees had received the day before (and their unwillingness to admit defeat) at Anthony's Hill, the unflinching determination of Wilson's cavalry would prove to be their final undoing. Another confrontation with the Army of Tennessee was looming, just a step away. This one would settle the issue once and for all.

Wilson's Cavalry Ambushed by Forrest's Rear Guard at Sugar Creek

The Confederate Ambush at Sugar Creek: A Confederate Memoir

About sunrise [just prior to the ambush] here, just in our front, Forrest convened the brigade and regimental officers, and giving instructions, said: "When the infantry break their lines, I'll turn Ross in on 'em." Col. (Hume Rigg) Feild—a wiry and heroic soldier, whose silvery voice could be heard in the roar of musketry, having under him his and Strahl's old brigades—immediately replied with spirit: "We have no such soldiers; we don't break our lines."

Forrest perceiving the double construction his words were capable of, said at once: "I don't mean that. I mean when you break the lines of the enemy, I'll throw Ross in on 'em and rout them."

We had rested and had hastily put up some breastworks and were in waiting. The fog still covered our front. Reynolds' still occupied the level valley between the gentle rise and the stream, our Tennessee forces [were situated on] the hillock and on to the left where the stream ran right up against the bluff. The Federals came in force, crossed the bridge, and moved in line of battle, and some came opposite Feild's left. When they came near enough, the firing commenced vigorously on our right and left, we holding our [position] until they came right near us … [as] the battle raged on both sides of us. Then the order to advance was given, and then the rapid charge was made that hurled back the impetuous foe, who had uncautiously come too near, and just where we wished them.[7]

Other than safeguarding the army from assaults from the rear, the encounter at Sugar Creek was conducted for the sole purpose of protecting the ordnance trains from capture and allowing them to safely cross to the other side, which it was in the process of doing. Accordingly, near sunup, Walthall's Brigades of Reynolds and Feild were placed a few hundred yards on either side of the creek with Featherston and Palmer stationed a half-mile to the rear, all under the cover of logs, rails, and whatever other material could be found. "[T]aking position, [we] awaited the onset of the well-equipped victorious legions of the North."[8]

Again Forrest's cavalry was discreetly posted on the infantry flanks. A dense morning fog had settled in and enshrouded them, giving the Confederates an even greater advantage. The scene at Anthony's Hill was about to be repeated. It was still quite early in the morning when several regiments of Union cavalry were observed crossing the creek not more than a hundred yards from the unseen Confederate front. Quickly dismounting, a segment of Federal troopers (Hammond's brigade) advanced through the fog to within fifty paces of the well-hidden Confederate breastworks, the Federal cavalry trailing behind. To the shock of Wilson's cavalrymen, a terrific volley of musketry suddenly exploded in the Union front, knocking them senseless and sending them fleeing for refuge to the rear as Walthall's infantry climbed over their works pouring fire into the enemy's ranks and putting the dispersing

Remains of a 19th-century home near Sugar Creek.

The Columbia Pike Highway bridge spanning Sugar Creek and intersecting the battlefield.

Federals into a total rout, chasing them down into the icy, waist-deep creek. On the flanks, the Confederate cavalry brigades of Ross and Dillon advanced, running over the fleeing bluecoats, surrounding and capturing many of them and driving the remnant back down the road.

Again out of respect for oncoming Federal cavalry support, Forrest soon called off the chase (but held his position until 12:00), securing the army's unhindered crossing of the Tennessee River. Seeing no intention of reprisal indicated by Federal movements, the guard was then put in motion to cross. With the fierce stand taken by Forrest's resolute rear guard at the banks of Sugar Creek the final sharp rattle of musketry had poured forth from the ice-covered rifles of the Army of Tennessee. The frightful cannon thunder, the furious desperate charge, the last, dying cheers to ever reverberate over the hills of Tennessee in the War for Southern Independence were at an end. Never again would the earth shake at the sound of national war in Tennessee.

The overall effects of the battles at Anthony's Hill and Sugar Creek, due particularly to the powerful striking effect of Confederate artillery, were severe in light of the consuming Federal objective: the capture and sacking of Hood's army. At Sugar Creek dozens of horses, officers, and soldiers (many of the men wearing precious Federal overcoats) had been killed, wounded, or seized with comparatively scant Confederate loss. An added bonus to Hood's depleted army came as a joy to many. The tough Union cavalry horses had been unable to scale the deep banks along the sides of Sugar Creek during the advance, resulting in many of them being captured for Confederate service. A veteran Texas infantryman remembered it well:

> At daylight we were aroused and informed that the Yankees were on our side of the creek. A dense fog rested upon the valley. After waiting some time for them to make an attack, which they failed to do, we were ordered to charge them, and did it successfully. In trying to cross the creek on their big cavalry horses, the banks on our side were so high they could not ascend them, and our boys captured many fine horses. When they were driven across the creek, Gen. Ross' Cavalry Brigade charged and drove them for miles. Our brigade got a good Yankee breakfast from the saddle pockets on horses killed and captured. From there to the pontoon bridge on the Tennessee River our brigade was largely mounted.[9]

Attempted Union Counterstroke Blocked at Sugar Creek

Ross's Report

Early the following morning [the 26th] the Yankees, still not satisfied, made their appearance, and our infantry again made dispositions to receive them. Reynolds' and Ector's brigades took position, and immediately in their rear I [Ross] had the Legion and the Ninth Texas drawn up in column of fours to charge, if an opportunity should

Looking eastward from Sugar Creek.

Looking westward from Sugar Creek.

occur. The fog was very dense and the enemy, therefore, approached very cautiously. When near enough to be seen, the infantry fired a volley and charged. At the same time the Legion and Ninth Texas were ordered forward, and passing through our infantry crossed the creek in the face of a terrible fire, overthrew all opposition on the farther side, and pursued the thoroughly routed foe nearly a mile, capturing twelve prisoners and as many horses, besides killing numbers of others. The force opposed to us here and which was so completely whipped, proved, from the statements of the prisoners, to be Hammond's brigade of cavalry. After this the Yankees did not again show themselves, and without further interruption we re-crossed the Tennessee River, at Bainbridge, on the evening of 27th of December[10] [Report of Brigadier General Lawrence S. Ross, CSA, commanding Ross's brigade, of operations October 24–December 27, 1864].

To the chagrin of Thomas's army the message had at last surfaced. Any further charges against Hood's rear guard would end in further mishap and failure. The Federal army had been thoroughly chastened. Any proposal for further attack was only a recipe for aggravated humiliation. With the succession of unbeaten standoffs achieved by the Confederates over the last several days, it had become painfully evident that the long-sought opportunity to bag the Army of Tennessee was fading fast. In the light of the numerous setbacks and failures, by the end of December Union morale must have become severely crippled.

For the weary Army of Tennessee, the smell of a much-needed change was in the air. A time of rest had, at last, finally arrived. "That bivouac, that grateful rest after the march, those hasty works, that fight and flight—they will not soon be forgotten. The spirit and vigor of our resistance satisfied our foes, and we had a quiet, peaceful, undisturbed march thence to the river."[11]

Although Hood was well on the way to making his escape, for one man in George Thomas's army there would be no stopping. Not yet. Federal cavalry commander Major General James Harrison Wilson, determined as ever, posted a message on the evening of the 26th stating his further intentions in continuing the pursuit. If he could not defeat Hood from the rear, he would hit him from the front: " [T]he [Confederate] enemy made a short stand at Sugar Creek, but soon retreated.... He [Wilson] also states that as soon as he crosses the creek he will send a brigade to fell trees in the Tennessee River to float down and destroy the enemy's pontoon bridge"[12] (Journal of the Fourth Army Corps).

Unfortunately for Wilson, that tactic was to become as unproductive as his former efforts. By the 26th he must have known his options for a successful termination of the conflict had narrowed to a very slim margin. Nevertheless, in spite of the obstacles that had nearly overwhelmed him, he would not relinquish his grasp on the fading hope. Ignoring the ever-present difficulties, he pushed on ahead, fully determined to see the thing through. Whether or not his plans could hold up under the strain of battle was a matter to be decided on the battlefield. Time would tell. Meanwhile, Forrest, in his typical matter-of-fact style, renders his account of the standoff at Sugar Creek and the failed Union attempt to produce a successful counterstroke:

> On the morning of the 26th the enemy commenced advancing, driving back General Ross' pickets. Owing to the dense fog he could not see the temporary fortifications which the infantry had thrown up and behind which they were secreted.
>
> The enemy therefore advanced to within fifty paces of these works, when a volley was opened upon him, causing the wildest confusion. Two mounted regiments of Ross' brigade and Ector's and Granbury's brigades of infantry were ordered to charge upon the discomfited foe, which was done, producing a complete rout.
>
> The enemy was pursued for two miles, but showing no disposition to give battle my troops were ordered back. In this engagement he sustained a loss of about 150 in killed and wounded; many prisoners and horses were captured and about 400 horses killed. I held this position for two hours, but the enemy showing no disposition to renew the attack, and fearing he might attempt a flank movement in the dense fog, I resumed the march, after leaving a picket with orders to remain until 4 o'clock.
>
> The enemy made no further attack between Sugar Creek and Tennessee River, which stream I crossed on the evening of the 27th of December. The infantry were ordered to report back to their respective corps, and I moved with my cavalry to Corinth[13] [Report of Maj. Gen. Nathan B. Forrest, CSA].

Before long Wilson and Forrest would lock horns for one final round of fighting, resulting in Forrest's surrender to the Federal authorities in Selma, Alabama in May, 1865.

At the conclusion of the standoff at Sugar Creek the terrible rounds of fighting in Tennessee were all but over. It now remained for the survivors to carry their departed comrades and the war they waged in remembrance and honor for the generations to come. For the time being, with both armies on the brink of exhaustion, a temporary moment of rest was met with open arms, although, strictly from the Confederate perception, any sense of elation had been completely submerged, drowned in a sea of profound astonishment. "[M]arched in rear of General Hammond's command to Sugar Creek, and encamped for the night"[14] (Report of Col. Datus Coon, 2nd Iowa Cavalry, Commanding Second Brigade, of operations from September 30, 1864, to January 15, 1865).

"I [Chaplain Quintard] crossed the [Tennessee] river at nine o' clock. On crossing the river on our forward march I had sung 'Jubilate.' Now I was chanting 'De Profundis.'"[15] "Jubilate" is essentially the 100th Psalm, a psalm of joy and thankfulness in God's faithful, providential care. "De Profundis" (Out of the Depths," Psalm 130) is a psalm of repentance and faith. The centuries-old psalms of David that have brought comfort to millions throughout millennia were a fitting source for the chaplain to quote from as the army trudged its way farther south. The deeply moving, ancient tenor of King David's words echo the inner turmoil that the army had been thrown into: "Out of the depth's have I cried unto thee." Doubtless the intense agony of soul David had experienced on a personal level was deeply mirrored in the lives of the rank and file of Hood's crippled army, an army laden with more questions than answers.

My God! My God! Why hast thou forsaken me? Why art thou so far from helping me, and from the words of my groaning?

O my God, I cry in the daytime, but thou answerest not; and in the night season, and am not silent.

But thou art holy, O thou that inhabitest the praises of Israel.

Our fathers trusted in thee: they trusted, and thou didst deliver them.

They cried unto thee, and were delivered: they trusted in thee, and were not put to shame.

But I am a worm, and no man; a reproach of men, and despised of the people.

All they that see me laugh me to scorn: they shoot out the lip, they shake the head, saying,

Commit thyself unto Jehovah; let him deliver him: let him rescue him, seeing he delighteth in him.

But thou art he that took me out of the womb; thou didst make me trust when I was upon my mother's breasts.

I was cast upon thee from the womb; thou art my God since my mother bare me.

Be not far from me; for trouble is near; for there is none to help.

Many bulls have compassed me; strong bulls of Bashan have beset me round.

They gape upon me with their mouth, as a ravening and a roaring lion.

I am poured out like water, and all my bones are out of joint: my heart is like wax; it is melted within me.

My strength is dried up like a potsherd; and my tongue cleaveth to my jaws; and thou hast brought me into the dust of death.

For dogs have compassed me: a company of evil-doers have enclosed me; they pierced my hands and my feet.

I may count all my bones; they look and stare upon me." [Psalm 22:1–16].

Those emaciated, wounded souls passing by the pillaged homes and towns of Middle Tennessee were slowly fading into an uncertain history. Barely visible, their devastated homes, with their astonished, gaunt inhabitants staring blindly, as if into some darkened, nameless void, were solemn testimonies of the ravages of war. Throughout that bitter winter of 1864 Middle Tennessee and the soldiers who tramped its roads could well relate to the anguished cries of ancient King David and share in the intensity of his internal struggles. For he also was a mighty warrior, a man of tremendous faith and valor, a man who bore the constant pain of great personal suffering and the loss of all things. He was immersed in affliction and well acquainted with grief and sorrow. Those skeletal, bent forms, pressing through the blasts of icy wind in huddled form, threw themselves forward with every sunken step, a pitiable, starving mass of heroic mien.

"I may count all my bones; they look and stare upon me."

12

Tuesday, December 27, 1864
Tuscumbia

The Army of Tennessee Enters Tuscumbia, Alabama

"The [Confederate] Army, having nearly all crossed, we moved on through Tuscumbia, and bivouacked in the mud that night, in the vicinity of Cane Creek, ten miles from Tuscumbia"[1] (Itinerary of Cheatham's Army Corps).

My [Confederate Infantry] command was stopped on the afternoon of December 27, 1864, about four miles from the [Tennessee] river, and a detail was called for from the regiment to go to the river. It fell to a boy from my home and a former school-mate to go, and I volunteered to take his place, as he was practically barefooted and had been unwell for several days. We did not know, of course, what we were to do till we arrived at the bridge. Two men were detailed to each boat, one at the upper end not to allow anything to lodge against the boat, and the man at the lower end was to keep the water bailed out; and both were to see that the plank floor was kept in place, which was, by the way, no easy task. It fell my lot to be placed in the lower end, and, unfortunately for me, our boat was about amid stream. The night was so black that we couldn't see anymore than the unfortunate British in the "black hole of Calcutta." The weather was bitterly cold, which was intensified threefold on account of our boat being about the middle of the stream. I thought I would freeze in spite of myself before midnight, and when the thought struck me that I had to remain there till sunrise I was tempted to give up in despair. Yet, duty being the watchword of a true soldier, I determined to stay at my post regardless of the weather; so when I began to feel the numb, sleepy feeling I would shake myself vigorously and stamp my feet till I overcame the awful sensation of freezing. All this time the troops were passing over the bridge, and it is a miracle that there were no casualties, as the black darkness, coupled with the loose bridge floor constantly shifting about, rendered the crossing extremely hazardous even in the day time; and to think that an army of about nineteen thousand men, requiring two days and nights to cross, did not lose a man sounds almost incredible. Notwithstanding fifty-six long years have passed since that

179

dreadful night, and notwithstanding I have passed my allotted three score and ten, being now seventy-six years old, yet the incidents of that night are as indelibly imprinted on my mind as if they were but yesterday.[2]

Regardless of Hood's evident success at getting the greater part of his army over the river, "the [Federal] major general commanding" had not succumbed to the pressure of caving in to circumstances beyond his control. The day before, Thomas had ordered Wood "to push on and support the cavalry as fast as you can and drive the rebels into the Tennessee River." His policy of pushing ahead "as long as there is a chance of doing anything" remained at the forefront of his tactics. Even at this final stage of the drama when all seemed lost, Thomas held fast.

Headquarters Department of the Cumberland
Pulaski, December 26th, 1864
Brig. Gen. T.J. Wood
Commanding Fourth Army Corps:

General: Yours of 4 p.m. today received. The major general commanding has no orders for you except to push on and support the cavalry as fast as you can and drive the rebels into the Tennessee River. Send word back from time to time with information as to the state of your supplies, and your wagons will be sent forward as fast as possible.[3]

Respectfully, WM. D. Whipple,
Assistant Adjutant General [Journal of the Fourth Army Corps].

December 27, received orders to march at daylight, my division marching in the rear. The rain continued heavily yesterday and during the night, rendering an advance extremely tedious and difficult; the loose nature of the soil of the country through which we passed rendered locomotion with artillery and trains almost impossible without the assistance of infantry to extricate them from the deep cuts and gullies, caused by heavy rains since and during the passage of the rebel army and trains. We succeeded in advancing eleven miles, passing a large number of abandoned ammunition wagons of the enemy and large quantities of ammunition partially destroyed, but did not encounter the enemy[4] [Report of Brigadier General Samuel Beatty, USA, Commanding Third Division].

On the 27th at his Headquarters in Pulaski, General Thomas temporarily refrained from the pursuit of the Confederates, taking precious time to consider the sacrifice and valor of the soldiers under his command who had fought at the battle of Franklin, both those who perished and those who had survived. Although he had not been on the field during that awful night, Thomas deemed it a worthy contribution to bear in mind those of his army who were.

Circular Hdqrs. Department Of The Cumberland,
Pulaski, Tenn., December 27, 1864

Corps commanders and the commanding officers of all detachments of troops in the field will collect together the battle flags, swords, &c., captured by their various commands at the battle of Franklin, and since entering upon this campaign, and forward them to these headquarters, with a full and complete list of the same, giving a description of the captured article, the name of the captor, his company, and regiment, the date and place of capture, and, whenever possible, the incidents connected therewith. In case where the name of the captor is not definitely known, and the trophy be held either by the regiment or company making the capture as an organization, it is advisable for such company or regiment to elect, from among the most brave and deserving in the command, one who shall be deemed worthy of the honor to be conferred on him. Wherever the name of the captor is known, even though he may not have survived the conflict, this fact should also be stated, and, as in all other cases, be inscribed upon the trophy. It is the design of the major general commanding, at the termination of the present campaign against the enemy, and the completed collection of the captured articles herein mentioned, to forward the same, in charge of a capable officer, and accompanied by the parties making the capture, to the Department at Washington, recommending that each may receive a medal of honor, or some other fitting acknowledgment of their gallant services. In order that this design may be fully carried out, it is hoped that all commanding officers will cause such prompt and proper efforts to be made as will insure to his command its due proportion of honor.[5]

By command of Major General Thomas

Wood's Fourth Corps Reaches Sugar Creek

By midday of the 27th Wood had crossed Sugar Creek and met with Wilson. Without doubt irritated, Wilson informed the Fourth Corps commander that he (Wilson) could go no farther without the necessary supplies. His men and horses had passed the limit of endurance. They needed rest, as much as possible, before continuing. Wood's swift reply was certainly not a surprise to Wilson or anyone else. It would be absolutely out of the question to expect the wagons anytime soon. Movement over the "impassable" roads was predicted to take some twelve hours to complete a mere six-mile advance. Even if the wagons were on hand, it would make little difference. Recent reports indicated that the "bulk of the enemy's army" had crossed the Tennessee River at Bainbridge. If the reports were accurate, Wilson stated he would "go no further" without orders, preferring to hear from headquarters rather than continue his present course without them. On the 27th Wood updated Thomas on the current state of affairs, as seen by him and Wilson.

> Dec. 27 12.15 p.m., General Wood and staff reach General Wilson's headquarters at Pinhook Town, about two miles beyond Sugar Creek. General Wilson states that he is unable to move farther, as he has not forage for his horses nor rations for his men. A little forage can be procured from the country, and the cavalry is now bringing it in. It is impossible to bring rations up from Pulaski (or rather, it is impracticable), as the road from that point is almost impassable. It will take twelve hours to haul a wagon

six miles. General Wilson also reports that he believes that the enemy is now over the Tennessee River; that he crossed at Bainbridge, where he laid down his pontoon bridge. (Bainbridge is on the shoals between Lamb's Ferry and Florence.)

Dec. 27 1.30 p.m., General Wood sent word to General Thomas that he has conferred with General Wilson, who is of the opinion that the bulk of the enemy's army is over the river, and he has sent parties out on various roads to ascertain certainly whether this supposition is correct. If he learns from these parties that the enemy has not crossed he [Wilson] will move on and we will follow and support the cavalry. If the enemy has crossed we will go no farther, but wait further orders in our present position. He also stated that the roads between here and Pulaski are intolerably bad, and suggests that arrangements be made to feed us from some other point[6] [Journal of the Fourth Army Corps].

"We had better push on"

By 2:00 p.m. on the 27th Wood's entire corps had reached Sugar Creek, passing over twelve miles of "the worst road, perhaps, that an army ever marched," and went into camp. Early in the evening Wood received a communiqué. Wilson had further news of the Confederate army's progress. According to the latest dispatch, the "rebels" were not completely out of range, having had trouble with the laying of their bridge at Bainbridge. With some extra effort and a few rations it still might be possible to overtake them. "At all events, we had better push on, as far and as fast as possible. I shall move everything, beginning at 5 A.M.," he declared, regardless of the lack of supplies.

Shortly afterward Wood notified Thomas of Wilson's plan to move out in pursuit the following morning, informing him also that the infantry "would push on in support, as fast as the condition of the road will allow" and gently reminding him of "the necessity of pushing forth rations and forage to this [infantry] command, and full instructions for the guidance of our movements when we reach the Tennessee River." Wood, however, was not at all convinced of the accuracy of the reports, nor of the wisdom of Wilson's overeager response to them:

> The fact the enemy had not finished laying his pontoon bridge on the evening of the 25th … is no evidence that the enemy, or the bulk of his army, is not now over the river.... Knowing when the enemy's pontoon train left Pulaski, we must conclude that the enemy has done well to get his pontoon train to Bainbridge as soon as the 25th instant. General Wilson's proposed movement for tomorrow is not at all judicious, as the rear of the enemy will have crossed the river some time before he can reach it, even if they do not commence to cross until today, December 27. His horses will be without forage and his men without rations, and he is going into a barren country. Under orders from General Thomas we are obliged to follow up the cavalry closely and support it.

Wood followed up his message with a slight display of reluctance, nevertheless reaffirming his commitment and obligation to "follow wherever Wilson leads" and to be on the march the following day, trailing Wilson's cavalry[7] (Journal of the Fourth Army Corps).

Wood's estimation was the correct one. The Confederate Army Corps of Generals B.F. Cheatham and S.D. Lee had crossed safely over the previous day. Having earlier secured a number of Federal pontoons near Decatur, a certain General Roddey had worked in advance of the main body and had floated the pontoons downriver for Confederate use. Soon after that—at sunrise on the 26th—the bridge had been constructed and the crossing commenced. While Wood and Wilson were planning their movements, Stewarts' Corps had tramped across the rushing Tennessee unmolested. Forrest's cavalry corps and infantry rear guard made their passing on the evening of the 27th and the morning of the 28th, leaving the battle-weary men under Walthall's command to again cover the rear of the army until all had crossed.

The Confederate Rear Guard Passes Over Shoal Creek

In the afternoon of the next day [the 27th] we marched to Shoal Creek, and after passing over I [Walthall] was ordered to take a position to guard the crossing till I should be directed to withdraw. Here the Cavalry passed us and moved on toward the river. The order to halt at Shoal Creek and my subsequent orders were received from Lieutenant General Stewart, by whose directions I crossed the river with my command on the morning of the 28th, leaving a detail of 200 men to assist in taking up the pontoon bridge.... During the whole time covered by this report the weather was excessively severe, and the troops subjected to unusual hardships.

For several days the ground was covered with snow, and numbers of the men made the march without shoes, some had no blankets, and all were poorly clad for the season. What they had to endure was borne without complaint, and the march was conducted in an orderly manner, though there was much in the surroundings to test severely the discipline of the troops. When the main Army had been moving for forty-eight hours, and they were yet at Columbia and threatened by a heavy force, it was known, of course, to them that their situation was of extreme peril and the serious and discouraging disasters which had but recently befallen us were well calculated to bring all commands into a state of disorganization. For their fine conduct, despite these difficulties and disadvantages and the depression which then pervaded the whole Army, the officers under my command are entitled to no little praise. I need not comment on it, as Major General Forrest was present to witness it in person[8] [Major General E.C. Walthall].

"Chalmers' [Cavalry] command brought up the rear after night, and there was not a man of all that battle and well tempered band who did not feel a sense of supreme relief at the moment."[9]

Federal Gunboats Fail to Check Hood's Crossing

Up to this point, the contest had been between cavalry and rear guard. That was about to change. Several miles distant in Hood's front, the Federal navy under the command of Admiral S.P. Lee had been actively involved in hampering the enemy's capability to cross the river, evidently aware of Hood's forces already in progress. In conjunction with Thomas, the Federal navy had been very busy destroying a Confederate fort and its munitions, along with "all the enemy's visible means of crossing below Florence," including the demolition of over a dozen pontoons located at a nearby ferry. As earlier cited, Lee's attempts to block Hood's crossing had been aggressively moving ahead since the 24th.

Major General Thomas:

Today [the 27th] I destroyed two guns and caissons at Florence Landing.... Enemy is doubtless coming in, seeking crossing.... I will immediately dispatch an iron clad and gun boats to convoy your troops up from Paducah. If any are there, or expected, [I] shall keep up active patrol of river, above and below.[10]

S.P. Lee Acting Rear Admiral, Commanding

Concluding from dispatches recently received, Admiral Lee felt quite certain that his movements downriver would coincide with Hood's attempt to cross it. However, another unpredictable Federal obstacle hampered the way. The river was falling at such a rapid rate that the admiral found it "impracticable today to reach the crossing which the enemy is said to be using."[11] Unwilling to risk the hazard, and to the dismay of the Union troops, Admiral Lee held back from advancing as Hood's worn troopers continued their way across. "Foggy weather and a rapidly falling river prevented my reaching and destroying Hood's pontoons at Bainbridge, six miles above Florence."[12]

"Feeling the disaster"

The crossing of the river of the greater part of the Confederate forces must have dealt a crushing blow to Federal morale—so little accomplished at the hands of such tremendous effort. The major threats had, for the most part, been put behind the Southerners (except for the looming specter of the Federal navy.) The army, with its commander, could begin to unwind. The time had arrived for sober reflection on the momentous months that had passed. Traveling with them through the campaign, Dr. Quintard had recorded a few of Hood's words during a private exchange between them that had taken place previously, in Georgia during the summer months: "On the 10th of August, at headquarters, I presented a class to Bishop Lay for confirmation. It included General Hood and some officers of his staff. In speaking to me the night before his confirmation, the General said: 'Doctor, I have two objects in life that engage my supreme regard. One is to do all I can for my country. The other is to be ready and prepared for death whenever God shall call me.'" Upon reaching Tuscumbia on December 27th, Hood's physician "found the General feeling the disaster more [acutely] since he reached Tuscumbia than at any time since the retreat began."[13]

13

Wednesday, December 28, 1864
The Final Chapter—
Hood Crosses the Deep River

[We] Marched from Cane Creek, through Barton Station, to Bear Creek, a distance of sixteen miles.... Bear Creek swimming: have to pontoon it.[1] —Itinerary of Cheatham's Army Corps

The Infantry Rear Guard Crosses Over

"[A]t [the] Tennessee River, at Bainbridge, this [Confederate Army] Corps covered the operations, and was the last to cross, which it did on the morning of December 28th. At Columbia, a rear guard composed of several Brigades from this and the other Corps was organized and placed under the command of Major General Walthall. This force, in connection with the Cavalry, covered the retreat from Columbia to the Tennessee River."[2] (Lieutenant General Alexander P. Stewart, Circular, Hdqrs. Infty. Forces of the Rear Guard, December 28, 1864–3 a.m.). "Featherston's Brigade will move promptly ... at daybreak across the bridge, to be followed by Feild and then Palmer. General Reynolds will withdraw his command from Shoal Creek [in] time to reach the main line by daybreak and leave a skirmish line behind for a half hour.... Ector's Brigade will cover the road until the whole command has passed, then will follow leaving a line of skirmishers behind until the rear of the brigade has passed onto the bridge"[3] (By command of General Walthall). "It was the intention and expectation of our commanders to stop the stragglers and reorganize our commands. Consequently, guards were placed upon the bridge, and up and down the river to arrest all stragglers. But, so many were wounded, barefooted and sick that [the] guards would not stop them."[4] "Deep River, my home is over Jordan. Deep River, Lord. I want to cross over into campground" (African American spiritual, author unknown).

Hood's Crossing of the Tennessee River Completed

Early on the morning of the 28th of December 1864 the final remnants of the Army of Tennessee were passing over the Tennessee River. Predictably, the army's rear guard under Walthall filed over last, covering the rear. The 39th North Carolina Infantry Regiment commanded by Col. David Coleman was the final unit of Hood's Army to cross the Tennessee, "while half clad and half starved and barefooted and fighting three to one."[5] Once the closing ranks of Walthall's rear guard had crossed over, the pontoon bridge was taken up and the march immediately resumed in the direction of Burnsville, Mississippi, Lee's, Cheatham's, and Stewart's Corps under orders to move in the following days by separate routes to their respective destinations. "The march will be resumed tomorrow morning [the 29th] at sunrise, left in front, passing through Tuscumbia and going toward Iuka. The division of General Walthall will move in front, that of General Loring following. General Loring will place two regiments in his rear as a rear guard. The trains will move in advance of the troops."[6] (By command of Lieutenant General Stewart).

Although harassed by a substantial Federal cavalry force across the river at Decatur, the Confederate army was at relative ease. Hood's soldiers began to breathe freely. At last, and with good reason, the Federals were finally pulling back, calling off the chase.

Thomas Brings the Running Engagement to a Halt; The Majority of the Fighting in the West Ended

"Six miles south of Lexington [Alabama] Brevet Major General Wilson learned certainly, on the 28th, the rear of the enemy had crossed the Tennessee River on the 27th, and that his bridge was taken up the morning of the 28th. These facts were reported to the commanding general, who ordered that the pursuit be discontinued"[7] (Report of Brig. Gen. T.J. Wood, USA, commanding Fourth Army Corps). "December 28, [the Federal infantry] marched at 8 AM., following the Second Division, and marching thirteen miles, reached Lexington, Ala., eleven miles from the Tennessee River and sixteen miles from Florence, where intelligence reached us that the enemy had succeeded in crossing the Tennessee River, and the pursuit was abandoned"[8] (Report of Brigadier General Samuel Beatty, USA, commanding Third Division). "The pursuit of Hood's retreating army was discontinued by my main forces on the 29th of December, on reaching the Tennessee River; however, a force of cavalry, numbering 600 men, made up from detachments of the Fifteenth Pennsylvania, Second Michigan, Tenth, Twelfth, and Thirteenth Indiana Regiments, under command of Col. William J. Palmer, Fifteenth Pennsylvania, operating with Steedman's column, started from Decatur, Alabama in the direction of Hood's line of retreat in Mississippi. The enemy's cavalry, under Roddey, was met at Leighton, with whom Colonel Palmer skirmished and pressed back in small squads toward the mountains"[9] (Report of Maj. Gen. George H. Thomas, USA, commanding Department of the Cumberland).

Col. Palmer's thrust at Roddey's cavalry had proven satisfactory for the Union, as they destroyed up to 83 of Hood's pontoon trains and 150 of his wagons and caused the loss of 400 mules. Nevertheless, Hood pushed on, with or without these assets, as the ferocious winter weather continued in its brutality:

> We continued our retreat unmolested on the 28th and 29th, and camped near Bear Creek. On the 30th we continued our retreat. There was rain, sleet, and snow at night. On the 31st, the last of the long to be remembered year of 1864, we continued our retreat, passing through Iuka and Burnsville.
>
> January 1st, 1865, a beautiful Sabbath day, was not a day of rest for us. We marched five and a half miles and camped. The next day we marched thirteen miles.... We were leaving the Federals in the rear but continued our heavy and tiresome marching. I was so tired at night I could hardly move. The Federals were paying no attention to us, but were resting from their successful battles in Tennessee.... [I]n the summer of 1862 we had a fine Army, now nearly half of our soldiers were sick.... How different now! A wrecked and shattered Army with nothing but gloom before us. Comment is unnecessary.[10]

Although it was not possible for a soldier from either side to avoid the unusually harsh conditions on the harried march from Nashville to the Tennessee River, the civilian population fared no better. It was a setting that seemed calculated to produce the highest casualties. The South—in this case, particularly the region of Middle Tennessee—had been ravaged so completely that by the winter of 1864 it was barely recognizable. What had once been a prosperous, fertile land was now a vacant, wasted territory, unfit for human habitation:

> The Tennessee Valley and Buzzard Roost country had been noted as the finest country in the South. Fertile lands, fine dwellings, large farms, where peace, plenty, and prosperity once existed. [By late 1864 it had become] almost a desert waste. Hardly one house in ten were left [untouched]. Cotton gins, fencing, everything was destroyed, and once happy and contented families were scattered and refugeed. In fact, the entire country from Tuscumbia to Corinth was almost entirely depopulated and devastated.
>
> We could but note the changes at Corinth ... made memorable in 1862 by the battle of Shiloh.... We looked in vain for scenes and places with which we had been familiar ... [but] few residences were left. What had been in 1862 the most thickly settled portion of the town was [now] a fort and a graveyard. Every vestige of a house had disappeared.[11]

There is a remarkable feature within these tributes, common to most, if not all of them. With slight exception, the authors of these reports recount the sufferings of the retreat more often and in greater detail than those of the battles of Franklin and Nashville that immediately preceded them. Although the ghastly memories of Franklin followed by the crushing disaster at Nashville could hardly be forgotten by anyone remotely associated with them, it was the bitter severity experienced on the retreat from Tennessee that tried them to the bone.

These were without doubt, "the sternest trials of the war."

As the last week of December 1864 drew to a close, the Army of Tennessee pushed its battered ranks to the limits of endurance, taking up a staggered march to Iuka and Burnsville, bivouacking along the roadside in a march of twelve miles, then to Corinth Mississippi, another fourteen miles. By Tuesday, January 10, the army had "started from Corinth at daylight," by use of the railroad, "and made our quarters at Rienzi, fifteen miles distant, that night." With the arrival of the first two weeks of January 1865, the army had covered the territory stretching from Corinth to Tupelo, avoiding the "impassable roads" as much as possible, and reached Tupelo on the 13th by means of an alternative route passing through a swamp. The army remained there for several days[12] (Itinerary of Cheatham's Army Corps, October 31, 1864–January 17, 1865).

"We then quietly moved to Corinth, MS., January 5th, 1865, with the other West Tennesseeans; we had a thirty day's furlough, with orders to reassemble at West Point, MS. And to their lasting honor, be it said, almost to a man they met at the time and place."[13] "And so ends the year.... Alas for my poor, bleeding land!/Alas for the friends I mourn—/Darkest of all Decembers ever my life has known./How dear, yet oh, how painful too;/that joy how near to grief allied/When thoughts of loved ones now no more;/ come rushing on me like the tide."[14]

With the arrival of 1865 the Southern Confederacy was breathing its last breath. The devastating stroke that had crushed the life out of the Army of Tennessee had announced not only the end of the war but the end of the Confederate government as well. With the heart taken out of its army, the Confederacy's end was only a matter of time. By the arrival of 1865, with both of its armies caught in the throes of death, the Confederate States of America was tottering on the brink of disaster. Not given to caving under pressure, the Confederate government acted quickly. In order to counteract the recent turn of events in Tennessee, Georgia, and Northern Alabama, the Confederate congress adopted a particular resolution, requesting President Davis to appoint General Joseph E. Johnston once again to full command of the Army of Tennessee, a decision that suited many of Hood's men. Both the congress and the Confederate states viewed the appointment as one to "be hailed with joy by the army and ... receive the approval of the country." Consequently, on the 22nd of February, General Robert E. Lee appointed General Joseph

E. Johnston to full command of the Army of Tennessee, including all troops in the department of Georgia, South Carolina, and Florida, with instructions to concentrate them and "drive back Sherman."

But the excitement was not to last. No amount of fiery rhetoric or emotional fervor could bring victory out of military defeat or restore to wholeness a nation's shattered soul. Johnston's appointment offered little more than a momentary respite from the enormous loss of men and morale suffered in those final days of 1864. Yet, even in the presence of such dark circumstances, perhaps there was still a ray of hope to be found. With the right amount of concentrated effort, one combined, final, national exertion could restore the historic right of independence. One more round of sacrifice might bring it all together. Lives and lost fortunes, vanished and gone, could never be reclaimed. But with one, concluding, overwhelming victory, the crushing losses would obtain not only meaning and purpose but would also provide the grounds for justification and validation. However, the intense fighting around Atlanta and the recent tragedies taking place in Tennessee had forced the conviction upon the mind of the army that ultimate victory was unattainable. Nevertheless, to the honor of the Southern soldier, the majority of survivors entered upon the final campaign in North Carolina under Johnston "with loyalty and unmatched constancy."[15]

The nightmare in Middle Tennessee was over. What had begun with such promise, dedication, and desperate self-sacrifice had ended in a disaster that no Southerner would have thought possible or could have imagined. The sole consolation to be found was in the army's narrow escape from complete overthrow and capture over the icy fields and rivers of mud covering the impoverished territory of Middle Tennessee in the winter of 1864. Hood's proud divisions had, a mere month before, crossed the Tennessee River at Tuscumbia and Florence with an army of some 30,000 hardened veterans of Confederate service, prepared to give the last ounce of blood for the liberation of Tennessee. At the never-to-be-forgotten village of Franklin on November 30, 1864, they established for all time that this was no vain boast. With banners snapping in the breeze and bayonets glistening in the sun's dying rays, and surely aware that many a compatriot would not outlast the day, waves of Confederate infantry marching in perfect order flooded the fields south of town. Hood's army, charging heroically into those rough-hewn Federal lines, those "formidable" works, on that fatal, blood-red afternoon would go down in the annals of history as among the most extraordinary military encounters the world has yet witnessed. After five solid hours of battle and a series of desperate charges the darkness of night had closed in upon a scene of unmatched horror, leaving thousands of Confederates killed, wounded, captured, or missing, with Union losses relatively few in number. The Confederate army's loss of men and officers on those memorable fields left the Army of Tennessee significantly depleted of men in arms ready for battle only days ahead.

In mid–December of 1864 the surviving remnants of Hood's army dug in on the frozen hillsides south of Nashville, pitting themselves against the resolute powers of nature and Thomas's vast array of rested troopers eager for the fray, all waiting for their chance to burst from quarters, swoop down upon the thin grey lines, and finish them off. Before it was over, Thomas had been reinforced to twice his original strength, increasing the numerical odds again in his favor three to one. Following the humiliating defeat at Nashville, the Army of Tennessee had limped from its state wounded and broken, fighting from Nashville to Bainbridge, Alabama, against all that man and an untamable nature could hurl against them. On December 29, 1864, General George Thomas, unable to proceed further in pursuit of Hood, finally brought the running engagement to a halt. General Orders No. 169, sent from the Headquarters of the Department of the Cumberland at Pulaski, Tennessee: "Soldiers: The Major General commanding announces to you that the rear guard of the flying and dispirited enemy was driven across the Tennessee River on the night of the 27th instant. The impassable state of the roads and consequent impossibility to supply the army compels a closing of the campaign for the present."[16]

In a rather embellished statement, General Thomas congratulated his drained army as "brilliant in its achievements and unsurpassed in its results … although your forces were inferior to it [the Confederate Army] in numbers." Continuing his address, Thomas chose to refrain from any mention of the resounding tactical defeats brought upon his army during the retreat. Despite the extraordinary efforts of his troops, both infantry and cavalry, in the end he was unable to accomplish his ultimate goal. For the moment it would be impossible to finish what many a Union man must have previously considered a relatively easy task: to inflict the finishing blows upon a defeated foe, one that supposedly had neither the will nor means to defend itself.

Wilson (and his fellow officers), surely crestfallen and somewhat despondent as to the ultimate turn of events, nevertheless joined Thomas and the bulk of the officer corps in tribute and admiration for his indefatigable cavalry corps and the men on the ground: "[I]t may not be improper to say that throughout the entire campaign the bravery and steadiness of the Cavalry troops, new and old, were most conspicuous. Nothing could have been more admirable than their conduct on the Harpeth [at Franklin], in the two days battle at Nashville, in the affair on the West Harpeth, or in the pursuit which followed. I know of no battles in the war where the influence of Cavalry was more potent, nor of any pursuit sustained as long and well."[17] "Of the officers and men of their command who deported themselves so bravely and entered so heartily into the actions and fierce assaults and bore up so manfully in the subsequent pursuit, I cannot speak in too high praise. The nation can safely trust its honor and safety to the courage and endurance of such men. The officers of my staff performed their duty well, both on the battlefield and the subsequent arduous campaign, and it is due to them to record their names in my official report"[18] (Report of Brigadier General Samuel Beatty, USA, commanding Third Division). "Of the pursuit it may be truly remarked that it is without a parallel in this war. It was continued for more than a hundred miles at the most inclement season of the year, over a road the whole of which was bad, and thirty miles of which were wretched, almost beyond description. It were scarcely an hyperbole to say that the road from Pulaski to Lexington was bottomless when we passed over it. It was strewn with the wrecks of wagons, artillery carriages, and other material abandoned by the enemy in his flight.... Thus was closed for the Fourth Corps one of the most remarkable campaigns of the war"[19] (Report of Brig. Gen. T.J. Wood, USA, commanding Fourth Army Corps). "I would state the men of this command accompanying me from Memphis have been nearly 100 days in the saddle, more than half the time without rations. Both men and officers have been conspicuous for gallantry. No instance of cowardice has been reported by the brigade commanders, and none have come under my notice"[20] (Report of Brigadier General Edward Hatch, USA, commanding Fifth Division, of operations October 29–December 27, 1864).

Confederate cavalry commander Nathan Bedford Forrest initially refrained from speaking his mind in matters relating to the campaign, choosing rather to commend the exceptional behavior of the men under his command:

> The campaign was full of trial and suffering, but the troops under my command, both cavalry and infantry, submitted to every hardship with an uncomplaining patriotism; with a single exception, they behaved with commendable gallantry.... I am also indebted to Major General Walthall for much valuable service rendered during the retreat from Columbia. He exhibited the highest soldierly qualities. Many of his men were without shoes, but they bore their sufferings without murmur and were ever ready to meet the enemy. From the day I left Florence, on the 21st of November, to the 27th of December my cavalry were engaged every day with the enemy. My loss in killed and wounded has been heavy [Report of Maj. Gen. Nathan B. Forrest, CSA, Commanding Cavalry, of operations in North Alabama and Middle Tennessee Relating to the Battle of Nashville].

"Never were soldiers placed in a more trying position than were the men of Hood's army. No records show more shining courage and valor than was displayed by Forrest's Cavalry from Nashville to Shoal Creek."[21]

Brigadier General J.T. Holtzclaw, in recalling the horrors of that fateful winter, recounted the achievements of his battle-hardened brigades during the retreat in the most modest of terms: "I will say nothing of the hardships and exposures endured by my command; they but bore their part of the general burden; yet that part they bore with cheerfulness and spirit, and repulsed the enemy with loss whenever they encountered him on the soil of Tennessee. My officers and men conducted themselves to my entire satisfaction throughout all the fights and marches."[22] Major General E.C Walthall was more expansive in his summation:

> I have been able to furnish but an inadequate idea of what was done and endured by my brave and faithful troops in the arduous and eventful campaign here imperfectly sketched. The limits of such a report as is expected at this time do not enable me to make full mention of the hard marches and severer duties, in night time as well as in day, accomplished by my command during the time to which it refers, nor to do more than refer to the privations and trials bravely borne by my troops, ill clad and often shoeless, campaigning in the depths of a rigorous winter in Tennessee; but it is due to the officers who commanded the several Brigades under me, and the artillery battalion which served with me, and the men they commanded, having witnessed their courage and endurance, their self sacrifice and their fidelity, during the trials and dangers of this severe campaign, that I should here record my high appreciation of their conduct and services, and accord to them with my thanks my unqualified approval. All that their skill and courage, their labor and sufferings, could accomplish was freely given to reach results which could not be attained.[23]

"It is due to the officers and men of this corps that I should bear testimony to their patient endurance of fatigue and privation, their cheerfulness and alacrity in obeying orders, and, above all, their heroic valor as displayed on many occasions since I have had the honor to command them, but preeminently at Franklin"[24] (Lt. General Alexander P. Stewart).

Barely had the Army of Tennessee crossed over in safety and found a measure of rest when another major event transpired. After bearing the burden of accountability (and, in the minds of many, the blame) for the formation, planning, and outcome of the Tennessee Campaign with all its ensuing atrocious hardships and losses, General Hood, worn, exhausted, and surely overwhelmed by the unexpected turn of events, had to face the music. The grim reality had to be reckoned with. With the failure of the campaign to take the war into Northern soil after the proposed liberation of Tennessee from Federal occupation, the war in the Western Theatre had come to its ultimate, bitter end, and with it possibly the finishing blow to the Confederacy. Whether or not the commanding general believed the end had come, he well knew that his tenure with the Army of Tennessee was finished. Having accepted the full weight of responsibility of the Tennessee Campaign and its outcome, General Hood knew that the time had arrived for his departure. Consequently, on January 23, 1865, he respectfully resigned his command:

Headquarters, Army of Tennessee
Tupelo, Miss. January 23rd, 1865

Soldiers: At my request I have this day been relieved from the command of this Army. In taking leave of you, accept my thanks for the patience with which you have endured your many hardships during the recent campaign. I am alone responsible for its conception, and strived hard to do my duty in its execution. I urge upon you the importance of giving your entire support to the distinguished soldier who now assumes command, and I shall look with deep interest upon all your future operations and rejoice at your successes.[25]

J.B. Hood General

At the moment of great trial and absolute failure, yet consistent with his sense of duty, Hood sought further initiatives, suggesting to President Davis a renewal of the conflict with the aid of reinforcements from the Trans-Mississippi. This too, however, was more optimistic idealism than a thing that was workable. Endless replacements and vast Federal resources had overwhelmed the Confederate states for four long, bloody years. The final toll the Confederacy had taken in its defense had all but drained the South's lifeblood to its last drop. Although a meager remnant of Hood's former army would make its way into North Carolina for the final round of fighting in the months ahead, the Army of Tennessee in contrast to its former glory was finished, perhaps foreshadowing the ultimate end of the Confederacy as a national entity. Nevertheless, Hood's praise of his worn and tattered army was absolute: "The Tennessee troops entered the State with high hopes as they approached their homes; when the fortunes of war were against us the same faithful soldiers remained true to their flag, and, with rare exceptions, followed it in retreat as they had borne it in advance."[26]

Hood's praise of his army was justified by all accounts. Supportive of the general's tribute, Luke Finlay, in his regimental history of the Fourth Tennessee, draws a resemblance of martial excellence between the renowned Tenth Legion of the ancient Gallic wars and his band of ragged Confederates, comrades "no less distinguished for their soldierly qualities [than the Tenth Legion]. That fought for conquest; this for honor."[27] "Though few in numbers (truly the skeleton of a once grand regiment), it maintained its history at Nashville, and followed the ragged but beloved flag in the retreat, which, for hardship, hunger, and actual suffering, was only equaled by (Napoleon's) retreat from Moscow."[28]

Colonel Ellison Capers of the 24th South Carolina, in his official report, vividly described the entry of the Army of Tennessee into its home state in the fall of 1864. These were heady days of soaring expectation, commitment, and dedication to principle, long-held beliefs that had carried them through the most trying of times. Capers' clear description of the disaster that had befallen the private sectors of the country was unmistakable evidence of the Union army's intentions. Everyone, civilians included, had become targeted. Evidently no crime was too low for the soldiers of Lincoln's army. The desolate sights that met the eyes of the Confederates served only to further the army's convictions of the righteous purpose of their cause. "The beautiful valley of the Tennessee, through which we marched, was desolated by the enemy, and the commanding general published a field circular to the army, calling attention of the troops to the ruined homes on every hand, and exhorting every man and officer resolutely to vow the redemption of Tennessee from the grasp of the foe. The circular was received by the Twenty-fourth [South Carolina] with a hearty cheer, though many of the gallant soldiers who cheered were absolutely suffering for clothing and shoes."[29]

Nothing in American Civil War history quite resembles the Army of Tennessee's withdrawal from Nashville to Tuscumbia. The collective forces of prolonged intolerable weather with its impossible traveling conditions in combination with an enraged foe unleashed without restraint upon them created a never to be forgotten or possibly repeated scenario, a picture that can by no means be fully grasped or appreciated in its scope.

Regardless of the intensity of enemy pursuit, the resolute, fierce stands of prolonged Confederate rear guard actions over a distance of a hundred miles displayed by Lee's corps, Forrest's band of cavalry, and Walthall's infantry brigades literally saved the Army of Tennessee from certain capture and extinction. As the Federal government preferred to view it, Hood's retreat was simply a demonstration of defeat, having driven him from the state in a complete rout—an indisputable, undeniable Federal victory on all sides. Other voices remember the courage, the ever-present sense of duty to principle that overcame the most excruciating of trials, the final summing up of an extraordinary legacy:

> The Army of Tennessee had made its last retreat. With all its flags streaming; with all its bugles blowing and its drums beating, with its strong files as unbroken in that final retreat as when facing its first fight; with not a commander away, not an officer absent, not a private forgotten from its proud story, the army of Tennessee, in serried ranks, horse, foot and artillery, marched in shadowy column victoriously from its last Confederate field of December 16, 1864, straight through the golden portal leading to the transcendent roadway of history.
>
> Within five months, its elder brother, the army of Northern Virginia, holding within its skeleton ranks every man, general, officer, or private, who had in its day of greatest glory belonged to it, was to retreat from Petersburg to Appomattox, and from that culminating height of heroic effort, to march without let or challenge through those same golden portals, behind which the Confederate armies, great or small, were to meet, one in birth as in endeavor; one in hope as in failure; one in failure as in unending fame!
>
> It was April, 1865, that the rings of that Titanic curtain which had hidden within its heavy folds the thrilling epoch of so much valor and so much devotion, noiselessly shaken by some hand mightier far than man's, and rattling off from their pole, fell with a crash upon the land sodden with the blood of an entire people, never to rise again over our Union of States, "one and indivisible."
>
> Never in the course of this war have the best qualities of our soldiers been more conspicuously shown, never more enthusiasm evinced than when our troops once

more crossed the Tennessee river; never greater gallantry than that which was so general at Franklin; never higher fortitude than was displayed on the retreat from Nashville to Tupelo[30] [Beauregard's Report, April 15, 1865].

The contrast to former days soon became too difficult to dwell upon. By the first week of 1865 the Army of Tennessee was all but finished for further active service:

In 1862, Wade's 1st Mo. Battery, and Gen. Little's 1st Mo. Brig. spent about four months of pleasant soldier life at Tupelo, at that time our commissary and quartermaster departments were at their best, and no man had any complaint to offer, if he so desired. They had a well-arranged camp and drill and parade grounds, arbors arranged by every regiment for preaching and thousands made profession of faith in the Lord Jesus Christ, and their hopes in the success of our cause, was bright. They returned with less than one tenth of their former number, with an empty commissary, and no quartermaster department, and nothing in view, but to fight from now on, many times their number, with no hopes of success.[31]

Pvt. Dozier, Co. B, 18th Alabama, spoke for many of his former comrades in his closing remarks recorded in an early edition of *Confederate Veteran*: "I know our cause was just, and desire to honor it as best I can.... I was wounded in the battle of Chickamauga, and again wounded at New Hope, Ga. I had three brothers in the same Company; but when the surrender came, I was the only one."[32]

With the crushing defeats of the 1864 Tennessee campaign the fortunes of the Confederacy were all but lost. For generations to come, the distant echoes of that mighty struggle would linger over the land, permeating it with its mystery, captivating the attention like nothing before or since. History must, by all means, give a just, honest, and reasonable portrayal of these astounding events, how and why they occurred, and at what cost. Those terrible days of trial and bloodshed, the wanton, wholesale destruction of personal property committed under the hand of cruel and base persons, the honor of supreme sacrifice for a common just cause, the endless suffering endured by the country as a whole—all these and more must be kept close to the nation's heart. "The heroic dead of that campaign will ever be recollected with honor by their countrymen, and the survivors have the proud consolation that no share of the disaster can be laid to them, who have so worthily served their country, and have stood by their colors even to the last dark hours of the republic"[33] (General P.G.T. Beauregard).

Having never been returned home, the remains of lost and forgotten American soldiers outfitted in blue and grey alike lie hidden in obscurity, covered by unmarked graves throughout the farmlands and cities of the South. In the quiet woods of Shiloh, the fields and streams of Chickamauga, the bustling thoroughfares encompassing Atlanta, and along the routes of Middle Tennessee from Nashville to the Alabama border and beyond the countryside of a thousand battles lies still. With few exceptions, the finest of American manhood lie beneath it, entombed where they fell. These valiant, dauntless, extraordinary yet common men must never be forgotten.

"The survivors were few when the end came; their comrades slept wherever brave men had fought and died; to the State of Tennessee they will be ever living men of heroic memory."[34]

Appendix I:
Casualties from the 1864 Tennessee Campaign Retreat, December 17–26, 1864

Saturday, December 17, 1864

Confederate

17TH ALABAMA INFANTRY

Milton aka Melton, William L.—Private—Co. C—Captured December 17, 1864, at Franklin, Tennessee; sent to Camp Chase Prison, Ohio; released upon taking oath of allegiance, June 12, 1865.

Tomlinson, William B.—Private—Co. A—Captured December 17, 1864, at Franklin, Tennessee; sent to Camp Chase Prison, Ohio; died March 18, 1865, of pneumonia; buried: grave #1701, Camp Chase Confederate Cemetery, Columbus, Ohio.

31ST ALABAMA INFANTRY

Harrison, Hiram S.F.—Private/Musician—Co. —Captured December 17, 1864, at Franklin, Tennessee; sent to Camp Chase Prison, Ohio; released June 12, 1865; light hair, hazel eyes, florid complexion, age 33.

55th Alabama Infantry

Chambers, William M.—Private—Co. D—Captured December 17, 1864, at Franklin, Tennessee; sent to Camp Chase Prison, Ohio; released upon taking oath of allegiance, June 12, 1865; black hair, brown eyes, dark complexion, height 5'11".

Grammer, John T.—Corporal—Co. G—Captured December 17, 1864, at Franklin, Tennessee; sent to Camp Chase Prison, Ohio; released upon taking oath of allegiance, June 12, 1865; black hair, hazel eyes, dark complexion, height 5'7".

Harp, Phillip—Sergeant—Co. I—Captured December 17, 1864, at West Harpeth, Tennessee; sent to Camp Chase Prison, Ohio; released upon taking oath of allegiance, June 12, 1865; dark hair, blue eyes, fair complexion; height 5' 7½".

Raines, John W.—Private—Co. I—Captured December 17, 1864, at Franklin, Tennessee; sent to camp Chase Prison, Ohio; died April 10, 1865; buried: unknown.

9TH ARKANSAS INFANTRY

Grose, Columbus Carson—Bradley County, Arkansas–Private—Co. D— Captured December 17, 1864, at Franklin, Tennessee; sent to Camp Chase Prison, Ohio; released upon oath of allegiance, June 13, 1865; light hair, blue eyes, florid complexion; height 5'9"; age 21.

Johnson, Felix G.—Bradley County, Arkansas–Private–Co. D–Wounded in right ankle and Captured December 17, 1864, at Franklin, Tennessee; admitted to Hospital #1, Nashville, Tennessee, February 10, 1865, due to smallpox; sent to Louisville, Kentucky; released upon taking oath of allegiance, June 16, 1865; light hair, blue eyes, fair complexion; height 5'7".

15TH ARKANSAS INFANTRY

Kennedy, James B.—Captain—Co. D, "Napoleon Greys"—Wounded in left arm and Captured December 17, 1864, at Franklin, Tennessee; sent to Camp Chase Prison, Ohio; released March 27, 1865.

1ST GEORGIA INFANTRY

Turner, Joseph H.—Private—Co. E—Captured December 17, 1864, at Franklin, Tennessee.

34TH GEORGIA INFANTRY

Brooks, James—Private—Co. C—Killed December 17, 1864, at Franklin, Tennessee.

Cawthon, Chesley C.—Private—Co. I—Captured December 17, 1864, at West Harpeth, Tennessee; sent to Camp Chase Prison, Ohio; released June 6, 1865.

Childs, Orasha G.—Private—Co. G—Captured December 17, 1864, at Franklin, Tennessee; sent to Camp Chase Prison, Ohio; released June 12, 1865.

Gilbert, Isaac S.—Private—Captured December 17, 1864, at Franklin, Tennessee; sent to Camp Chase Prison, Ohio; released June 13, 1865.

Meade, John M.—Private—Co. H—Captured December 17, 1864; sent to Camp Chase Prison, Ohio; died February 22, 1865, of variola; buried: grave #1380, Camp Chase Confederate Cemetery, Columbus, Ohio.

Walters, William T.—Private—Co. I—Captured December 17, 1864, at Franklin, Tennessee; sent to Camp Chase Prison, Ohio; released June 12, 1865.

36TH GEORGIA INFANTRY

Beck, William A.—Private—Co. H—Captured December 17, 1864, at Franklin, Tennessee; sent to Camp Chase Prison, Ohio; died March 11, 1865, of variola; buried: grave #1623, Camp Chase Confederate Cemetery, Columbus, Ohio.

39TH GEORGIA INFANTRY

Keith, Joel M.—Hall County, Georgia—Private—Co. K, "Walker County Volunteers"—Captured December 17, 1864, at Franklin, Tennessee; sent to Camp Chase Prison, Ohio.

42ND GEORGIA INFANTRY

St. Johns, James Randolph—Newton County, Georgia–Private—Co. F—Killed December 12 or 17?, 1864, at Franklin, Tennessee.

Thomas, Phillip W.—Private—Co. A—Captured December 17, 1864, at Franklin, Tennessee; sent to Camp Chase Prison, Ohio; released: June 12, 1865.

Victory aka Victor, Levi—Private—Co. E, "Harper Guards"—Captured December 17, 1864, at Franklin, Tennessee; sent to Camp Chase Prison, Ohio; died February 28, 1865, of chronic diarrhea; buried: grave #1489, Camp Chase Confederate Cemetery, Columbus, Ohio.

43RD GEORGIA INFANTRY

Field, Logan—Private—Co. B—Captured December 17, 1864, at Franklin, Tennessee; sent to Camp Chase Prison, Ohio; released May 2, 1865.

65TH GEORGIA INFANTRY

Williams, Nelson—Private—Co. F—Captured December 17, 1864, at Franklin, Tennessee; sent to Camp Chase Prison, Ohio; died April 8, 1865; buried: grave #1892, Camp Chase Confederate Cemetery, Columbus, Ohio.

POINTE COUPEE [LOUISIANA] BATTERY

Bourgeois, Henry—Private—Captured December 17, 1864, at Franklin, Tennessee; sent to Camp Douglas Prison, Illinois; paroled May 26, 1865; died on parole.

4TH LOUISIANA INFANTRY

Alain (aka Allen), Andrew—Private—Co. H—Captured December 17, 1864, at Franklin, Tennessee; sent to Camp Douglas Prison, Illinois; released June 18, 1865.

Babin, Joseph—Private—Co. E—Captured December 17, 1864, at Franklin, Tennessee; sent to Camp Chase Prison, Ohio; died February 7, 1865; buried: grave #1091, Camp Chase Confederate Cemetery, Columbus, Ohio.

Barron, J.W.—Private—Co. I—Captured December 17, 1864, at Franklin, Tennessee; sent to Camp Douglas Prison, Illinois; released upon taking oath of allegiance, June 18, 1865.

Bickham, T.A.—Caddo Parish, Louisiana–Sergeant—Co. I—Captured December 17, 1864, at Franklin, Tennessee; sent to Camp Douglas Prison, Illinois; released June 17, 1865, on taking oath of allegiance.

Bivins, John H.—Private—Co. G—Captured December 17, 1864, at Franklin, Tennessee; sent to Camp Chase Prison, Ohio.

Blanchard, Samuel—Private—Co. F—Captured December 17, 1864, at

Franklin, Tennessee; sent to Camp Chase Prison, Ohio; released upon taking oath of allegiance, June 6, 1865.

Bobbin, George F.—Private—Co. E—Captured December 17, 1864, at Franklin, Tennessee; sent to Camp Douglas Prison, Illinois; died February 7, 1865.

Bourquin, Jules—Bayou Sara, Louisiana—Sergeant—Co. D—Captured December 17, 1864, at Franklin, Tennessee; sent to camp Douglas, Illinois; released June 12, 1865, on taking oath of allegiance.

Brewer, P.R.—Natchez, Mississippi—Lieutenant—Co. F—Captured December 17, 1864, at Hollow Tree Gap; sent to Johnson's Island Prison, Ohio; released June 16, 1865, on taking oath of allegiance; dark hair, brown eyes, dark complexion; height 5'6".

Crane, William J.—Feliciana, Louisiana—2nd Lieutenant—Co. D—Captured December 30, 1864, at Franklin, Tennessee; sent to Fort Delaware, Maryland; released June 17, 1865, on taking oath of allegiance; dark hair, brown eyes, fair complexion, height 5'6".

Getren, Traivill—Private—Co. B—Captured December 17, 1864, at Franklin, Tennessee; sent to Camp Chase Prison, Ohio; exchanged February 17, 1865.

Gipson, William—Private—Co. H—Captured December 17, 1864, at Franklin, Tennessee; sent to Camp Douglas Prison, Illinois; released upon taking oath of allegiance, June 12, 1865; height 5'4".

Hunter, Samuel E.—Colonel—F&S—Captured December 17, 1864, at Hollow Tree Gap; sent to Johnson's Island Prison, Ohio; dark hair, hazel eyes, dark complexion, height 5'11"; age 32.

Pennington, William F.—Lieutenant Colonel—F&S—Captured December 17, 1864, at Hollow Tree Gap.

Pullen, Edward J.—Major—F&S—Captured December 17, 1864, at Hollow Tree Gap.

Reid, James—Lake Providence, Louisiana—Captain—Co. D—Captured December 17, 1864, at Franklin, Tennessee; sent to Johnson's Island prison, Ohio; released on taking oath of allegiance, July 25, 1865; age 32; dark hair, hazel eyes, fair complexion, height 5'6".

13TH LOUISIANA INFANTRY

Barrow, Alexander D.—Baton Rouge, Louisiana—2nd Lieutenant—Co. B/G—Captured December 17, 1864, at Franklin, Tennessee; sent to Johnson's Island Prison, Ohio; released upon taking oath of allegiance, June 16, 1865; light hair, blue eyes, florid complexion, height 6'.

Georgy, William—New Orleans, Louisiana—1st Sergeant—Co. E—Captured December 18, 1864, at Franklin, Tennessee; sent to Camp Chase Prison, Ohio; exchanged February 17, 1865; age: 30; black hair, grey eyes, fair complexion, height 5' 9½".

14TH LOUISIANA BATTALION SHARPSHOOTERS

Martin, A.T.—1st Lieutenant—Wounded December 17th, 1864, at Franklin, Tennessee; captured December 18, 1864, at Franklin, Tennessee; died December 28, 1864, in Hospital #1, Nashville, Tennessee.

19TH LOUISIANA INFANTRY

Applewhite, Augustus C.—Bossier Parish, Louisiana—Private—Co. B—Captured December 17, 1864, at Franklin, Tennessee; sent to Camp Douglas Prison, Illinois; released June 18, 1865.

Banton, James C.—Sergeant—Co. B—Captured December 17, 1864, at Franklin, Tennessee; sent to Camp Chase Prison, Ohio; died January 15, 1865; buried: grave #781, Camp Chase Cemetery, Columbus, Ohio.

Hyde, W.J.—Private—Co. C—age 24—Wounded in left leg December 17, 1864; leg was amputated flap; gangrene developed; died November 20, 1865, typhoid fever.

20TH LOUISIANA INFANTRY

Aulfort, George—Private—Co. I—Captured December 17, 1864, at Franklin, Tennessee; sent to Camp Chase Prison, Ohio; released upon taking oath of allegiance, March 31, 1865 CSR.

Austizn, Zerro—Private—Co. K—Captured December 17, 1864, at Franklin, Tennessee; sent to Camp Chase Prison, Ohio.

Blust, Leopold—New Orleans, Louisiana–Musician—Co. B—Captured December 17, 1864, at Franklin, Tennessee; sent to Camp Douglas Prison, Illinois; released upon taking the oath May 12, 1865; light hair, blue eyes, fair complexion, height 5'7".

30TH LOUISIANA INFANTRY

Abbitz aka Albitz, Charles—St. Louis County, Missouri—Private—Co. C—Captured December 17, 1864, at Franklin, Tennessee; sent to Camp Douglas Prison, Illinois; released upon taking oath April 24, 1865; light hair, hazel eyes, fair complexion, height 5' 10 ½".

Back, George—Private—Co. C—Captured December 17, 1864, at Franklin, Tennessee; sent to Camp Douglas Prison, Illinois; died April 27, 1865; buried there.

Bambery, William—Private—Co. B—Killed December 17, 1864, at Franklin, Tennessee.

Barker, Augustus—Iberville Parrish, Louisiana—Private—Co. G—Captured December 17, 1864, at Franklin, Tennessee; sent to Camp Douglas Prison, Illinois; released upon taking oath of allegiance, June 12, 1865; light hair, hazel eyes, fair complexion, height 5'9".

Berra, Mechior—Orleans Parrish, Louisiana—Private—Co. A—Captured December 17, 1864, at Franklin, Tennessee; sent to Camp Chase Prison, Ohio; released upon taking oath of allegiance, May 13, 1865; dark hair, blue eyes, dark complexion, height 5'5".

Bosha, John—Private—Co. E—Captured December 17, 1864, at Franklin, Tennessee.

Boudreau, Louis—Private—Co. B, "St. James Guards"—Captured; sent to Camp Douglas Prison, Illinois; released May 18, 1865, upon taking oath of allegiance.

Dupuis, Joseph C.—Private—Co. A, "Algiers Guards"—Captured; sent to Camp Douglas Prison, Illinois; released June 19, 1865.

Gilbough, Joel—St. Martin, Louisiana—Private—Co. A—Captured December 17, 1864, at Franklin, Tennessee; sent to Camp Chase Prison, Ohio; released upon oath of allegiance, June 12, 1865; dark hair, hazel eyes, dark complexion, height 5'6".

Gravois aka Graves, Peter—Private—Co. A, "Algiers Guards"—Captured; sent to Camp Douglas Prison, Illinois; released June 6, 1865.

Guilbeau aka Gilbough, Joel—Private—Co. A, "Algiers Guards"—Captured; sent to Camp Chase Prison, Ohio; released on oath June 12, 1865.

Labauve, Louis Fenelon—Private—Co. F, "Orleans Guards"—Captured; sent to Camp Douglas Prison, Illinois; released May 17, 1865.

Landry, John H.—New Orleans, Louisiana—Lieutenant—Co. E, "Picket Guards"—Captured; sent to Johnson's Island Prison, Ohio; released June 16, 1865; dark hair, hazel eyes, dark complexion, height 5'6"; age 24.

Landry, Numa—Private—Co. A, "Algiers Guards"—Captured; sent to Camp Douglas Prison, Illinois; released June 19, 1865.

Landry, Uria—Private—Co. A, "Algiers Guards"—Captured.

Meeks, William—Private—Co. D—Captured December 17, 1864, at Franklin, Tennessee; sent to Camp Douglas Prison, Illinois; released June 19, 1865.

Poché, John—Private—Co. E—Captured; sent to Camp Chase Prison, Columbus, Ohio; released upon taking oath of allegiance, May 13, 1865.

Vienne, Lewis G.—New Orleans, Louisiana—Lieutenant—Co. D—Captured December 17, 1864, at Franklin, Tennessee; sent to Johnson's Island Prison, Ohio; released on taking oath of allegiance, June 17, 1865; age 28; dark hair, hazel eyes, dark complexion, height 5'11".

45TH MISSISSIPPI INFANTRY

Butler, Wiley J.—Private—Co. A, "The Duncan Riflemen"—Wounded December 15, 1864, at Nashville, Tennessee; captured there, December 17, 1864; sent to Camp Chase Prison, Ohio; released June 13, 1865.

Cobb, William B.—Sergeant—Co. C, "The Mississippi Rebels of Noxubee County"—Wounded in the right shoulder, November 30, 1864, at Franklin, Tennessee; captured there December 17, 1864; admitted to Hospital #1, Nashville, Tennessee; on April 3, 1865, sent to camp Chase Prison, Ohio; released on taking oath of allegiance June 13, 1865.

Doolittle, William E.—Sergeant—Co. D, "The Choctaw Rough and Readies"—Wounded November 30, 1864, at Franklin, Tennessee; captured there December 17, 1864; sent to Fort Delaware, Delaware; exchanged February 27, 1865.

Hodges, Samuel J.—Sergeant—Co. E, "The McNair Rifles"—Captured as a convalescent, December 17, 1864, at Franklin, Tennessee; admitted to Hospital #1, Nashville, Tennessee; sent to camp Chase Prison, Ohio.

London, A.R.—Private—Co. F, "The Tippah Highlanders"—Captured December 17, 1864, at Franklin, Tennessee; sent to Camp Chase Prison, Ohio; released June 13, 1865.

Miles, James J.—Private—Co. B, "The Insurgents of Itawamba County"—Wounded November 30, 1864, at Franklin, Tennessee; captured there December

17, 1864; on January 6, 1865, sent to Camp Chase Prison, Ohio; released June 13, 1865.

Pittman, H.R.—Private—Co. E, "The McNair Rifles"—Wounded November 30, 1864, at Franklin, Tennessee; captured there, December 17, 1864; sent to camp Chase Prison, Ohio; exchanged from Point Lookout, Maryland, March, 1865.

Spencer, William L.C.—Private—Co. F, "The Tippah Highlanders"— Wounded November 30, 1864, at Franklin, Tennessee; captured there December 17, 1864; sent to Camp Chase Prison, Ohio; sent to Point Lookout, Maryland, and released from there May 13, 1865.

Swindle, Joel—Private—Co. C, "The Mississippi Rebels of Noxubee County"—Captured December 17, 1864, at Franklin, Tennessee; sent to Camp Chase Prison, Ohio; released January 9, 1865.

Thomas, John—Private—Co. D, "The Choctaw Rough and Readies"—Captured December 17, 1864.

Towers, John—Private—Co. D, "The Choctaw Rough and Readies"—Captured December 17, 1864; sent to Camp Chase Prison, Ohio.

Varnado, Felix H.—Color Corporal—Co. E, "The McNair Rifles"—Captured December 17, 1864, at Franklin, Tennessee; sent to Camp Chase Prison, Ohio.

2ND TENNESSEE CAVALRY

Francis, C.C. "Dick"—Private—Co. C—"[H]e was the only member of Company C who was captured"—December 17, 1864, at Holly Tree Gap.

Knott, Tom—Private—Co. B—"Captured" December 17, 1864, at Holly Tree Gap.

McRae, F.M.—Lieutenant—Co. K—"[A]t Holly Tree Gap.... After making a gallant defense—emptying both his revolvers—Lieutenant F.M. McRae, who was in command of Company K, surrendered, and was afterward shot through the right shoulder by a drunken coward."

McRae, T.F.—Private ?—Co. ?—"Was knocked from his horse with a carbine and captured"—December 17, 1864, at Holly Tree Gap.

note: *Tennesseans in the Civil War* lists the following, only: "C.C. Francis, Pvt., Co. C, 22nd Tn. Cav. [Barteau's]"; "Thomas L. Knott, Sgt. Maj., Co. B, 22nd Tn. Cav." ; no "F.M. or T.F. McRae," by that spelling

20TH TENNESSEE CAVALRY

Poindexter, William J.—Private—Co. D—Captured December 17, 1864, at Franklin, Tennessee; sent to Camp Chase Prison, Ohio; died March 15, 1865, of pneumonia; buried there.

47TH TENNESSEE INFANTRY

Norvell, Joseph S.—Private—Co. B—Captured December 17, 1864, at Franklin, Tennessee.

DOUGLAS'S TEXAS BATTERY

Bloomer, Jacob—Private—Captured at West Harpeth.

Harmon, J.T.—Private—Captured at West Harpeth.

Smith, E.W.—Private—Captured at West Harpeth.
Speaker, B.K.—Private—Captured at West Harpeth.
Wilson, W.W.—Private—Captured at West Harpeth.
Williams, Edmond—Private—Wounded and captured at Harpeth.

Federal

7TH ILLINOIS CAVALRY

Cockrell, Royal—Canton, Illinois—Private—Co. K—Killed December 17, 1864, near Franklin, Tennessee.

16TH ILLINOIS CAVALRY

Dilg, Jacob—Private—Co. G—died December 30, 1864, from December 17, 1864, wounds.

9TH INDIANA CAVALRY

Arbuthnot, John—Dearborn County, Indiana—Private-Co. K—mortally wounded at Franklin, Tennessee.

Bristow, James S.—Southport, Indiana—Second Lieutenant—Co. L—Killed at West Harpeth, Tennessee.

Brown, William—Private—Marion County, Indiana—Co. L—Killed at Franklin, Tennessee.

Buskel, Willia—Private—Marion County, Indiana—Co. L—Killed at Franklin, Tennessee.

Hobson, Volney-Captain—Cadiz, Henry County, Indiana—Co. E—Killed beneath the railroad trestle on Liberty Pike, north of Franklin, Tennessee, on the morning of the 17th; buried: Batson Cemetery, Henry County, Indiana.

Lewis, Duane A.—Private—Fortville, Indiana—Co. B—Killed at Hollow Tree Gap.

Macy, Henry B.—Private—Dalton, Indiana—Co. C—Mortally wounded at Franklin, Tennessee; died March 9, 1865, at Nashville, Tennessee.

Parsons, Adrian—Private—Co. I—Severely wounded December 17, 1864, at West Harpeth, Tennessee; admitted to Hospital #8, Nashville, Tennessee.

Ricks, Benjamin F.—Private—Cadiz, Henry County, Indiana—Co. E—Killed at West Harpeth, Tennessee.

Watts, James S.—Private—Hendricks County, Indiana—Co. I—Killed at Franklin, Tennessee; buried: Franklin section, grave #445, Stones River National Cemetery, Murfreesboro, Tennessee.

Wine, J.—Private—Co. C—Wounded in left thigh December 17, 1864; leg was amputated the same day anterior post. flap, by Asst. Surgeon J.R. Culbertson, 10th Indiana Cavalry; discharged May 15, 1865; age 44.

10TH INDIANA CAVALRY

Banta, William J.—Switzerland County, Indiana—Private—Co. D—Captured December 17, 1864.

Ezell, Timothy—Private—Co. E—Killed December 17, 1864.

Howington, Polk—Private—Clarke County, Indiana—Co. E—Mortally wounded no place listed; died at New Albany, Indiana no date listed; buried: section B, grave #288, New Albany National Cemetery, New Albany, Indiana.

Jones, James T.—Gibson County, Indiana—Private—Co. K—Captured; survived the *Sultana*.

Jones, Thomas—Posey County, Indiana—Private—Co. A—Killed December 17, 1864.

Langwell, Malcom—Switzerland County, Indiana—Private—Co. D—Captured December 17, 1864.

Loyd, Henry W.—Gibson County, Indiana—Private—Co. ? ; missing December 17, 1864.

Northerland, Marion—Posey County, Indiana—Private—Co. K—Mortally wounded December 17, 1864; date of death unknown.

Stockings, Chester L.—Private—Pike County, Indiana—Co. F—Killed at Holly Tree Gap, Tennessee.

2ND IOWA CAVALRY

Anderson, William H.H.—Burlington, Illinois—Private—Co. K—Severely wounded at West Harpeth; mustered out June 9, 1865—"William Anderson escaped from a hand to hand encounter with an officer, with the loss of one eye."

Bennett Horace—Okobodji, Illinois—Private—Co. I—Captured at West Harpeth; escaped back to Federals December 18, 1864; mustered out September 19, 1865.

Black, Dominic—Iowa City, Iowa—Private—Co. C—Killed at West Harpeth—"As the contending forces came together, Private Dominic Black, of Company K, ordered the rebel color bearer to surrender; he refused, when Black followed by others, rushed upon him. Just as he was in the act of striking the color bearer down with his saber, one of the color guards shot him through the heart."

Bradfield, Joshua—Epworth, Iowa—Private—Co. I—Killed at West Harpeth.

Coulter, John—Louisa County, Iowa—Private—Co. H—Severely wounded at West Harpeth; mustered out September 19, 1865.

Dale, Joseph—Davenport, Iowa—Private—Co. I—Captured at West Harpeth; mustered out June 8, 1865.

Darlington, George B.—Northfield, Iowa—Private—Co. K—Captured at West Harpeth; mustered out June 7, 1865.

Gardner, Robert—Dallas County, Iowa—Private—Co. D—Captured at West Harpeth; mustered out June 14, 1865.

Givens, James H.—Keokuk County, Iowa—Private—Co. K—Captured at West Harpeth; mustered out August 17, 1865.

Hammitt, Benjamin F.—Cedar Rapids, Iowa—Private—Co. I—Captured at West Harpeth; escaped back to Federals December 18, 1864.

Klein, Theobald—Canton, Iowa–Private—Co. K—Captured at West Harpeth; mustered out June 7, 1865.

Mann, James—Davenport, Iowa—Private—Co. C—Severely wounded; discharged on account of wounds, June 14, 1865.

Margretz, Herman—Ottumwa, Iowa—Private—Co. F—Killed at West Harpeth.

Mason, Edwin D. Big Rock, Iowa—Private—Co. C—Captured at West Harpeth; mustered out September 19, 1865.

Prandy, Patrick—Ireland—Private—Co. M—Captured at West Harpeth; mustered out September 19, 1865.

Rooker, James W.—Rising Sun, Iowa—Private—Co. D—Severely wounded at West Harpeth; discharged on account of wounds, June 21, 1865—"One ball passed through the head of ... J.W. Rooker, of Company D, taking out both of his eyes. Rooker fell a prisoner and was left on the field, after being robbed."

Wynn, Milton B.—Private—Co.—Missing in action December 17, 1865, at West Harpeth.

19TH PENNSYLVANIA CAVALRY

Baker, Samuel—Quarter Master Sergeant—Co. L—Captured at Holly Tree Gap, Tennessee, December 17, 1864.

Blackstone, James—Private—Co. F—Wounded at Franklin, probably Holly Tree Gap, Tennessee, December 17, 1864.

Conkey, Thaddeus S.—Private—Co. D—Killed at Nashville, probably Holly Tree Gap, Tennessee, December 17, 1864.

Dougherty, Kennedy—Private—Co. F—Killed at Nashville, Tennessee, December 17, 1864.

Feehan, John—Private—Co. D—Captured, probably Holly Tree Gap, Tennessee, December 17, 1864; apparently exchanged April 29, 1865; discharged June 5, 1865.

Foster, James F.—Sergeant—Co. M—Captured at Nashville, probably Holly Tree Gap, Tennessee, December 17, 1864.

Harris, James B.—Private—Co. F—Wounded at Nashville, probably Holly Tree Gap, Tennessee, December 17, 1864.

Holhan, Amos J.—Major—F&S—Wounded at Franklin, probably Holly Tree Gap, Tennessee, December 17, 1864.

Hunt, Charles H.—Commissary Sergeant—Co. M—Captured at Nashville, probably Holly Tree Gap, Tennessee, December 17, 1864.

Montgomery, Matthew-Private—Co. C—Mortally wounded at Holly Tree Gap, Tennessee, December 17, 1864; died December 22, 1864; buried: grave #589, section L, Nashville, Tennessee National Cemetery.

Reeder, Frank—Captain—Co. B—Wounded at Franklin, probably Holly Tree Gap, Tennessee, December 17, 1864.

Smith, Norman M.—Adjutant—F&S—Wounded at Franklin, probably Holly Tree Gap, Tennessee, December 17, 1864.

2ND TENNESSEE CAVALRY

James, Arthur—Private—Co. I—Wounded in left ankle December 17, 1864; ball removed; gangrene developed; lower third of leg was amputated circa February 4, 1865, by Asst. Surgeon W.B. Trull, U.S.V.; age 20; died May 16, 1865; buried: section J, grave #1089; Nashville National Cemetery, Nashville, Tennessee.

Sunday, December 18, 1864
Confederate

55TH ALABAMA INFANTRY
   Sisk, Wesley E.—Private—Co. D—Captured December 18, 1864, at Franklin, Tennessee; sent to Camp Chase Prison, Ohio; released upon taking oath of allegiance no date; dark hair, brown eyes, dark complexion, age 24.

45TH MISSISSIPPI INFANTRY
   Boyd, Samuel—Private—Co. K, "The Charlton Rebels"—Wounded December 15, 1864, at Nashville, Tennessee; captured December 18, 1864, at Franklin, Tennessee; admitted to Hospital #1, Nashville, Tennessee; sent to Camp Chase Prison, Ohio; died there March 2, 1865, of pneumonia; buried: grave #1,500 Camp Chase Confederate Cemetery; age 42.
   Hackler, John P.—Private—Co. K, "The Charlton Rebels"—Wounded in left leg, November 30, 1864, at Franklin, Tennessee; captured there December 18, 1864; admitted to hospital in Nashville, Tennessee, where lower third of leg was amputated; sent March 10, 1865, to Camp Chase Prison, Ohio; sent to Point Lookout Prison, Maryland; released on taking oath of allegiance, June 6, 1865.
   Lockey, Amos S.—Private—Co. F, "The Tippah Highlanders"—Wounded November 30, 1864, at Franklin, Tennessee; captured there December 17, 1864; admitted to hospital in Nashville, Tennessee; leg was amputated; died April 27, 1865.
   Read, Joseph D.—Private—Co. K, "The Charlton Rebels"—Wounded November 29, 1864, at Spring Hill, Tennessee; captured there December 18, 1864; leg was amputated; sent to Camp Chase Prison, Ohio; released on taking oath of allegiance June 11, 1865.

Federal

None

Monday, December 19, 1864
Confederate

2ND TENNESSEE CAVALRY
   Cook, Frank—Private—Co. I—"Drowned in Duck River on Hood's Retreat," December 19, 1864.

Federal

1ST ILLINOIS BATTERY
   Shull, W.—Private—1st Illinois Artillery—age 19; Wounded in left forearm on December 19, 1864; arm was amputated the same day by Surgeon I.N. Barnes, 116th Illinois Infantry; discharged July 1, 1865.

Tuesday, December 20, 1864
Confederate

40TH GEORGIA INFANTRY
Phillips, Thomas F.—Sergeant—Co. D—Killed December 20, 1864, at Columbia, Tennessee.

Federal

16TH ILLINOIS CAVALRY
Hefelstein, Frederick—Private—Co. G—drowned in the Duck River, December 20, 1864.

Wednesday, December 21, 1864
Confederate

55TH ALABAMA INFANTRY
Grider, William M.—2nd Lieutenant—Co. F—Wounded and captured December 21, 1864, at Columbia, Tennessee; admitted to hospital at Nashville, Tennessee; sent to Ft. Delaware, Maryland; released June 17, 1865, upon taking oath of allegiance; dark hair, blue eyes, ruddy complexion; height 6'.

14TH LOUISIANA BATTALION SHARPSHOOTERS
Mehan, James—Private—Co. B—Captured December 21, 1864, at Columbia, Tennessee; sent to Camp Chase Prison, Ohio; released upon taking oath of allegiance, March 23, 1865.

Federal

None

Thursday, December 22, 1864
Confederate

55TH ALABAMA INFANTRY
Williams, James T.—Talladega, Alabama–Private—Co. C—Wounded and captured December 22, 1864, at Columbia, Tennessee; admitted to hospital in

Nashville, Tennessee, where he died March 19, 1865, of erysipalis; originally buried in grave #12631, Nashville City Cemetery, Nashville, Tennessee.

9TH ARKANSAS INFANTRY
Beasley, George W.—Private—Co. D—Captured December 22, 1864, at Columbia, Tennessee; sent to Camp Chase Prison, Ohio; released May 15, 1865.
Willeford, Joseph C.—Private—Co. D—Captured December 22, 1864, at Columbia, Tennessee; sent to City Point, Virginia, for exchange; admitted to hospital at Meridian, Mississippi, March 29, 1865.

12TH LOUISIANA INFANTRY
Brewster, Washington—Corporal—Co. I—Captured December 22, 1864, at Columbia, Tennessee; sent to Camp Chase Prison, Ohio; paroled February 25, 1865.

3RD MARYLAND ARTILLERY/STEPHEN'S GEORGIA LIGHT ARTILLERY
Barnes, Theophilus Jackson–Private—Captured December 22, 1864, at Columbia, Tennessee; sent to Camp Chase Prison, Ohio; released June 13, 1865.

Federal

None

Friday, December 23, 1864
Confederate

12TH LOUISIANA INFANTRY
Bridgeman, Thornton—1st Lieutenant—Co. G—Wounded and captured December 23, 1864, at Columbia, Tennessee; admitted to a Nashville hospital; sent to Fort Delaware, Maryland; released January 10, 1865, upon taking oath of allegiance; brown hair, hazel eyes, dark complexion, height 5'8".

Federal

None

Saturday, December 24, 1864
Confederate

17TH ALABAMA INFANTRY
Corley, Andrew B.—Private—Co. C—Captured December 24, 1864, near Columbia, Tennessee; sent to Camp Chase Prison, Ohio; paroled May 5, 1865.

GENERAL NATHAN BEDFORD FORREST'S ESCORT
    Black, Marcus—Private—"Killed near Pulaski," December 24, 1864.

7TH TENNESSEE CAVALRY
    Watkins, H.W.—Lieutenant—Co. A—"Killed at Richland Creek," December 24, 1864.

Federal

None

Sunday, December 25, 1864

Confederate

28TH MISSISSIPPI CAVALRY
    Montgomery, J.G.—2nd Lieutenant—Co. A—"Wounded near Pulaski," December 25, 1864.

45TH MISSISSIPPI INFANTRY
    Causey, Iley L.—Sergeant—Co. E, "The McNair Rifles"—Captured December 25, 1864, at Pulaski, Tennessee; sent to camp Chase Prison, Ohio; died January 16, 1865, of smallpox; buried: grave #788, Camp Chase Confederate Cemetery, Columbus, Ohio.

GENERAL NATHAN BEDFORD FORREST'S ESCORT
    Strickland, William–Private–Forrest's Escort—"Killed at Pulaski," December 25, 1864.

2ND TENNESSEE CAVALRY
    Briley, Elisha–Private–Co. F—"mortally Wounded at Pulaski."

Federal

7TH OHIO INFANTRY
    Danber, Fredrick—Corporal—Co. H—Wounded December 25, 1864, at Pulaski, Tennessee; mustered out May 22, 1865.
    McFarland, Samuel R.W.—Corporal—Co. H—Wounded December 25, 1864, at Pulaski, Tennessee; discharged on account of wounds, June 15, 1865.

4TH TENNESSEE CAVALRY, U.S.

Banner, Oliver—Private—Co. B, 4th Tennessee Cavalry, U.S.— Killed December 25, 1864, at Pulaski, Tennessee; age 24.

Jinkins, John—Private—Co. I—Killed at Pulaski, Tennessee; age 20.

Weedon, John—Private—Co. E, 4th Tennessee Cavalry, U.S.— Wounded at Pulaski, Tennessee; age 45.

Monday, December 26, 1864

Confederate

None

Federal

2ND TENNESSEE CAVALRY, U.S.

Morgan, Russell—Private-Co. D—Killed at Sugar Creek, Tennessee; age 31.

4TH TENNESSEE CAVALRY, U.S.

Darnell, William—Lieutenant-Co. G—Wounded at Sugar Creek, Tennessee; age 34.

Evans, James R.—Private-Co. M—Wounded at Sugar Creek, Tennessee; age 18.

Hoskins, William B.—Private-Co. A—Killed at Sugar Creek, Tennessee; age 26.

Kirby, Dolphus—Private-Co. M—Captured at Sugar Creek, Tennessee; age 39.

Weaver, Anthony—Private-Co. M—Captured at Sugar Creek, Tennessee; age 30.

Winthrop, Charles C.—Private-Co. L—Captured at Sugar Creek, Tennessee; age 18.

Appendix II:
Order of Battle: Confederate Rear Guard and Federal Advance

December 17–20, 1864, from Nashville, Tennessee, South to Columbia, Tennessee

Confederate Rear Guard

Including, but not limited to, elements of the following:

MAJOR GENERAL CARTER LITTLEPAGE STEVENSON'S DIVISION

Colonel Elihu P. Watkins's Brigade
24th Georgia Infantry
36th Georgia Infantry
39th Georgia Infantry
56th Georgia Infantry

Brigadier General Edmund W. Pettus's Brigade
20th Alabama Infantry
23rd Alabama Infantry
30th Alabama Infantry
31st Alabama Infantry
46th Alabama Infantry

MAJOR GENERAL HENRY D. CLAYTON'S DIVISION

Brigadier General Marcellus A. Stovall's Brigade
40th Georgia Infantry
41st Georgia Infantry
42nd Georgia Infantry
43rd Georgia Infantry
52nd Georgia Infantry

Brigadier General Randall L. Gibson's Brigade
1st Louisiana Infantry
4th Louisiana Infantry—Colonel S.E. Hunter, cmdg.—Captured at Hollow Tree Gap
4th Louisiana Battalion
13th Louisiana Infantry—Colonel Francis L. Campbell, cmdg.
14th Louisiana Battalion Sharpshooters—Lieutenant A.T. Martin, cmdg.
16th Louisiana Infantry—Colonel Robert Hume Lindsay, cmdg.; born 1833 in Scotland
19th Louisiana Infantry
20th Louisiana Infantry
25th Louisiana Infantry
30th Louisiana Infantry—Major Arthur Picolet, cmdg.

Brigadier General James Holtzclaw's Brigade
18th Alabama Infantry—Col. Peter Hunley, cmdg.
32nd Alabama Infantry
36th Alabama Infantry
38th Alabama Infantry
58th Alabama Infantry

BLEDSOE'S MISSOURI BATTERY, CSA

MORTON'S TENNESSEE BATTERY, CSA

DOUGLAS'S TEXAS BATTERY, CSA

CONFEDERATE CAVALRY CORPS ARMY OF TENNESSEE—DEC. 1864

MAJOR GENERAL NATHAN BEDFORD FORREST, CMDG.

CHALMER'S DIV—BRIGADIER GENERAL JAMES R. CHALMERS

Rucker's Brigade—Col. Edmund W. Rucker; Lt. Col. Raleigh R. White
7th Alabama Cavalry
5th Mississippi Cavalry
3rd Tennessee Cavalry
7th Tennessee Cavalry
12th Tennessee Cavalry
14th Tennessee Cavalry
15th Tennessee Cavalry

Biffle's Brigade—Colonel Jacob B. Biffle
4th Tennessee Cavalry
9th Tennessee Cavalry
10th Tennessee Cavalry

BUFORD'S DIV.—BRIGADIER GENERAL ABRAM BUFORD

Bell's Brigade—Colonel Tyree H. Bell
2nd/22nd Tennessee Cavalry

19th Tennessee Cavalry
20th Tennessee Cavalry
21st Tennessee Cavalry
Nixon's Tennessee, Cavalry Regiment

Crossland's Brigade—Colonel Edmond Crossland
3rd Kentucky Mounted Infantry
7th Kentucky Mounted Infantry
8th Kentucky Mounted Infantry
12th Kentucky Cavalry
Huey's Kentucky Battalion

JACKSON'S DIV.—BRIGADIER GENERAL WILLIAM H. JACKSON

Armstrong's Brigade—Brigadier General Frank C. Armstrong
1st Mississippi Cavalry
2nd Mississippi Cavalry
28th Mississippi Cavalry
Ballentine's Mississippi Regiment (2nd Partisan Rangers)

Ross's Brigade—Brigadier General Lawrence S. Ross
3rd Texas Cavalry
6th Texas Cavalry
9th Texas Cavalry
27th Texas Cavalry
1st Texas Legion

Federal Advance

FIRST DIVISION, BRIGADIER GENERAL EDWARD M. MCCOOK, CMDG.

First Brigade; Brigadier General John T. Croxton, cmdg.
8th Iowa Cavalry—Colonel Joseph B. Dorr, cmdg.
4th Kentucky Mounted Infantry—Colonel Robert M. Kelly, cmdg.
2nd Michigan Cavalry—Lieut. Colonel Benjamin Smith, cmdg.
1st Tennessee Cavalry—Lieut. Colonel Calvin M. Dyer, cmdg.

First Division Artillery
Chicago Board of Trade Battery Robinson's

FIFTH DIVISION, BRIGADIER GENERAL EDWARD HATCH, CMDG.

First Brigade, Colonel Robert R. Stewart, cmdg.
3rd Illinois Cavalry—Lieut. Colonel Robert H. Carnahan, cmdg.
11th Indiana Cavalry—Lieut. Colonel Abram Sharra, cmdg.
12th Missouri Cavalry—Lieut. Colonel Robert H. Brown, cmdg.
10th Tennessee Cavalry—Major William P. Story, cmdg.

SECOND BRIGADE, COLONEL DATUS COON, CMDG.
6th Illinois Cavalry—Lieut. Colonel John Lynch, cmdg.

7th Illinois Cavalry—Major John M. Graham, cmdg.
9th Illinois Cavalry—Captain Joseph W. Harper, cmdg.
2nd Iowa Cavalry—Major Charles C. Horton, cmdg.
12th Tennessee Cavalry—Colonel George Spaulding, cmdg.

Fifth Division Artillery
1st Illinois Battery "I" McCartney

SIXTH DIVISION, BRIGADIER GENERAL RICHARD W. JOHNSON, CMDG.

First Brigade, Colonel Thomas J. Harrison, cmdg.
16th Illinois Cavalry—Major Charles H. Beeres, cmdg.
5th Iowa Cavalry—Major J. Morris Young, cmdg.
7th Ohio Cavalry—Colonel Israel Garrard, cmdg.

SECOND BRIGADE, COLONEL JAMES BIDDLE, CMDG.
14th Illinois Cavalry—Major Francis M. Davidson, cmdg.
6th Indiana Cavalry—Major Jacob S. Stephens, cmdg.
8th Michigan Cavalry—Lieut. Colonel Grover S. Wormer, cmdg.

Sixth Division Artillery
4th U.S. Artillery, Battery "I"

SEVENTH DIVISION, BRIGADIER GENERAL JOSEPH F. KNIPE, CMDG.

First Brigade, Brevet Brigadier General John H. Hammond, cmdg.
9th Indiana Cavalry—Colonel George W. Jackson, cmdg., wounded by
falling horse at West Harpeth
10th Indiana Cavalry
19th Pennsylvania Cavalry
2nd Tennessee Cavalry—Colonel Daniel Ray, cmdg.
4th Tennessee Cavalry—Colonel R.M. Edwards, cmdg.

Appendix III:
Battle Flags Captured
on the Retreat

Saturday, December 17

Hollow Tree Gap (approximately 0800)

CONFEDERATE

Fourth and Thirtieth Louisiana Infantry Battle Flags: Gibson's Brigade, Clayton's Division:

"[C]ame up with the enemy at Hollow Tree Gap, four or five miles north of Franklin. After a sharp fight, in which Hammond's brigade with a part of his command passed around the enemy's right and struck them in the flank, the position was handsomely carried. Three colors and 413 prisoners, including 2 colonels and 2 lieutenant colonels, were captured" (No. 194, Reports of Bvt. Major General James H. Wilson, USA, commanding Cavalry Corps, Military Division of the Mississippi, of operations October 24, 1864–February 1, 1865, *Official Records of the War of the Rebellion*, Series I, Volume XLV, Part I, p. 565).

The *Nashville Journal* of the 24th is full of the Yankee accounts about Hood's reverse. It says: ["]It is said that, in passing through Franklin, the rebels gutted all the stores and a number of private residences. In Maury County they have been conscripting everybody able to go into the army, and confiscating the property of all who had fled the conscription. It is thought they will make a free use of whatever may be in the stores of Columbia, now that they have to leave. A citizen of Columbia informs us that nearly all the mills in Maury County had been burned by the Federals when they were evacuating that region, and when the rebels have left the county the citizens will find themselves poorer by several millions of dollars. Gen. James F. Knipe, of the Seventh Cavalry Division, made a lucky hit on Saturday afternoon near Brentwood, capturing two flags, belonging to the Fourth and Thirtieth Louisiana Cavalry [Infantry], together with about two hundred and fifty prisoners, including twenty commissioned officers, two brigade musicians, and two sets of musical instruments—one of silver and the other of brass. The flag of the Thirtieth Louisiana was faded and torn, red cotton ground, with blue cross, and twelve silver bullion stars on the cross. That of the Fourth Louisiana commanded by Colonel Hunter, who was also captured is a magnificent one. The ground is of red bunting, with a cross made of heavy blue silk, the border of yellow twilled silk, twelve gold stars being upon the cross. This flag bears the following inscription: '*Jackson, Port Hudson, Baton Rouge, and Shiloh*'" [*Charleston (SC) Mercury*, January 4, 1865, p. 1, c. 3].

"Part of the Tenth Indiana Cavalry, under Lieutenant-Colonel Gresham, captured in this movement 2 flags, 2 colonels, 1 major, a number of line officers and 110 enlisted men, mostly Louisiana troops" (No. 204, Report of Bvt. Brig. Gen. John H. Hammond, commanding First Brigade, Seventh Division, of operations December 15–27, 1864, *Official Records of the War of the Rebellion*, Series I, Volume XLV, Part I, p. 607).

1 Nondescript Confederate Flag:
"The regiments claim as follows: "[*]Nineteenth Pennsylvania Cavalry, 242 enlisted men prisoners and 1 color..." (No. 204, Report of Bvt. Brig. Gen. John H. Hammond, commanding First Brigade, Seventh Division, of operations December 15–27, 1864, *Official Records of the War of the Rebellion*, Series I, Volume XLV, Part I, page 608).

(*The researcher of this appendix ascribes the Nineteenth Pennsylvania Cavalry as having captured this flag at Hollow Tree Gap, as that is the battle in which they were most directly engaged and thus where they most likely were to have obtained it. Still, this is conjecture on the researcher's part, and is hereby noted as such.)

Franklin

CONFEDERATE

2 Nondescript Confederate Flags:
"The enemy having retreated [from Hollow Tree Gap] we followed rapidly, the Ninth Indiana in advance, to near Franklin, and drove the enemy across the river into the town, capturing, it is reported, 2 stand of colors and near 200 prisoners" (No. 204, Report of Bvt. Brig. Gen. John H. Hammond, commanding First Brigade, Seventh Division, of operations December 15–27, 1864, *Official Records of the War of the Rebellion*, Series I, Volume XLV, Part I, p. 607).

West Harpeth (just prior to sunset, approximately 1630)

FEDERAL

9th Indiana Cavalry Battle Flag: Hammond's First Brigade; Knipes' Seventh Division:
"Color Sergeant Ricks, of Company E, a noble boy, was killed and, in the darkness, the colors were lost" (*Ninth Cavalry: One Hundred and Twenty-first Regiment Indiana Volunteers*, Daniel Comstock, 1890).

Confederate

1 Nondescript flag belonging to Ross's Texas Brigade: Jackson's Division:
"On reaching and driving in the rebels left the Second Iowa [Cavalry] pressed its way around to their rear, when a hand-to-hand fight ensued, resulting in the capture of one stand of colors and several prisoners. In this engagement Sergt. John Coulter, Corpl. A.R. Heck, and Private Black, of Company K, captured and brought off a stand of division colors, after which Private Black and Corpl. A.R. Heck were killed and [*]Sergt. Coulter was severely wounded. The sergeant, however, succeeded in bringing away the rebel standard" (No. 197—Report of Col. Datus E. Coon, Second Iowa Cavalry, commanding Second Brigade, of operations September 30, 1864–January 15, 1865, *Official Records of the War of the Rebellion*, Series I, Volume XLV, Part I, p. 592).

"In this struggle, which for fierceness exceeded any the regiment ever engaged in, Company 'L,' Lieut. Crawford commanding, and Company 'K,' [*]Serg't. Coulter commanding, were the principle actors in a conflict over the colors of Ross' rebel brigade. As the contending forces came together, Private Dominic Black, of company 'K,' ordered the rebel color bearer to surrender; he refused, when Black, followed by others rushed upon him. Just as he was in the act of striking the color bearer down with his saber, one of the color guard shot him through the heart. Serg't. Coulter then seized the flag, wrenching it from the hands of the bearer; the moment Coulter got possession of the flag, he was shot through the shoulder by a rebel not three steps distant; through severely wounded he succeeded in escaping with the prize" (*History of the Second Iowa Cavalry*, Sergeant Lyman B. Pierce, former regimental color bearer, 1865).

"The colors of Ross' rebel brigade were captured by the Second Iowa Cavalry. First Sergeant Coulter, Company K, Second Iowa Cavalry, brought off the colors after a desperate fight, in which he was wounded in the shoulder. Around the flag and within a few feet of where it was captured seven rebels lay dead, as well as two Federal soldiers of the Second Iowa Cavalry, to attest the desperate nature of the conflict" (No 198, Report of Lieut. Sidney O. Roberts, Acting Provost-Marshall, of operations December 15–16, 1864, *Official Records of the War of the Rebellion*, Series I, Volume XLV, Part I, pp. 595–596).

[*Sergeant John Coulter received no Congressional Medal of Honor for this action.]

Sunday, December 18

None documented as captured.

Monday, December 19

None documented as captured.

Tuesday, December 20

None documented as captured.

Wednesday, December 21

None documented as captured.

Thursday, December 22

None documented as captured.

Friday, December 23

None documented as captured.

Saturday, December 24

CONFEDERATE

1 Nondescript guidon W.D. #210–193 belonging to Chalmers' Division:
This flag was Captured at Richland Creek, Giles County, Tennessee, by Corporal Harrison Collins, Co. A, 1st Tennessee Cavalry, who was awarded the Congressional Medal of Honor for doing so ("The Returned Battle Flags," presented to the Confederate veterans at their reunion, Louisville, Kentucky, June 14, 1905, with the compliments of the Passenger Department, "Cotton Belt Route" Railroad Company, p. 19).

Sunday, December 25

CONFEDERATE

HDQRS. FIRST BRIGADE, FIRST CAVALRY DIVISION
Near Richland Creek, December 25, 1864
Lieutenant Col. A.J. Alexander,
Chief of Staff, Cavalry Corps:
Colonel:

I have the honor to forward herewith a rebel battle-flag [guidon] Captured from Chalmers' division yesterday evening. The capture was made by [*]Corpl. Harrison

Collins, Company A, First Tennessee Cavalry. The corporal saw the rebel standard bearer, under the direction of a rebel major, trying to rally his men. He determined to have the flag; led a charge, Killed the major, routed his men, and secured the flag.

I am, colonel, very respectfully, your obedient servant,
John T. Croxton,
Brigadier General, Commanding [Addenda to No. 195, Report of Brig. Gen. John T. Croxton, USA, commanding First Brigade, First Division, of operations October 24, 1864–January 14, 1865, *Official Records of the War of the Rebellion*, Series I, Volume XLV, Part I, page 574].

Collins, Harrison—Corporal—Co. A, 1st Tennessee Cavalry Regt.; First Brigade Croxton's; First Division McCook's; Wilson's Cavalry Corps.

Born: March 10, 1834, Hawkins County, Tennessee.

Citation: Collins Captured Chalmer's Division Flag guidon; W.D. #210–193, near Richland Creek, Giles County, Tennessee, December 24, 1864; date of Congressional Medal of Honor issue: February 24, 1865.

Died: December 25, 1890; buried: Springfield National Cemetery, Springfield, Greene County, Missouri.

Monday, December 26

None documented as captured.

Appendix IV:
Biographical Sketches

Stephen Dill Lee

A native South Carolinian and West Point graduate in the class of 1854, S.D. Lee, a professional artillerist, entered Confederate service as an officer of artillery. By the late summer of 1863 he had received promotion to that of major general, commanding the Confederate cavalry of the Department of Mississippi, Alabama, West Tennessee, and East Louisiana. The following year Lee was again promoted, overseeing Hood's old infantry corps as a Lt. General, the youngest officer of that rank in the Confederate army.

Along with his other accomplishments, General Lee is to be particularly credited for his vital role in commanding the rear guard action of the Army of Tennessee during the traumatic first phase of its retreat from Nashville. Lee's courageous leadership in galvanizing the scattered ranks of fleeing Confederates after the Union breakthrough, combined with the formation of an effective rear guard during the initial rounds of conflict covering the army's retreat, were actions that may well have saved the army from capitulation and defeat. Lee's bold shout of command rallying the men in the face of certain disaster was doubtless remembered by many a veteran as the moment when the tide turned from near panic to stability and resolve.

After the conclusion of hostilities in 1865, Lee returned to his home state of Mississippi, serving as state senator and member of the Mississippi constitutional convention of 1890, as well as holding the presidency of Mississippi Agricultural and Mechanical College for a number of years. S.D. Lee is most notably remembered as an honored spokesman for post–Confederate affairs and a guardian of historical accuracy of Southern history.

Stephen D. Lee passed from this life on May 28, 1908, in Vicksburg, Mississippi, at the age of 75, and was buried in the city of Columbus, Mississippi.

Nathan Bedford Forrest

Tall, quiet, and possessing an imposing presence, Nathan Bedford Forrest, the Confederacy's most fearsome and ingenious cavalry officer, stands foremost among the few military prodigies generated by the war.

Unencumbered with formal military training, Forrest moved freely and instinctively possessd as much and at times more inherent knowledge of military strategy and tactics as his well-trained contemporaries. Uniquely capable of accurately analyzing and interpreting ongoing battlefield developments, Forrest quickly earned the admiration of the Confederate army and a formidable reputation for military skill, cunning, and intensely aggressive exploits among his enemies. Bold, unstoppable, and unyielding in resolution, his sudden presence on the field was certain to produce inspiration and dread, mingled with a definite sense of sober apprehension. He was "a man of few words and intense action," as recorded in the annals of Confederate military history.

Following hard on the heels of numerous victories, in late 1864 Forrest's cavalry linked up with Hood's army fighting through the battles of the Tennessee Campaign. His role as commander of Hood's rear guard from Columbia, Tennessee, to the army's crossing of the Tennessee River was a major factor in the survival of the Confederate army.

John Bell Hood

A graduate of West Point Military Academy in the class of 1853, John Bell Hood is universally recognized as a bold and courageous fighter. Possessing a rugged physique and endowed with a handsome appearance, Hood's friendly, open demeanor attracted the admiration of a wide range of personal acquaintances.

Following a rapid series of promotions in the early years of the war during his service in the Army of Northern Virginia, on July 18, 1864, Hood was promoted to the command of the Army of Tennessee as a full general with temporary rank. Upon taking command, Hood was entrusted with the responsibility of protecting Atlanta from military occupation by driving the Federal forces of W.T. Sherman out of Georgia. By September of that year Hood's attempt to halt Sherman's advance on Atlanta had failed, leaving Georgia and the Carolinas open to Federal depredations. As a bait to lure the Federal army out of Southern territory Hood embarked upon a bold maneuver. With the consensus of his superiors, the Confederate commander marched his army northwest into Tennessee, where he was eventually repulsed at the battles of Franklin and Nashville.

Following the failed Tennessee Campaign and the arduous retreat to Alabama, Hood was relieved of command at his own request in January 1865, surrendering to the Federal forces in Natchez, Mississippi, the following May.

At war's end General Hood moved to New Orleans, where on August 30, 1879, he died of yellow fever. His memoirs, *Advance and Retreat: Personal Experiences in the United States and Confederate States Armies,* is his account of his military career in both armies.

Edward Cary Walthall

Edward C. Walthall was a Confederate officer of well-earned distinction. Subsequent to a continual stream of promotions, and prevailing through some of the most intense fighting of the war including an effort of "desperate resistance" as noted by Confederate commander Braxton Bragg at Lookout Mountain in the fall of 1863, Walthall had proven himself a worthy opponent to Federal military aggression. By the summer of 1864 he had risen to the rank of major general. Throughout the successive battles for Atlanta, North Georgia, and Tennessee, Walthall's involvement was significant, particularly in the retreat from Nashville in the winter of 1864, where, in concert with Forrest, his role in covering the army's withdrawal to the Tennessee River rendered an invaluable service.

Following the army's retreat into Alabama, Walthall accompanied the remnant of the Army of Tennessee's fighting force into North Carolina for its final round of warfare. Paroled in Greensboro, North Carolina on May 1, 1865, Walthall returned to practice law in his home state of Mississippi, where he served as U.S. senator from 1885 until his death in 1898.

Edward Hatch

Edward Hatch, brigadier general of the 5th Division of Wilson's vast cavalry corps of 1864 was indefatigable. Throughout the long weeks of Federal resistance to Hood's invasion of Tennessee, Hatch's division could be found pressing forward the colors. Aggressive and unrelenting, it seemed that nothing could hold him in check. Frigid temperatures, strong enemy fortifications, swollen rivers, downed bridges, hand-to-hand combat in pitch darkness, or lack of supplies—none of this daunted him. From the breakthrough of the Confederate lines to the final hours of Federal pursuit of Hood's forces, Hatch's 5th Division was in the forefront of the action.

A characteristic description of his fortitude is contained in the following quotation regarding the Federal charge against the far left of the Confederate line on the afternoon of December 16, 1864, at Nashville, Tennessee:

> While McMillen's brigade was preparing for this wonderful charge [upon the Confederate left], Hatch's division of cavalry, dismounted, had also pushed its way through the woods, and had gained the tops of two hills that commanded the rear of the enemy's works. Here, with incredible labor, they had dragged, by hand, two pieces of Artillery, and, just as McMillen began his charge, these opened on the hill where Bate was, up the opposite slope of which the infantry were scrambling. At the same time Coon's brigade of Hatch's division with resounding cheers charged upon the enemy and poured such volleys of musketry from their repeating rifles as I have never heard equaled. Thus beset on both sides, Bate's people broke out of the works, and ran down the hill [*Battles and Leaders*, vol. 4, part 2, pp. 463–464].

Hatch's role in the subsequent retreat is no less significant. Following the fierce night fighting at West Harpeth, where Hatch's 5th Division was heavily involved, General Wilson summed up his estimation of Edward Hatch in a single line: "Hatch is a brick!" he declared.

James Harrison Wilson

James Harrison Wilson, a West Point graduate, was an energetic, active man, evidenced by a notable military career spanning several decades. Devoted to the Union and the army that fought to preserve it, throughout the early years of the war Wilson was awarded various responsibilities including an appointment as member of Grant's staff during the Vicksburg Campaign; as aide-de-camp to McClellan during the Peninsula Campaign; as Federal cavalry commander under Sheridan and Sherman; and finally in an independent capacity as chief of cavalry in "absolute command" of the "Cavalry Corps of the Military Division of the Mississippi," an amalgamation of the combined cavalry forces of the three branches of the Federal army then operating in the Western Theatre of operations. In the latter months of 1864 Wilson would utilize "all the mounted forces of the three armies" under his command to their utmost capacity, playing the decisive role in the Federal advance and breakthrough of the Confederate left during the second day of the Battle of Nashville, in addition to subsequent events of the following two weeks in pursuit of Hood's army. Throughout the long retreat of Hood's forces from the slopes of the Confederate battle line on the hills of Nashville, Wilson's immense cavalry corps, numbering some 12,000 mounted troopers, would be called upon to exert every ounce of strength and resilience required to pursue and overtake the retreating ranks of Hood's battered army before they could make good their escape over the Tennessee River.

If the Union army possessed the kind of cavalry officer endowed with the necessary military skill, determination, and qualifications to accomplish such a task, it would be found in Major General James H. Wilson, chief of cavalry, in overall command of the vast mounted forces of the Cavalry Corps of the Military Division of the Mississippi.

George Henry Thomas

George Henry Thomas, a graduate of the U.S. Military Academy at West Point in the class of 1840, was born on a family plantation in Southampton County, Virginia. A veteran of the war with Mexico, Thomas also rose to become an instructor of cavalry and artillery at West Point from 1851 to 1854 under the watchful eye of the academy superintendent, Lt. Col. Robert E. Lee.

With the outbreak of civil war in 1861 Thomas made a bold decision, one that would profoundly affect his life, legacy, and military career. Against the advice of family and friends, Thomas turned his back on his native state, choosing rather to remain loyal to the Union than align himself with the secessionist movement. Tough, disciplined, and methodical to the point of agonizing slowness, "Old Slow Trot" proved his worth in the heat of battle. Commissioned a brigadier general in 1862, Thomas played an active role in the battles of Stones River and Chickamauga in September of 1863, where his stubborn refusal to abandon the field in the face of an overpowering Confederate assault gained him the reputation as the Rock of Chickamauga.

As the commander of the Army of the Cumberland in November of that year, Thomas achieved greater acclaim in the Battle of Chattanooga, followed by influential roles in the Atlanta and Tennessee campaigns of 1864, including the Confederate defeat at Nashville and the fiercely aggressive pursuit of Hood's fleeing army. Following the war, from 1865 to 1869 Thomas occupied important administrative positions in Tennessee and Kentucky. In June of 1869 he was assigned oversight of the Military Division of the Pacific, located in San Francisco, California, where he died of a stroke in 1870.

Appendix V:
Medal of Honor Recipients

December 1864, Middle Tennessee

Beaumont, Eugene Beauharnais—Lieutenant and A.A.G., 4th U.S. Cavalry; Wilson's Cavalry Corps; born: August 2, 1837, Luzerne County, Pennsylvania.

Graduated: Class of 1861; USMA Citation: On December 17, 1864, at West Harpeth, Tennessee, he obtained permission from Corps commander to advance upon the enemy's position with the 4th U.S. Cavalry, of which he was a lieutenant; his attack upon a battery, dispersed the enemy and captured the guns.

Date of issue: March 30, 1898.

Died: August 17, 1916, Harvey's Lake, Pennsylvania; buried: Hollenbeck Cemetery, Wilkes-Barre, Pennsylvania.

Eugene Beauharnais Beaumont, United States Cavalry officer and the son of Andrew and Julia Colt Beaumont, was born in Wilkes-Barre, Luzerne County, Pennsylvania, on August 2, 1837, and was appointed to the United States Military Academy at West Point on July 1, 1856. His father had served in the United States Congress from 1832 to 1836 and was descended from a line of *Mayflower* colonists. His classmates included Confederate major general Thomas L. Rosser of Texas. Beaumont graduated thirty-second in his class and was commissioned a second lieutenant in the First United States Cavalry on May 6, 1861. From then through June he drilled volunteer troops in Washington, D.C., and participated in the battle of First Manassas, or Bull Run, as a volunteer aide-de-camp to Col. Ambrose E. Burnside in the First Cavalry.

After transfer to the Fourth United States Cavalry on August 3, 1861, he served as acting adjutant general of the regiment. He was promoted to first lieutenant on September 14, 1861, and on February 1, 1862, was assigned as aide-de-camp to Gen. John Sedgwick. In this capacity he took part in guarding the upper Potomac River and was engaged in the Peninsular campaign from March through May of 1862. He was posted as aide-de-camp to Gen. Henry W. Halleck on August 7, 1862, but was promoted to captain in the volunteer army and returned to Sedgwick's staff on May 13, 1863. Beaumont served in the Rappahannock campaign with the Army of the Potomac in the spring of 1863 and in the Gettysburg cam-

227

paign in July. He was brevetted to captain in the regular army on November 7, 1863, for "gallant and meritorious service" in the battle of Rappahannock Station, Virginia. After fighting in the battles of the Wilderness and Spotsylvania, where General Sedgwick was killed in May 1864, Beaumont was transferred as aide-de-camp to Gen. James H. Wilson. He served in the Petersburg campaign and in the Shenandoah Valley in the summer of 1864 before transferring with Wilson on October 1 to the cavalry corps of the Army of the Mississippi, where he served as assistant adjutant general.

On October 20 he was promoted to major of volunteers. He subsequently saw action in the battle of Nashville December 1864 and the battle of Harpeth River, Tennessee December 17, 1864. For his performance at Harpeth River he was awarded a Medal of Honor on March 30, 1898. Beaumont was brevetted lieutenant colonel of volunteers on March 13, 1865, for "gallant and meritorious service" during the pursuit of John Bell Hood's army in Tennessee. On April 2, 1865, his attack on the Confederate breastworks at Selma, Alabama, won him a brevet to major in the regular army and to colonel of volunteers for "gallant and distinguished service" as well as a second Medal of Honor. When Confederate president Jefferson Davis was captured in Georgia, he was placed in Beaumont's charge.

At the end of the war Beaumont was mustered out of the volunteer army, on March 19, 1866. He retained his prewar rank in the regular army and was advanced to captain of the Fourth Cavalry on July 25, 1865. He commanded Troop A, which garrisoned San Antonio from April through October 1866, and served at Camp Sheridan, Texas, in November and December. The following months saw him at Fredericksburg, Fort Mason, Fort Chadbourne, and Fort McKavett. After a brief leave of absence he returned to the regiment in May 1869 as commander of the garrison at Lampasas. After recruiting service in 1871 and 1872, he was stationed at Fort Richardson and Fort Clark in 1873 and 1874. On May 18, 1873, he took part in Col. Ranald S. Mackenzie's raid on Kickapoo and Lipan villages at Remolino, Mexico. When Beaumont observed that his officers and men would be "justified in refusing to obey your orders, which you now admit as being illegal, and exposing them to such peril," Mackenzie replied that he would have any officer or man shot who refused to follow him across the Rio Grande. From August 18 through December 29, 1874, Beaumont accompanied Mackenzie on his expedition into Indian Territory after the Warren Wagontrain Raid, and on September 28, 1874, he commanded the advance battalion that attacked Quanah Parker's Comanche encampment in the battle of Palo Duro Canyon.

On March 1, 1875, Beaumont was appointed assistant instructor at the United States Military Academy, where he taught cavalry tactics until August 1879. He was promoted to major on November 12, 1879, and subsequently served in Indian Territory, Colorado, New Mexico, Arizona, and Kansas. On December 24, 1888, he was appointed acting inspector general of Texas, a post he held until 1892, when he was promoted to lieutenant colonel of the Third United States Cavalry. Beaumont retired from active service on May 16, 1892, and settled in Wilkes-Barre, Pennsylvania.

He was married to Margaret Rutter on September 18, 1861. She died on April 22, 1879, and he married Maria Lindsley Orton on December 20, 1883. After the death of his second wife on November 19, 1901, he married her sister, Stella S. Orton Rushing, in 1905. Beaumont was the father of four children. According to Robert Goldthwaite Carter, an officer in his regiment, Beaumont was "one of the finest types of an 'all around,' efficient" cavalry officer in the army. "With his jet black hair and moustache, soldier's slouch hat, riding pants tucked into his boots, pistols in his belt, and off-hand soldierly way of putting things," Beaumont "favorably impressed" the men of his troop. He died at Harvey's Lake, Pennsylvania, on August 17, 1916 (Bibliography: Robert G. Carter, *On the Border with Mackenzie, or Winning West Texas from the Comanches* Washington: Eynon, 1935; Francis B. Heitman, *Historical Register and Dictionary of the United States Army*, 2 vols., Washington: GPO, 1903; rpt., Urbana: University of Illinois Press, 1965).

Hedges, Joseph S.—1st Lieutenant—Co. ?, 4th U.S. Cavalry Regt.

Born: June 12, 1836, Mansfield, Richland County, Ohio.

Citation: At the head of his regiment, Hedges charged a field battery with strong infantry supports, broke the enemy's line and, with other mounted troops, captured three guns and many prisoners, December 17, 1864, at West Harpeth, Tennessee; Date of issue: April 5, 1898.

Died: August 12, 1910; buried: Mansfield City Cemetery, Mansfield, Richland County, Ohio.

Collins, Harrison—Corporal—Co. A, 1st Tennessee Cavalry Regt.; First Brigade Croxton's; First Division McCook's; Wilson's Cavalry Corps.

Born: March 10, 1834, Hawkins County, Tennessee.

Citation: Collins captured Chalmer's Division Flag guidon, near Richland Creek, Giles County, Tennessee, December 24, 1864; Date of issue: February 24, 1865.

Died: December 25, 1890; buried: Springfield National Cemetery, Springfield, Greene County, Missouri.

Appendix VI:
Voices from the Past

Our rear guard was engaged all the time and met him the enemy with the same unflinching courage shown in attacking him at the Battle of Franklin. The men were distressed by hunger and exhaustion. Bloody foot tracks in the frozen snow and upon the icy roads were to be seen in many places. Yet, like Napoleon's Old Guard on the retreat from Moscow, they presented a front for fight at all times. The weather was not as severe as a Russian winter, it is true, but the hardships our poor fellows had to endure were similar, because they were so poorly clad and fed. The patriotism of the Confederate soldier can never be doubted by anyone familiar with the horrors of the retreat. All his troubles would end if he were to fall out of the ranks and allow himself to be taken. The Federals would clothe him, feed him, administer the oath of loyalty or royalty, as we used to call it, and send him to his home. In fact, many a man marched wearily along within sight of his home. No; he would rather die than desert his flag. Those who were taken fell overcome by fatigue and hunger. After many days of hardships and nights of suffering, the command reached Bainbridge and recrossed the Tennessee River. At this point the enemy abandoned the pursuit, and Hood and his suffering men proceeded on their way unmolested ["Missourians in Battle of Franklin," by Captain Joseph Boyce, formerly of the 1st/4th Missouri Infantry Consolidated, CSA, Volume 24, no. 3 March 1916].

February 28, 1865: "[A]t the depot Fri. evening was the box containing remains of H.B. Macy, Co. C, 9th In. Cavalry ... [who] was shot through the lungs at Franklin, Tenn. December 17, 1864 and died ... [and] was brother of Lewis Macy of Hagerstown and Dr. Jesse Macy of Knightstown" *Indiana True Democrat*, Centreville, February 28, 1865.

The invasion of Tennessee, the final, grand attempt of aggressive military action by the Southern Confederacy had ended in bitter defeat. There would be no threat of a victorious Rebel army advancing on the Ohio River, no Confederate battle flags waving over Northern cities. The battle of Nashville had decided otherwise.

Hood had risked all, and lost. His only hope after so thorough a defeat was to survive as an army, to reach the safety of crossing the Tennessee River before being cut off, Captured, destroyed, or a combination of all the above.

The ten day period of Federal pursuit of Hood's army following in the wake of the Confederate defeat at Nashville remains a wholly unique drama in the history of the American Civil War; a matchless spectacle of tragedy, courage, and punishing fortitude in the face of the most trying experiences our men in arms have ever had to encounter and overcome ["Great Battles of the Civil War," by the editors of *Civil War Times Illustrated*, statement by Stanley Horn, p. 506]

The winter of 1864–5 was the coldest that had been known for many years. The ground was frozen and rough, and our soldiers were poorly clad, while many, yes, very many, were entirely barefooted. Our wagon trains had either gone on, we knew not whither, or had been left behind.

Everything and nature, too, seemed to be working against us. Even the keen, cutting air that whistled through our tattered clothes and over our poorly covered heads, seemed to lash us in its fury. The floods of waters that had overflowed their banks, seemed to laugh at our calamity, and to mock us in our misfortunes. All along the route were weary and footsore soldiers. The citizens seemed to shrink and hide from us as we approached them. And, to cap the climax, Tennessee River was overflowing its banks, and several Federal gunboats were anchored just below Mussel Shoals, firing at us while crossing.

The once proud Army of Tennessee had degenerated to a mob. We were pinched by hunger and cold. The rains, and sleet, and snow never ceased falling from the winter sky, while the winds pierced the old, ragged, grayback Rebel soldier to his very marrow. The clothing of many were hanging around them in shreds of rags and tatters, while an old slouched hat covered their frozen ears. Some were on old, rawboned horses, without saddles…. [O]ur country is gone, our cause is lost [Sam Watkins; Co. Aytach, *A Side Show of the Big Show,* chapter 16].

Alas, for Hood!

Chapter Notes

Preface

1. *Official Records of the War of the Rebellion*, Series I, Part II, Vol. XLV, p. 653.
2. "Evolution of the American Cavalry," *Photographic History of the Civil War*, Vol. IV, pp. 19–21.
3. Job 39:19–25, *The Holy Bible*.

Introduction

1. *OR*, Series I, Part II, Vol. XLV, pp. 639–640.
2. *OR*, Series I, Part I, Vol. XLV, p. 650.
3. Matthew Forney Steele, *American Campaigns*, Vol. I, p. 561.
4. Robert Underwood Johnson and Clarence Clough Buel, eds., *Battles and Leaders of the Civil War*, Vol. IV, pp. 425–427.
5. Robert Underwood Johnson and Clarence Clough Buel, eds., *Battles and Leaders of the Civil War*, Vol. IV, p. 441.
6. *OR*, Series I, Part II, Vol. XLV, p. 143.
7. *OR*, Series I, Part II, Vol. XLV, p. 155.

Chapter 1

1. J.A. Dozier, *Confederate Veteran*, Vol. XVI, No. 4.
2. *OR*, Series I, Part I, Vol. XLV, p. 747.
3. *OR*, Series I, Part I, Vol. XLV, p. 673.
4. Rev. Edgar W. Jones, "18th AL. Inf. Reg.," *The Jones Valley Times*, 1905.
5. *OR*, Series I, Part I, Vol. XLV, p. 128.
6. *Confederate Military History*, Vol. VIII, Ch. X, p. 163.
7. *OR*, Series I, Part I, Vol. XLV, p. 154.
8. *OR*, Series I, Part I, Vol. XLV, p. 503.

9. *OR*, Series I, Part I, Vol. XLV, p. 37.
10. *OR*, Series I, Part I, Vol. XLV, p. 561.
11. *OR*, Series I, Part I, Vol. XLV, p. 688.
12. *OR*, Series I, Part I, Vol. XLV, pp. 688–689.
13. *OR*, Series I, Part I, Vol. XLV, p. 695.
14. J.A. Dozier, *Confederate Veteran*, Vol. XVI, No. 4.
15. Rev. Edgar W. Jones "18th AL. Inf. Reg.," *The Jones Valley Times*, 1905.
16. *OR*, Series I, Part I, Vol. XLV, p. 705.
17. *OR*, Series I, Part I, Vol. XLV, p. 40.
18. *OR*, Series I, Part I, Vol. XLV, p. 133.
19. *OR*, Series I, Part I, Vol. XLV, p. 706.
20. *OR*, Series I, Part I, Vol. XLV, p. 655.
21. W.J. Murray, *History Of The Twentieth Tennessee Regiment Volunteer Infantry*.
22. *OR*, Series I, Part I, Vol. XLV, p. 706.
23. *Ibid*.
24. *OR*, Series I, Part I, Vol. XLV, p. 689.
25. *OR*, Series I, Part II, Vol. XLV, p. 695.
26. Matthew Forney Steele, *American Campaigns*, Vol. I, p. 576.
27. Gen. J.B. Hood—*Battles and Leaders*, Vol. IV, p. 437.
28. Alex. P. Stewart, "The Army of Tennessee: A Sketch," *Military Annals of Tennessee*, 1886.
29. A.D. Rape, "Some Thrilling War Experiences," *Confederate Veteran*, Vol. XXXV, No. 5 (May 1927).
30. Capt. George E. Brewer, "Incidents of the Retreat from Nashville," *Confederate Veteran*, Vol. XVIII, No. 7, (July 1910), pp. 328, 329.
31. G.T. Cullens, "Our Second Campaign to Nashville," *Confederate Veteran*, Vol. XII, No. 9, (September 1904), p. 436.

32. Col. R.H. Lindsay, "The Retreat from Nashville," *Confederate Veteran*, Vol. VII, No. 7, (July 1899), p. 311.
33. *Confederate Veteran*, Vol. XII, No.7, p. 750.
34. OR, Series I, Part I, Vol. XLV, p. 134.
35. *Battles and Leaders of the Civil War*, Vol. IV, p. 469.
36. OR, Series I, Part I, Vol. XLV, p. 131.
37. OR, Series I, Part I, Vol. XLV, p. 552.
38. *Battles and Leaders of the Civil War*, Vol. IV, p. 469.
39. OR, Series I, Part I, Vol. XLV, p. 695.
40. Levi T. Schofield, *The Retreat from Pulaski*, 1909, p. 65.
41. J.A. Dozier, *Confederate Veteran*, Vol. XVI, No. 4.
42. Rev. Edgar W. Jones, "18th AL. Inf. Reg.," *The Jones Valley Times*, 1905.
43. OR, Series I, Part I, Vol. XLV, p. 40.
44. OR, Series I, Part I, Vol. XLV, p. 695.
45. "Report of the Operations of Clayton's Div.," *Southern Historical Society Papers*, Vol. VI, (August 1878), p. 88.
46. *Confederate Military History*, Vol. VIII, Ch. X, p. 167.
47. Sumner A. Cunningham, *Reminiscence of the 41st Tennessee*, 1872. p. 107
48. OR, Series I Part II, *Vol. XLV*, p. 222.
49. OR, Series I Part II, *Vol. XLV*, p. 210.
50. Gen. Thomas Jordan and J.P. Pryor, *The Campaigns of Lt. Gen. N.B. Forrest*, p. 643.
51. Rev. Edgar W. Jones, "18th AL. Inf. Reg.," *The Jones Valley Times*, Vol. VIII, Ch. X, 1905, p. 168.
52. *Battles and Leaders of the Civil War*, Vol. IV, p. 469.
53. Matthew Forney Steele, *American Campaigns*, Vol. I, p. 576.
54. Luke W. Finlay, "Fourth Tennessee Infantry," in *Military Annals of Tennessee*, Vol. I, ed. John Berrien Lindsley, 1886, p. 190.
55. *Confederate Military History*, Vol. VIII, Ch. X, p. 167.
56. Gen. J.B. Hood—*Battles and Leaders*, Vol. IV, p. 437.
57. *Confederate Military History*, Vol. VIII Ch. X, pp. 167–8.
58. *Confederate Military History*, Vol. VIII Ch. X, pp. 168–9.
59. *The Memoir and Civil War Diary of Charles Todd Quintard*, p. 200.
60. Douglas John Carter, *As It Was: Reminiscences of a Soldier of the Third Texas Cavalry and the Nineteenth Louisiana Infantry*, p. 202.
61. Captain James Dinkins, "How Forrest Saved the Army of Tennessee," *Confederate Veteran*, Vol. XXXV, No. 2, (February 1927).
62. *Report of Maj. Gen. Nathan B. Forrest*, January 24, 1865.
63. W. L. Truman, *Memoirs of the Civil War*, pp. 577.
64. OR, Series I, Part I, Vol. XLV, p. 134.
65. Ezekiel 7:10, 11, *The Holy Bible*.

Chapter 2

1. OR, Series I, Part I, Vol. XLV, p .655.
2. OR, Series I, Part I, Vol. XLV, p. 673.
3. Dr. Samuel Mims Thompson, "Annotations on the 41st TN," *Reminiscences of the 41st TN*, p. 111.
4. W. L. Truman, *Memoirs of the Civil War*, p. 577.
5. M.B. Morton, "The Battle of Nashville," *Confederate Veteran* (January 1909).
6. Sam Watkins, *Co. Aytch*, p 241.
7. Robert Gates, "Sixth Tennessee Infantry," in *Military Annals of Tennessee*, Vol. I, ed. John Berrien Lindsley, 1886.
8. Capt. George E. Brewer, "Incidents of the Retreat from Nashville," *Confederate Veteran*, Vol XVIII, No. 7, (July 1910), pp. 328, 329.
9. Samuel Robinson, "First Tennessee Infantry," in *Military Annals of Tennessee*, ed. John Berrien Lindsley, 1886.
10. Captain O.B. Hayden, *Ninth Cavalry: One Hundred and Twenty-first Regiment, Indiana Volunteers*, 1890, p. 35.
11. "Report of Surgeon George E. Cooper, April 7, 1865," *The Official Records of the War of the Rebellion*, p. 111.
12. Rev. Edgar W. Jones, "The History of the 18th Alabama Infantry Regiment," 1905, page 50.
13. "Report of the Operations of Clayton's Div.," *Southern Historical Society Papers*, Vol. VI, (August 1878), p. 88.
14. OR, Series I, Part II, Vol. XLV, p. 230.
15. *Ibid.*
16. OR, Series I, Part II, Vol. XLV, p. 231.
17. *Battles and Leaders of the Civil War*, Vol. IV, pp. 470.
18. OR, Series I, Part II, Vol. XLV, pp. 239–240.

19. "The Cavalry Leaders North and South," *Photographic History of the Civil War*, Vol. IV, p. 285.

20. "Equipment Organization of the Federal Cavalry," *Photographic History of the Civil War*, Vol. IV p. 41.

21. "The Union Cavalry in the Hood Campain," *Battles and Leaders of The Civil War*, Vol. IV , pp. 465, 467.

22. *OR*, Series I, Part II, p. 232.

23. *OR*, Series I, Part I, Vol. XLV, p. 134.

24. *Battles and Leaders of the Civil War*, Vol. IV, pp. 470.

25. *OR*, Series I, Part II, Vol. XLV, p. 237.

26. *Ibid.*

27. Rev. Edgar W. Jones, "The History of the 18th Alabama Infantry Regiment," 1905.

28. *OR*, Series I, Part I, Vol. XLV, p. 157.

29. Captain O.B. Hayden, *Ninth Cavalry: One Hundred and Twenty-first Regiment*, 1890, p. 35

30. *OR*, Series I Part II Vol XLV, pp. 243, 252.

31. *OR*, Series I Part II Vol XLV, p. 251.

32. *Official Records of the War of the Rebellion*, Series I, Part I, Vol. XLV, p. 689.

33. Captain O.B. Hayden, *Ninth Cavalry: One Hundred and Twenty-first Regiment*, 1890, p. 35

34. *OR*, Series I, Part I, Vol. XLV, p. 699.

35. Alexander Eckel, *History of the Fourth Tennessee Cavalry 1861–1865*, 1929, p. 75,.

36. Capt. George E. Brewer, "Incidents of the Retreat from Nashville," *Confederate Veteran*, Vol XVIII, No. 7, (July 1910), pp. 328, 329.

37. Samuel P. Bates, "19th Pennsylvania Cavalry portion," *History of Pennsylvania Volunteers 1861-6*, Vol. IX, 1871, pp. 3, 4.

38. Capt. George E. Brewer, "Incidents of the Retreat from Nashville," *Confederate Veteran*, Vol XVIII, No. 7, (July 1910), pp. 328, 329.

39. "Report of Brevet Major General James H. Wilson," *Official Records of the War of the Rebellion*, Series I, Part I, Vol. XLV, No. 194, p. 553.

40. Samuel P. Bates, "19th Pennsylvania Cavalry portion," *History of Pennsylvania Volunteers 1861-6*, Vol. IX, 1871, pp. 3, 4.

41. Capt. George E. Brewer, "Incidents of the Retreat from Nashville," *Confederate Veteran*, Vol XVIII, No. 7, (July 1910), pp. 328, 329.

42. "Report of Major General Henry D. Clayton," *Official Records of the War of the Rebellion*, Series I, Part I,Vol. XLV, No. 240, p. 697.

43. "Report of Brevet Major General James H. Wilson," *Official Records of the War of the Rebellion*, Series I, Part I, Vol. XLV, No. 194 p. 553.

44. "Report of Major General Henry D. Clayton," *Official Records of the War of the Rebellion*, Series I, Part I,Vol. XLV, No. 240, p. 697.

45. Rev. Edgar W. Jones, "The History of the 18th Alabama Infantry Regiment," 1905, p. 50.

46. *OR*, Series I, Part I, Vol. XLV, p. 689.

47. Alexander Eckel, *History of the Fourth Tennessee Cavalry 1861–1865*, 1929, p. 75.

48. *OR*, Series I, Part I, Vol. XLV, p. 553.

49. *The Charleston Mercury*, January 4, 1865, p. 1, c3.

50. *Official Records of the War of the Rebellion*, Series I, Part I, Vol. XLV, p. 703.

51. "Clayton's Brigade," *The Dubose Manuscript*.

52. "Report of the Operations of Clayton's Div.," *Southern Historical Society Papers*, Vol. VI, (August 1878), p. 89.

53. Gen. J.B. Hood,—*Battles and Leaders*, Vol. IV., p. 437.

54. Luke W. Finlay, "Fourth Tennessee Infantry," in *Military Annals of Tennessee*, Vol. I, ed. John Berrien Lindsley, 1886, p. 191.

55. W.J. McMurray, *History of the 20th TN. Regiment Volunteer Inf.*, p. 350.

56. *OR*, Series I, Part I, Vol. XLV, p. 565.

57. *Battles and Leaders of the Civil War*, Vol. IV, p. 469.

58. *OR*, Series I, Part I, Vol. XLV, p. 601.

59. *OR*, Series I, Part II, Vol. XLV, p. 241.

60. Captain O.B. Hayden, *Ninth Cavalry: One Hundred and Twenty-first Regiment*, 1890, p. 35.

61. Col. R.H. Lindsay, "The Retreat from Nashville," *Confederate Veteran*, Vol. VII, No. 7, (July 1899), p. 311.

62. Capt. R.N. Rea, "A Mississippi Soldier of the Confederacy," *Confederate Veteran*, Vol. XXX (1922); No. 8 (August).

63. Capt. George E. Brewer, "Incidents of the Retreat from Nashville," *Confederate Veteran*, Vol XVIII, No. 7, (July 1910), pp. 328, 329.

64. Capt. W.A. Polk, "Gallant Col. William F. Taylor," *Confederate Veteran*, Vol. XVI, No. 3, (March 1908), pp. 124–125.

65. W.J. McMurray, *History of the 20th TN. Regiment Volunteer Inf.*, p. 350.

66. Rev. Edgar W. Jones, "The History of the 18th Alabama Infantry Regiment," 1905, p. 51.

67. OR, Series I, Part I, Vol. XLV, p. 690.

68. *"Official Report of Brig. Gen. Randall L. Gibson," Official Records of the War of the Rebellion*, Series I, Part I, Vol. XLV, p. 703.

69. *"Official Report of Brig. Gen. James T. Holtzclaw," Official Records of the War of the Rebellion*, Series I, Part I, Vol. XLV, pp. 704–706.

70. Captain O.B. Hayden, *Ninth Cavalry: One Hundred and Twenty-first Regiment*, 1890

71. Daniel W. Comstock, Adjutant, F&S, 9th Indiana Cavalry, "Letter to the Editor," *The Cincinnati Commercial*, December 29, 1864.

72. "Official Report of Bvt. Brig. Gen. John H. Hammond," *Official Records of the War of the Rebellion*, Series I, Part I, Vol. XLV, No. 204, p. 607.

73. R.J. Black, "How Three Men Held An Army In Check," *Confederate Veteran*, Vol. XVI, No. 6, (June 1908), p. 268.

74. OR, Series I, Part I, Vol. XLV, p. 699.

75. Rev. Edgar W. Jones, "The History of the 18th Alabama Infantry Regiment," 1905,.

76. *Official Records of the War of the Rebellion*, Series I, Part I, Vol. XLV, pp. 704–706.

77. Alexander Eckel, *History of the Fourth Tennessee Cavalry 1861–1865*, 1929, p. 75.

78. Capt. W.A. Polk, "Gallant Col. William F. Taylor," *Confederate Veteran*, Vol. XVI, No. 3, (March 1908), pp. 124–125.

79. *Official Records of the War of the Rebellion*, Series I, Part I, Vol. XLV, p. 703.

80. Col. R.H. Lindsay, "The Retreat from Nashville," *Confederate Veteran*, Vol. VII, No. 7, (July 1899), p. 311.

81. *Official Records of the War of the Rebellion*, Series I, Part I, Vol. XLV, p. 699.

82. Capt. James Dinkins, "How Forrest Saved the Army of Tennessee," *Confederate Veteran*, Vol. XXXV, No. 2, (February 1927).

83. OR, Series I, Part I, Vol. XLV, p. 601.

84. OR, Series I, Part I, Vol. XLV, pp. 573–4.

85. Captain O.B. Hayden, *Ninth Cavalry: One Hundred and Twenty-first Regiment*, 1890.

86. OR, Series I, Part I, Vol. XLV, p. 565.

87. OR, Series I, Part I, Vol. XLV, p. 157.

88. OR, Series I, Part I, Vol. XLV, p. 135.

89. Rev. Edgar W. Jones, "The History of the 18th Alabama Infantry Regiment," 1905, p. 51.

90. P.D. Stephenson, *The Civil War Memoir of Phillip Daingerfield Stephenson*, 1894, p. 340.

91. Rev. Edgar W. Jones, "The History of the 18th Alabama Infantry Regiment," 1905.

92. OR, Series I, Part I, Vol. XLV, pp. 706–7.

93. OR, Series I, Part I, Vol. XLV, p. 135.

94. OR, Series I, Part II, Vol. XLV, p. 233.

95. OR, Series I, Part I, Vol. XLV, p. 157.

96. OR, Series I, Part II, Vol. XLV, p. 233.

97. OR, Series I, Part I, Vol. XLV, p. 135.

98. OR, Series I, Part II, Vol. XLV, p. 233.

99. *Official Records of the War of the Rebellion*, Series I, Part II, Vol. XLV, pp. 237–8.

100. W.J. McMurray, *History of the 20th TN. Regiment Volunteer Inf.*, p. 350.

101. G.H. Nixon, "Twentieth Tennessee Cavalry," *in Military Annals of Tennessee*, Vol. I, ed. John Berrien Lindsley, 1886, p. 740.

102. OR, Series I, Part II, Vol. XLV, p. 238.

103. OR, Series I, Part I, Vol. XLV, p. 565.

104. OR, Series I, Part I, Vol. XLV, p. 553.

105. OR, Series I, Part I, Vol. XLV, p. 553.

106. *Official Records of the War of the Rebellion*, Series I, Part I, Vol. XLV, p. 690.

107. OR, Series I, Part I, Vol. XLV, p. 157.

108. Daniel Comstock, Ninth Cavalry: *One Hundred and Twenty-first Regiment Indiana Volunteers*, 1890.

109. OR, Series I, Part I, Vol. XLV, p. 553.

110. *Official Records of the War of the Rebellion*, Series I, Part I, Vol. XLV, p. 696.

111. OR, Series I, Part I, Vol. XLV, p. 565.

112. Gen. Thomas Jordan and J.P. Pryor, *The Campaigns of Lt. Gen. N.B. Forrest*, p. 644.

113. *The Life of Major General George H. Thomas by Thomas Van Horne*, 1882.

114. *Official Records of the War of the Rebellion*, Series I, Part I, Vol. XLV, p. 696.

115. Capt. George E. Brewer, "Incidents of the Retreat from Nashville," *Confederate Veteran*, Vol XVIII, No. 7, (July 1910), pp. 328, 329.

116. OR, Series I, Part I, Vol. XLV, p. 699.

117. *Ibid*.

118. *Official Records of the War of the Rebellion*, Series I, Part I, Vol. XLV, p. 690.

119. Alexander Eckel, *History of the Fourth Tennessee Cavalry 1861–1865*, 1929, p. 76.

120. A.D. Rape, "Some Thrilling War Experiences," *Confederate Veteran*, Vol. XXXV, No. 5 (May 1927).

121. Daniel Comstock, *Ninth Cavalry: One Hundred and Twenty-first Regiment Indiana Volunteers*, 1890..

122. *Ibid.*

123. *OR*, Series I, Part I, Vol. XLV, p. 553.

124. *Battles and Leaders of the Civil War*, Vol. *IV*, p. 470.

125. *OR*, Series I, Part I, Vol. XLV, p. 700.

126. Capt. James Dinkins, "How Forrest Saved the Army of Tennessee," *Confederate Veteran*, Vol. XXXV, No. 2, (February 1927).

127. *OR*, Series I, Part I, Vol. XLV, p. 566.

128. R.J. Black, "How Three Men Held An Army In Check," *Confederate Veteran*, Vol. XVI, No. 6, (June 1908).

129. *Official Records of the War of the Rebellion*, Series I, Part I, Vol. XLV, p. 553.

130. Sergeant Lyman B. Pierce, *History of the Second Iowa Cavalry*, 1865.

131. *Official Records of the War of the Rebellion*, Series I, Vol. XLV, p. 592.

132. Rev. Edgar W. Jones, "The History of the 18th Alabama Infantry Regiment," 1905, p. 51.

133. Edward A. Davenport ed., *"Ninth Regiment Illinois Cavalry Volunteers,"* Historical Committee of the Regiment: John H. Carpenter, Anthony R. Mock, Charles L. Pullman, Hiram A. Hawkins, Harry B. Burgh, Joseph W. Harper, Patrick V. Fitzpatrick, John T. Showalter., Chicago, 1888, pp. 162, 163.

134. *Official Records of the War of the Rebellion*, Series I, Part I, Vol. XLV, p. 690.

135. *Battles and Leaders of the Civil War*, Vol. IV, p. 470.

136. *OR*, Series I, Part I, Vol. XLV, p. 696.

137. Alexander Eckel, *History of the Fourth Tennessee Cavalry 1861–1865*, 1929, p. 76.

138. *OR*, Series I, Part I, Vol. XLV, p. 553.

139. *OR*, Series I Part II, *Vol.* XLV, p. 238.

140. *OR*, Series I, Part II, Vol. XLV, p. 239.

141. *OR*, Series I, Part II, Vol. XLV, pp. 238–9.

142. *OR*, Series I, Part II, Vol. XLV, p. 239.

143. *Official Records of the War of the Rebellion*, Series I, Part II, Vol. XLV, p. 707.

144. Gen. Thomas Jordan and J.P. Pryor, *The Campaigns of Lt. Gen. N.B. Forrest*, p. 644.

145. Rev. Edgar W. Jones, "The History of the 18th Alabama Infantry Regiment," 1905.

146. *OR*, Series I, Part I, Vol. XLV, p. 700.

147. *OR*, Series I, Part I, Vol. XLV, p. 766.

148. *OR*, Series I, Part II, Vol. XLV, p. 229.

149. *OR*, Series I, Part I, Vol. XLV, p. 158.

150. *OR*, Series I, Part II, Vol. XLV, p. 240.

Chapter 3

1. *OR*, Series I, Part I, Vol. XLV, p. 673.

2. *OR*, Series I, Part I, Vol. XLV, p. 135.

3. *OR*, Series I, Part I, Vol. XLV, p. 158.

4. *Ibid.*

5. *Official Records of the War of the Rebellion*, Series I, Vol. XLV, p. 592.

6. *Official Records of the War of the Rebellion*, Series I, Part I, Vol. XLV, p. 578.

7. *Official Records of the War of the Rebellion*, Series I, Part II, Vol. XLV, p. 256.

8. *Official Records of the War of the Rebellion*, Series I, Part I, Vol. XLV, p. 766.

9. *OR*, Series I, Part I, Vol. XLV, p. 135.

10. Rev. J.H. McNeilly, *49th TN. Inf.*, Vol. XXVI, No. 7, p. 305.

11. W.J. McMurray, *History of the 20th TN. Regiment Volunteer Inf.*, p. 350.

12. *OR*, Series I, Part II, Vol. XLV, p. 256.

13. *OR*, Series I, Part I, Vol. XLV, pp. 553–4, 566.

14. *Official Records of the War of the Rebellion*, Series I, Part I, Vol. XLV, p. 578.

15. *Official Records of the War of the Rebellion*, Series I, Part I, Vol. XLV, p. 592.

16. Capt. James Dinkins, "How Forrest Saved the Army of Tennessee," *Confederate Veteran*, Vol. XXXV, No. 2, (February 1927).

17. *OR*, Series I, Part I, Vol. XLV, p. 158.

18. *Ibid.*

19. *OR*, Series I, Part II, Vol. XLV, p. 253.

20. *OR*, Series I, Part II, Vol. XLV, p. 263.

21. *OR*, Series I, Part II, Vol. XLV, p. 284.

22. *OR*, Series I, Part II, Vol. XLV, p. 253.

23. *OR*, Series I, Part II, Vol. XLV, p. 254.

24. *OR*, Series I, Part II, Vol. XLV, p. 699.

25. *OR*, Series I, Vol. XLV

26. *OR*, Series I, Part I, Vol. XLV, p. 724.

27. *OR*, Series I, Part II, Vol. XLV, p. 256.

28. W.J. McMurray, *History of the 20th TN. Regiment Volunteer Inf.*, p. 351.

29. Gen. Thomas Jordan and J.P. Pryor, *The Campaigns of Lt. Gen. N.B. Forrest*, p. 645.

Chapter 4

1. *OR*, Series I, Part I, Vol. XLV, p. 731.
2. *Official Records of the War of the Rebellion*, Series I, Vol. XLV, p. 592.
3. Edward A. Davenport ed., *"Ninth Regiment Illinois Cavalry Volunteers,"* Historical Committee of the Regiment: John H. Carpenter, Anthony R. Mock, Charles L. Pullman, Hiram A. Hawkins, Harry B. Burgh, Joseph W. Harper, Patrick V. Fitzpatrick, John T. Showalter., Chicago, 1888, pp. 162, 163.
4. Dr. Samuel Mims Thompson, "Annotations on the 41st TN," *Reminiscences of the 41st TN*, p. 112.
5. *OR*, Series I, Part I, Vol. XLV, p. 158.
6. *Battles and Leaders of the Civil War*, Vol. IV, p. 470.
7. *OR*, Series I, Part II, Vol. XLV, p. 275.
8. *Battles and Leaders of the Civil War*, Vol. IV, p. 470.
9. *OR*, Series I, Part I, Vol. XLV, p. 159.
10. *OR*, Series I, Part I, Vol. XLV, p. 135.
11. *OR*, Series I, Part II, Vol. XLV, p. 270.
12. *OR*, Series I, Part II, Vol. XLV, p. 271.
13. *Ibid.*
14. *OR*, Series I, Part I, Vol. XLV, p. 566.
15. Henry Stone, "The Battle of Nashville, December 15, 16, 1864," *The Papers of the Military History Society of Massachusetts*, Vol. VII, 1908.
16. *OR*, Series I, Part II, Vol. XLV, p. 271.
17. *OR*, Series I, Part II, Vol. XLV, p. 278.
18. *OR*, Series I, Part II, Vol. XLV, p. 271.
19. *OR*, Series I Part *II, Vol.* XLV, p. 272.
20. *Official Records of the War of the Rebellion*, Series I, Part II, Vol. XLV, p. 276.
21. *Ibid.*
22. W. L. Truman, *Memoirs of the Civil War*, p. 577.
23. Fenner's Battery "An Incident of Hood's Campaign" *Southern Bivouac*, Vol. III, No. 3, (November 1884), pp. 131–132.
24. J. Harvey Mathies, "The Old Guard in Gray: Researches in the Annals of the Confederate Historical Association," 1897, p. 124.
25. "Confederate Disaster at Nashville—Another Letter from Col. W.D. Gale to His Wife After Hood's Defeat Before Nashville," *Confederate Veteran*, Vol. II, No. 2 (February 1894).

26. *OR*, Series I, Part I, Vol. XLV, p. 661.
27. Maj. David Ward Sanders, "Autobiography of Maj. D.W. Sanders," *Confederate Veteran*, Vol. XVIII, No. 8, (August 1910).
28. Luke W. Finlay, "Fourth Tennessee Infantry," in *Military Annals of Tennessee*, Vol. I, ed. John Berrien Lindsley, 1886, p. 191.
29. *Ibid.*
30. J.P. Young, 7th Tennessee Cavalry.
31. Rev. Edgar W. Jones, "The History of the 18th Alabama Infantry Regiment," 1905, p. 51.
32. Dr. Samuel Mims Thompson, "Annotations on the 41st TN," *Reminiscences of the 41st TN*, p. 112.
33. *The Memoir and Civil War Diary of Charles Quintard*, p. 200.
34. *OR*, Series I, Part I, Vol. XLV, pp. 711–12.
35. Lt. General Alexander P. Stewart, "Reminiscences of Hood's Tennessee Campaign," *Southern Historical Society Papers*, Vol. IX. (Oct.-Dec. 1881), p. 522.
36. W. L. Truman, *Memoirs of the Civil War*, p. 577.
37. James H. Wilson, *Under the Old Flag: Recollections of Military Operations in the War for the Union, the Spanish War, the Boxer Rebellion, Etc.*, Vol. II, 1912, pp. 28, 30, 44–5.
38. *OR*, Series I, Part II, Vol. XLV, p. 270.
39. *OR*, Series I, Part I, Vol. XLV, pp. 160–1.
40. *OR*, Series I, Part I, Vol. XLV, p. 159.

Chapter 5

1. *Official Records of the War of the Rebellion*, Series I, Part II, Vol. XLV, p. 291.
2. *Official Records of the War of the Rebellion*, Series I, Vol. XLV, p. 593.
3. J.P. Young, 7th Tennessee Cavalry.
4. Douglas John Carter, *As It Was: Reminiscences of a Soldier of the Third Texas Cavalry and the Nineteenth Louisiana Infantry.*
5. *The Memoir and Civil War Diary of Charles Todd Quintard*, p. 203.
6. "Forrest and his Campaigns," *Southern Historical Society Papers*, Vol. VII No. 10, (Jan.—Dec. 1879), pp. 482–483.
7. *OR*, "Summary of Principle Events"—No. 252, p. *757*
8. *Ibid.*
9. *Confederate Veteran*, Vol. XV, p. 401.
10. *OR*, Series I, Part I, Vol. XLV, pp. 715, 726.

11. Gen. Thomas Jordan and J.P. Pryor, *The Campaigns of Lt. Gen. N.B. Forrest*, pp. 646–7.

12. *The Memoir and Civil War Diary of Charles Todd Quintard*, p. 201.

13. Gen. Thomas Jordan and J.P. Pryor, *The Campaigns of Lt. Gen. N.B. Forrest*, p. 647.

14. *OR*, Series I, Part I, Vol. XLV, p. 661.

15. *OR*, Series I, Part I, Vol. XLV, p. 726.

16. *Confederate Military History*, Vol. VIII, Ch. X, p. 170.

17. *Battles and Leaders*, Vol. IV, p. 437.

18. *Confederate Military History*, Vol. VIII, Ch. X, p. 170.

19. *Ibid.*

20. *OR*, Series I, Part I, Vol. XLV, p. 566.

21. *OR*, Series I, Part I, Vol. XLV, p. 578.

22. Gen. Thomas Jordan and J.P. Pryor, *The Campaigns of Lt. Gen. N.B. Forrest*, p. 647.

23. *Official Records of the War of the Rebellion*, Series I, Part II, Vol. XLV, p. 291.

24. Edward A. Davenport ed., "*Ninth Regiment Illinois Cavalry Volunteers*," Historical Committee of the Regiment: John H. Carpenter, Anthony R. Mock, Charles L. Pullman, Hiram A. Hawkins, Harry B. Burgh, Joseph W. Harper, Patrick V. Fitzpatrick, John T. Showalter., Chicago, 1888, pp. 162, 163.

25. "Official Report of Lt. Gen. N.B. Forrest of operations November 16, 1864—January 23, 1865".

26. *OR*, Series I, Part I, Vol. XLV, p. 726.

27. *OR*, Series I, Part I, Vol. XLV, p. 136.

28. *OR*, Series I, Part II, Vol. XLV, p. 287.

29. *Official Records of the War of the Rebellion*, Series I, Part II, Vol. XLV, p. 161.

30. *Official Records of the War of the Rebellion*, Series I, Part II, Vol. XLV, p. 295.

Chapter 6

1. Dr. Samuel Mims Thompson, "Annotations on the 41st TN," *Reminiscences of the 41st TN*, pp. 112.

2. W. L. Truman, *Memoirs of the Civil War*, pp. 577.

3. *Official Records of the War of the Rebellion*, Series I, Part I, Vol. XLV, p. 593.

4. *Official Records of the War of the Rebellion* Series I, Part I, Vol. XLV, p. 720.

5. *The Memoir and Civil War Diary of Charles Todd Quintard*, p. 204.

6. *The Memoir and Civil War Diary of Charles Todd Quintard*, pp. 204–5.

7. *OR*, Series I, Part I, Vol. XLV, p. 136.

8. *OR*, Series I, Part I, Vol. XLV, p. 161.

9. *Ibid.*

10. *Ibid.*

11. *Battles and Leaders of the Civil War*, Vol. IV, p. 470.

12. *OR*, Series I, Part II, Vol. XLV, p. 295.

13. *OR*, Series I, Part II, Vol. XLV, pp. 295–6.

14. *OR*, Series I, Part II, Vol. XLV, p. 307.

15. *Ibid.*

16. *OR*, Series I, Part II, Vol. XLV, p. 329.

17. *Battles and Leaders of the Civil War*, Vol. IV, p. 467.

Chapter 7

1. *OR*, Series I, Part I, Vol. XLV, p. 136.

2. *OR*, Series I, Part II, Vol. XLV, pp. 307–8.

3. *OR*, Series I, Part I, Vol. XLV, p. 673.

4. *Official Records of the War of the Rebellion*, Series I, Part I, Vol. XLV, p. 766.

5. *Official Records of the War of the Rebellion*, Series I, Part I, Vol. XLV, p. 721.

6. *Ibid.*

7. *Ibid.*

8. Douglas John Carter, *As It Was: Reminiscences of a Soldier of the Third Texas Cavalry and the Nineteenth Louisiana Infantry.*

9. *OR*, Series I, Part I, Vol. XLV, p. 136.

10. *OR*, Series I, Part I, Vol. XLV, p. 162.

11. *Ibid.*

12. *OR*, Series I, Part II, Vol. XLV, p. 309.

13. *OR*, Series I, Part I, Vol. XLV, p. 162.

14. *OR*, Series I, Part II, Vol. XLV, p. 314.

15. *OR*, Series I, Part I, Vol. XLV, p. 162.

16. *OR*, Series I, Part I, Vol. XLV, pp. 162–3.

17. B. W. Holcomb, *Reminiscences of the Boys in Gray, 1861–1865*, 1912, pp. 293–294.

18. *Official Records of the War of the Rebellion*, Series I, Part II, Vol. XLV, p. 307.

Chapter 8

1. *OR*, Series I, Part I, Vol. XLV, p. 732.

2. *OR*, Series I, Part II, Vol. XLV, p. 319.

3. *OR*, Series I, Part II, Vol. XLV, p. 321.

4. *OR*, Series I, Part I, Vol. XLV *No. 5*, p. 69.

5. *OR*, Series I, Part I, Vol. XLV, p. 136.

6. Richard K. and Geraldine M. Rue ed.,

In Song and Sorrow: The Daily Journal of Thomas Hart Benton McCain of the Eighty-Sixth Indiana Volunteer Infantry, 1998.

7. *Official Records of the War of the Rebellion*, Series I, Vol. XLV, p. 593.

8. OR, Series I, Part I, Vol. XLV No. 66, p. 292.

9. OR, Series I Part *II, Vol.* XLV, p. 726.

10. *Report of Maj. Gen. Nathan B. Forrest, C.S. Army, Commanding Cavalry, Of Operations In North Alabama and Middle Tennessee Relating to The Battle of Nashville.*

11. OR, Series I, Part I, Vol. XLV, p. 163.

12. OR, Series I, Part II, Vol. XLV, p. 324.

13. OR, Series I, Part II, Vol. XLV, p. 726.

Chapter 9

1. OR, Series I, Part I, Vol. XLV, p. 732.

2. Rev. Edgar W. Jones, "The History of the 18th Alabama Infantry Regiment," 1905.

3. Douglas John Carter, *As It Was: Reminiscences of a Soldier of the Third Texas Cavalry and the Nineteenth Louisiana Infantry.*

4. W.J. McMurray, *History of the 20th TN. Regiment Volunteer Inf.*, p. 352.

5. OR, Series I, Part I, Vol. XLV, p. 137.

6. OR, Series I, Part I, Vol. XLV, p. 163.

7. *Battles and Leaders of the Civil War*, Vol. IV, p. 470.

8. OR, Series I, Part I, Vol. XLV, p. 163.

9. Richard K. and Geraldine M. Rue ed., *In Song and Sorrow: The Daily Journal of Thomas Hart Benton McCain of the Eighty-Sixth Indiana Volunteer Infantry*, 1998.

10. "Confederate Disaster at Nashville—Another Letter from Col. W.D. Gale to his new wife after Hood's Defeat before Nashville," *Confederate Veteran*, Vol. II, No. 2, (February 1894).

11. *Official Records of the War of the Rebellion*, Series I, Part I, Vol. XLV, p. 593.

12. OR, Series I, Part II, Vol. XLV, p. 331.

13. OR, Series I, Part I, Vol. XLV, p. 567.

14. *Battles and Leaders of the Civil War*, Vol. IV, p. 471.

15. OR, Series I, Part I, Vol. XLV, p. 593.

16. OR, Series I, Part II, Vol. XLV, p. 334.

17. OR, Series I, Part I, Vol. XLV, pp. 757–8.

18. OR, Series I, Part II, Vol. XLV, p. 335.

19. *Ibid.*

20. OR, Series I, Part I, Vol. XLV, p. 727.

21. OR, Series I, Part II, Vol. XLV, p. 655.

22. OR, Series I, Part I, Vol. XLV, p. 774.

23. OR, Series I, Part II, Vol. XLV, p. 371.

24. Gen. Thomas Jordan and J.P. Pryor, *The Campaigns of Lt. Gen. N.B. Forrest*, pp. 648–9.

25. OR, Series I, Part I, Vol. XLV, p. 567.

26. OR, Series I, Part II, Vol. XLV, p. 331.

27. OR, Series I, Part I, Vol. XLV, p. 163.

28. OR, Series I, Part II, Vol. XLV, p. 334.

29. Rev. Arthur Howard Noll ed., *Doctor Quintard Chaplain C.S.A. and Second Bishop of Tennessee*, 1905.

Chapter 10

1. OR, Series I, Vol. XLV, Part I, p. 674.

2. OR, Series I, Part I, Vol. XLV, p. 732.

3. W. L. Truman, *Memoirs of the Civil War*, p. 577.

4. *The Memoir and Civil War Diary of Charles Todd Quintard*, p. 206.

5. OR, Series I, Part I, Vol. XLV, pp. 163–4.

6. Dr. Samuel Mims Thompson, "Annotations on the 41st TN," *Reminiscences of the 41st TN*, p. 112.

7. Douglas John Carter, *As It Was: Reminiscences of a Soldier of the Third Texas Cavalry and the Nineteenth Louisiana Infantry..*

8. Lundberg, John W. *The Finishing Stroke: Texans in the 1864 Tennessee Campaign.* Abilene, Texas: McWhiney Foundation Press, 2002., p. 19.

9. J.A. Dozier, *Confederate Veteran*, Vol. XVI, No. 4,(April), p. 192

10. James H. Wilson, *Under the Old Flag: Recollections of Military Operations in the War for the Union, the Spanish War, the Boxer Rebellion, Etc.*, Vol. II, 1912, p. 143.

11. *Official Records of the War of the Rebellion*, Series I, Part I, Vol. XLV, p. 603.

12. "Gen. Nathan Bedford Forrest," *Confederate Veteran*, Vol. V, No. 6, (June 1897), pp. 277–278.

13. *Official Records of the War of the Rebellion*, Series I, Part I, Vol. XLV, p. 603.

14. OR, Series I, Part I, Vol. XLV, p. 163.

15. OR, Series I, Part I, Vol. XLV, p. 137.

16. OR, Series I, Part I, Vol. XLV, p. 164.

17. OR, Series I, Part II, Vol. XLV, p. 348.

18. *Battles and Leaders of the Civil War*, Vol. IV, p. 471.

19. OR, Series I, Part I, Vol. XLV, p. 758.

20. *OR*, Series I, Part II, Vol. XLV, p. 342.
21. *OR*, Series I, Part I, Vol. XLV, p. 163.
22. *OR*, Series I, Part I, Vol. XLV, p. 603.
23. "Forrest and his Campaigns," *Southern Historical Society Papers*, Vol. VII No. 10, (Jan.—Dec. 1879) , p. 483.
24. *OR*, Series I, Part I, Vol. XLV, p. 164.
25. *OR*, Series I, Part I, Vol. XLV, p. 603.
26. "Forrest and his Campaigns," *Southern Historical Society Papers*, Vol. VII No. 10, (Jan.—Dec. 1879), p. 483.
27. Edward A. Davenport ed., "*Ninth Regiment Illinois Cavalry Volunteers*," Historical Committee of the Regiment: John H. Carpenter, Anthony R. Mock, Charles L. Pullman, Hiram A. Hawkins, Harry B. Burgh, Joseph W. Harper, Patrick V. Fitzpatrick, John T. Showalter., Chicago, 1888, pp. 162, 163.
28. *Official Records of the War of the Rebellion*, Series I, Vol. XLV, p. 593.
29. Ed. Richard K. and Geraldine M. Rue, *In Song and Sorrow: The Daily Journal of Thomas Hart Benton McCain of the Eighty-Sixth Indiana Volunteer Infantry*, 1998.
30. J.T. Tunnell, "Ector's Brigade in Battle of Nashville," *Confederate Veteran*, Vol. XII, No. 7, (July 1904).
31. Major General James Harrison Wilson, "The Union Cavalry in the Hood Campaign," in *The Battles and Leaders of the Civil War*, Vol. IV, 1956.
32. "Confederate Disaster at Nashville—Another Letter from Col. W.D. Gale to his new wife after Hood's Defeat before Nashville," *Confederate Veteran*, Vol. II, No. 2, (February 1894).
33. Rev. Arthur Howard Noll ed., *Doctor Quintard Chaplain C.S.A. and Second Bishop of Tennessee*, 1905.
34. "Forrest and his Campaigns," *Southern Historical Society Papers*, Vol. VII, No. 10, (Jan.—Dec. 1879), p. 483.
35. John Berrien Lindsley, *Military Annals of Tennessee*, Vol. I, 1886, pp. 191–2.
36. *OR*, Series I, Part I, Vol. XLV, p. 603.
37. *OR*, Series I, Part II, Vol. XLV, p. 342.
38. *OR*, Series I, Part I, Vol. XLV, p. 164.
39. *OR*, Series I, Part II, Vol. XLV, p. 349.
40. *OR*, Series I, Part II, Vol. XLV, p. 351.

Chapter 11

1. *OR*, Series I, Part I, Vol. XLV, p. 674.
2. *OR*, Series I, Part I, Vol. XLV, p. 732.

3. Dr. Samuel Mims Thompson, "Annotations on the 41st TN," *Reminiscences of the 41st TN*, p. 113.
4. *OR*, Series I, Part I, Vol. XLV, p. 735.
5. *Battles and Leaders of the Civil War*, Vol. IV, p. 471.
6. *OR*, Series I, Part I, Vol. XLV, No. 66, p. 292.
7. Luke W. Finlay, "Fourth Tennessee Infantry," in *Military Annals of Tennessee*, Vol. I, ed. John Berrien Lindsley, 1886, p. 191, 192.
8. John Berrien Lindsley, *Military Annals of Tennessee*, Vol. I, 1886, p. 192.
9. J.T. Tunnell, "Ector's Brigade in Battle of Nashville," *Confederate Veteran*, Vol. XII, No. 7, (July 1904).
10. *OR*, Vol. XLV, Part I, p. 772.
11. John Berrien Lindsley, *Military Annals of Tennessee*, Vol. I, 1886, pp.192.
12. *OR*, Series I, Part I, Vol. XLV, p. 165.
13. *OR*, Series I, Part I, Vol. XLV, p. 758.
14. *Official Records of the War of the Rebellion*, Series I, Vol. XLV, p. 593.
15. Rev. Arthur Howard Noll ed., *Doctor Quintard Chaplain C.S.A. and Second Bishop of Tennessee*, 1905.

Chapter 12

1. *OR*, Series I, Part I, Vol. XLV, p. 732.
2. I.W. Fowler, "Crossing the Tennessee River," *Confederate Veteran*, Vol. XXVIII No. 10, (October 1920), pp. 379, 398.
3. *OR*, Series I, Part I,Vol. XLV, p. 165.
4. *OR*, Series I, Part I, Vol. XLV, p. 292.
5. *OR*, Series I, Part II, Vol. XLV, p. 375.
6. *OR*, Series I, Part I, Vol. XLV, pp. 165–166.
7. *OR*, Series I, Part I, Vol. XLV, p. 166.
8. *OR*, Series I, Part I, Vol. XLV, p. 728.
9. Gen. Thomas Jordan and J.P. Pryor, *The Campaigns of Lt. Gen. N.B. Forrest*.
10. *OR*, Series I, Part II, Vol. XLV, p. 371.
11. *Ibid*.
12. *OR*, Series I, Part II, Vol. XLV, p. 507.
13. *The Memoir and Civil War Diary of Charles Todd Quintard*, pp. 88, 207.

Chapter 13

1. *OR*, Series I, Part I, Vol. XLV, p. 732.
2. *OR* Series I, Part I, Vol. XLV, p. 711.
3. *OR*, Series I, Part II,, Vol. XLV, p. 744.

4. Dr. Samuel Mims Thompson, "Annotations on the 41st TN," *Reminiscences of the 41st TN*, p. 113–114.

5. W.J. McMurray, *History of the 20th TN. Regiment Volunteer Inf.*, p. 352.

6. *OR*, Series I, Part II, Vol. XLV, p. 744.

7. *OR*, Series I, Part I, Vol. XLV, p. 137.

8. *OR*, Series I, Part I, Vol. XLV, No. 66, p. 292.

9. *OR*, Series I, Part I, Vol. XLV, p. 45.

10. Douglas John Carter, *As It Was: Reminiscences of a Soldier of the Third Texas Cavalry and the Nineteenth Louisiana Infantry.*

11. Dr. Samuel Mims Thompson, "Annotations on the 41st TN," *Reminiscences of the 41st TN*, pp. 115–116.

12. *OR*, Series I, Part I, Vol. XLV, p. 732.

13. John Berrien Lindsley, *Military Annals of Tennessee*, Vol. I, 1886.

14. *The Memoir and Civil War Diary of Charles Todd Quintard*, pp. 208–9.

15. *Confederate Military History*, Vol. VIII, Ch. X, p. 172.

16. *OR*, Series I, Part I, Vol. XLV, p. 50.

17. *OR*, Series I, Part I, Vol. XLV, p. 568.

18. *OR*, Series I, Part I, Vol. XLV, No. 66, p. 293.

19. *OR*, Series I, Part I, Vol. XLV, pp. 137–8.

20. *OR*, Series I, Part I, Vol. XLV, p. 579.

21. George F. Hager of the 2nd Tennessee Cavalry, C.S.A., *in Military Annals of Tennessee*, Vol. I, ed. John Berrien Lindsley, 1886, page 622.

22. *OR*, Series I, Part I, Vol. XLV, p. 707.

23. *OR*, Series I, Part I, Vol. XLV, pp. 724–725.

24. *OR*, Series I, Part I, Vol. XLV, p. 711.

25. *OR*, Series I, Part II, Vol. XLV, pp. 781, 805.

26. *OR*, Series I, Part I, Vol. XLV, p. 656.

27. Luke W. Finlay, "Fourth Tennessee Infantry," in *Military Annals of Tennessee*, Vol. I, ed. John Berrien Lindsley, 1886, p. 191, 192.

28. Captain C.W. Frazier, "5th Confederate Infantry; Granbury's Brigade; Cleburne's Division," in *Military Annals of Tennessee*, Vol. I, ed. John Berrien Lindsley, 1886, p. 146.

29. *OR*, Series I, Part I, Vol. XLV, p. 735.

30. *Confederate Military History*, Vol. X, Ch. XIX, pp. 202, 203.

31. W. L. Truman, *Memoirs of the Civil War*, pp. 577.

32. J.A. Dozier, *Confederate Veteran*, Vol. XVI, *No. 4.*

33. *OR*, Series I, Part I, Vol. XLV, p. 651.

34. *Confederate military History*, Vol. VIII, Ch. XI, p. 216.

Bibliography

Archival Material

The Confederate Veteran Magazine.
Boyce, Captain Joseph. "Missourians in the Battle of Franklin." Volume XXIV, No. 3 (March 1916).
Brewer, Capt. George E. "Incidents of the Retreat from Nashville." Volume XVIII No. 7 (July 1910).
The Civil War Memoir of Phillip Daingerfield Stephenson. D.D., 1894.
Confederate Military History: A Library of Confederate States History in Twelve Volumes, Written by Distinguished Men of the South and Edited by General Clement A. Evans of Georgia. Atlanta: Confederate Publishing Co., 1899.
Cullens, G.T. "Our Second Campaign to Nashville." Volume XII, No. 9 (September 1904), p. 436.
Diary of G.L. Griscom, 9th Texas Cavalry.
Dinkins, James. "How Forrest Saved the Army of Tennessee." Volume XXXV, No. 2 (February 1927).
Fowler, I.W. "Crossing the Tennessee River." Volume XXVIII, No. 10 (October 1920), pp. 379, 398.
Gale, Col. W.D. "Confederate Disaster at Nashville—Another Letter from Col. W.D. Gale to His New Wife After Hood's Defeat Before Nashville." Volume II, No. 2 (February 1894).
"Gen. Nathan Bedford Forrest." Volume V, No. 6 (June 1897), pp. 277–278.
J.P. Young, 7th Tennessee Cavalry.
Lindsay, R.H. "The Retreat from Nashville." Volume VII, No. 7 (July 1899), p. 311.
Truman, W.L. Memoirs of the Civil War.
Military Annals of Tennessee. Confederate First Series. Compiled From Original and Official Sources. Edited by John Berrien Lindsley. Volume 1. J.M. Lindsley & Co., Publishers, 1886.
The Official Records of the War of the Rebellion: A Compilation of the Union and Confederate Armies. Washington, D.C.: Government Printing Office, 1901.
The Photographic History of the Civil War. Portland House, 1997.
Polk, W.A. "Gallant Col. William F. Taylor." Volume XVI, No. 3 (March 1908), pp. 124–125.
Rape, A.D. "Some Thrilling War Experiences." Volume XXXV, No. 5 (May 1927).
Rea, R.N. "A Mississippi Soldier of the Confederacy." Volume XXX, No. 8 (August 1922).
Sanders, D.W. "Autobiography of Maj. D.W. Sanders" (Dictated by Maj. David Ward Sanders on April 12, 1906). Volume XVIII, No. 8 (August 1910).

The Southern Historical Society Papers.
Tunnell, J.T. "Ector's Brigade in Battle of Nashville." Volume XII, No. 7 (July 1904).

Books and Periodicals

Carter, Douglas John. *As It Was; Reminiscences of a Soldier of the Third Texas Cavalry and the Nineteenth Louisiana Infantry.* State House Press, 1990.

The Charleston Mercury. January 4th, 1865.

The Cincinnati Commercial. Letter to the editor by Adjutant Daniel W. Comstock, F&S, 9th Indiana Cavalry. December 29, 1864,

Comstock, Daniel. *Ninth Cavalry; One Hundred and Twenty-first Regiment, Indiana Volunteers,* Richmond, IN: J.M. Coe, 1890.

The Courier. New Castle, Henry County, Indiana. Thursday, January 5, 1865.

Cunningham, Sergeant Major Sumner A. *Reminiscences of the 41st TN.; The Civil War in The West.* Shippensburg, PA: White Mane Books, 2001.

Davenport, Edward A., *Ninth Regiment Illinois Cavalry Volunteers.* Published under the auspices of the Historical Committee of the Regiment: John H. Carpenter, Anthony R. Mock, Charles L. Pullman, Hiram A. Hawkins, Harry B. Burgh, Joseph W. Harper, Patrick V. Fitzpatrick, John T. Showalter. Chicago: Donohue & Henneberry, Printers, 1888.

Eckel, Alexander. *History of the Fourth Tennessee Cavalry, U.S.A., 1861–1865.* Knoxville, TN: Stubley Printing Co., 1929.

Elliot, Sam Davis, ed. *The Memoir and Civil War Diary of Charles Todd Quintard.* Baton Rouge: Louisiana State University Press, 2003.

Holcomb, Surgeon B.W., and Miss Mamie Yeary, compiler. *Reminiscences of the Boys in Gray, 1861–1865.* 1912.

*The Holy Bible—*Cambridge University Press (KJV, NASV).

Johnson, Robert Underwood, and Clarence Clough Buel, eds. *Battles and Leaders of the Civil War: Being for the Most Part Contributions by Union and Confederate Officers.* New York: Century Co., 1884.

Jones, Rev. Edgar W. "History of the 18th Alabama Infantry Regiment." *The Jones Valley Times,* 1905.

Jordan, Gen. Thomas, and J.P. Pryor. *The Campaigns of Lt. Gen. N.B. Forrest.* Dayton, OH: Morningside Bookshop, 1977 (rpt.).

Mathes, J. Harvey. *The Old Guard in Gray; Researches in the Annals of the Confederate Historical Association.* Memphis, TN: N.p., 1897.

McMurray, W.J., M.D. *History of the 20th Tennessee Volunteer Infantry, C.S.A.* Nashville, TN: The Publication Committee, 1904.

Pierce, Sergeant Lyman B. *History of the Second Iowa Cavalry.* Burlington, IA: Hawkeye Steam Book and Job Printing Establishment, 1865.

Preston, N.D. *History of the Tenth Regiment of Cavalry, New York State Volunteers.* New York: D. Appleton and Co., 1892

Quintard, C.T., and Rev. Arthur Howard Noll. *Doctor Quintard, Chaplain C.S.A. and Second Bishop of Tennessee.* Sewanee, TN: The University Press of Sewanee, Tennessee, 1905.

Rue, Richard K., and Geraldine M. Rue. *In Song and Sorrow: The Daily Journal of Thomas Hart Benton McCain of the Eighty-Sixth Indiana Volunteer Infantry.* Carmel, IN: Guild Press of Indiana, 1998.

Schofield, Levi. *The Retreat from Pulaski.* Cleveland, OH: Press of the Caxton Co., 1909.

Steele, Matthew Forney. *American Campaigns,* 2 vols. Washington: Byron S. Adams, 1909.

Stephenson, Philip Daingerfield. *Civil War Memoir of Philip Daingerfield Stephenson, D.D.* Baton Rouge: Louisiana State University Press, 1998 [1894].

Van Horne, Thomas. *The Life of Major General George H. Thomas*. New York: Charles Scribner's Sons, 1882.

Watkins, Sam R. *Co. Aytch: A Confederate Memoir of the Civil War*. New York: Touchstone, 1997.

Welsh, Jack D., M.D. *Medical History of Confederate Generals*. Kent, OH: Kent State University Press, 2013.

Wilson, James H. *Under the Old Flag: Recollections of Military Operations in the War for the Union, the Spanish War, the Boxer Rebellion, Etc., Volume II*. New York: D. Appleton and Company, 1912.

Index